D1717129

ANCIENT
COINS
THROUGH
THE
BIBLE

To Patrick

I HOPE YOU ENJOY READING MY BOOK AS MUCH AS I
ENJOYED COLLECTING THE COINS FOR IT

BEST WISHES AND GOD BLESS

1/9/2012

ANCIENT COINS THROUGH THE BIBLE

JOSEPH A. DOW

TATE PUBLISHING & Enterprises

Published by Tate Publishing & Enterprises, LLC
127 E. Trade Center Terrace | Mustang, Oklahoma 73064 USA
1.888.361.9473 | www.tatepublishing.com

Tate Publishing is committed to excellence in the publishing industry. The company reflects the philosophy established by the founders, based on Psalm 68:11,
"The Lord gave the word and great was the company of those who published it."

Book design copyright © 2011 by Tate Publishing, LLC. All rights reserved.
Cover design by Leah LeFlore
Interior design by Lindsay B. Behrens

Published in the United States of America

ISBN: 978-1-61777-135-4
1. Religion / Biblical Studies / History & Culture
2. Antiques & Collectibles / Coins, Currency & Medals
11.06.29

To my family; my wife, Marjorie; and our sons, Philip and James.

Acknowledgments

I am indebted to countless people, articles, historians, and scholars who have written many important works on ancient history and ancient coins. They deserve most of the credit. This book would be incomplete without the continuous help of Classical Numismatic Group in Lancaster, Pennsylvania. Over 80 percent of the coins shown in this book were purchased from CNG mail bid or electronic auctions and from their mother company, Seaby of London, over the past twenty-seven years. I thank CNG for their immeasurable generosity in granting me the right to use some of Seaby's publication maps as needed. Proper credit is given as each map had been used from the publications throughout the book. In addition to that, I would like to thank CNG's very knowledgeable numismatists, manager, controller, and photographer for the pride they take in their work and for their endless patience in answering many complicated questions I asked to determine the course of writing this book. However, any factual description or other error presented in this book is the sole responsibility of the author.

I would like to take the opportunity to express my thanks to Julie Malcolm of Zondervan Publishing Company for her efforts in securing me the right to use up to 500 Bible verses, nine biblical maps, and an armored statue and table known as "Visions in Daniel." These items were taken from the NIV Bible, copyright 1995, are credited to Zondervan, and can be seen occasionally throughout the book.

I also would like to offer my thanks to my wife, Marjorie, who read and provided feedback on the book's first draft; our two boys, Philip, who took photographs of almost 1,000 coins pictured in this book; and James, who typed my original manuscript on the computer; and all our friends for the continuing encouragement to compile this book.

Table of Contents

Introduction

There have been millions of books written in the past 2,500 years, but not a single book has ever been more effective in developing and shaping world civilization than the Bible. Many religions of the world—Christians, Muslims, and Jews—consider the Bible as inspired by God and written by many different scholars over thousands of years. Others regard both the Old and the New Testaments as the undiluted word of God, spoken by God, and written down by man. The Bible is a book of relationships between God and human, God and nature, and human and human. It is God's infallible word to mankind.

Readers of the Bible don't always comprehend the geographical extent to where its stories took place. They initially began in the ancient Near East, particularly the Fertile Crescent, which extends from Egypt to Mesopotamia through Syria and Judaea. In the middle of the crescent lies a narrow strip of land squeezed between the Syrian Desert and the Mediterranean Sea, which was known as Canaan, Judaea, and Palestine. This narrow strip became the Holy Land, where Judaism and Christianity sank their roots. Christianity spread its roots to Asia Minor (present-day Turkey), Greece, Italy, and Spain in the first century AD when the Apostle Paul made his missionary journeys, which cover many different countries and provinces.

I am not a historian. I am a petroleum engineer and also a numismatist. I have been collecting coins and studying numismatic books for about forty-two years, of which twenty-six years were devoted to ancient coins. I have always been fascinated by the history and the stories of the Bible, ancient Egypt, Abraham, Moses, the Israelites, the Assyrians, the Babylonians, the Persians, the Greeks, the Romans, and the birth of Christianity. All the wars and the rise and fall of all these nations have made the outlines of our world and developed our borders today. The biblical world events for all these nations were concentrated in one area from Mesopotamia to the Mediterranean Sea, and later the Greek and the Romans conquered a wider horizon that spread from east of the Mediterranean to Spain.

All these nations mentioned in the Bible created their own governments; built their own cities, temples, armies, and weapons; and made their own money. They made their money in the shape of coins from gold, electrum, silver, bronze, and copper. They placed their stories, ways of life, events, their own portraits, and even their wives portraits on some coins. They commemorated on their coins wars, peace treaties, their victorious battles, their gods and goddesses, their true and given names, and any other important events in their dynasties. We cannot see these nations' leaders in person nor the way they lived, but we can, in fact, see them, relate to them, and learn about them and their way of life through their coins, which speak abundantly about them. Coins are effective witnesses to our forefathers' trials and struggles to promote the beliefs that gave them strength to persevere. These tangible bits of history should be seen, touched, and appreciated for what they tell us of the past and what they can assure us today. Their coins are a living proof of ancient times. They have been buried for 2,500 years and held in our hands today. Trust me. Most of these coins are a joy to behold.

This book, *Ancient Coins through the Bible,* briefly discusses the history, geography, and religions of the biblical world, in some cases, a little more detailed just enough to cover the period discussed. Many books have been written about biblical coins, but they were limited to the Holy Land and the immediate surrounding areas where Jesus carried out most of his teachings. Some of the books covered the Bible stories from different perspectives using ancient, medieval, and modern coins to describe the events in the Bible. This book, in my opinion, is one of a kind; it retells the Bible stories and presents photographs of real ancient coins for the biblical stories following the Bible sequence of events from Genesis to Revelation. This book presents ancient coins and the brief history for the cities, villages, provinces, kings, emperors, and leaders of the ancient world. It also shows ancient maps where all the stories took place, which makes the biblical land become more real and alive and the biblical stories become more meaningful. The book covers the time from Abraham's journey to the promised land to the crusaders' wars in an effort to liberate Jerusalem from the Islamic invasion. This time frame offers a tremendous amount of coins minted in all of these cities, reflecting the patriarchs who roamed around the Bible land, the prophets' predictions, the Israelites' exile to Babylon, the Assyrians/Babylonians, the Persians, the Greeks, the Romans, the Parthians, the Maccabeans, the Herodians, and the spread of Christianity through the Byzantine Empire. This book also presents coins for the Jewish nation during the Greek and Roman empires, Jewish revolts against the Romans, persecutions of Christians, and the oppositions of nations against Christianity, such as the Roman and Sasanian empires. In addition to the coins for all these nations, this book presents coins for the cities where Jesus Christ performed most of his teachings and ministries, Philip and Peter's early travels, and the Apostle Paul's four missionary journeys. These journeys alone amount to about 150 different cities and places. The cities and provinces that have coins in this book are supported by verses from the NIV Bible and/or by scholars' commentaries in the Bible.

Based on archeological discoveries, coin hoards discoveries, numismatists all over the world, kings' reigns and scholars, it was agreed upon that the earliest date for minting coins was circa 650–600 BC. The coins minted in that period were struck in Lydia and Ionia from electrum (a natural mixture of gold and silver) and shaped like ingots. This book presents a few pieces of them, and they are considered to be the earliest coins on earth. The coins minted later proved to be a very artful, thus attracting both numismatists and the general population. Of course there were no coins minted during the time of the patriarchs; however, the cities they visited, the provinces they conquered, and the places they built and lived were later rebuilt by the Greeks, the Romans, and other dynasties who minted coins in these cities. In my opinion, ancient coins are priceless. How can we place a value on the experience of holding a little fragment of the ancient past in our hands? These coins offer tremendous history of the Bible land.

About the Coins in This Book

All the coins presented in this book are from my private collection. All the coins are guaranteed to be genuine, and they are resting safely in a local bank. All the photographs in this book are not the actual size for the coins. Some of them appear to be the actual size, but this is incidental. However, the actual size in millimeters and the exact weight in grammes are shown in the description under each coin.

Ancient coin collecting has long been a hobby rich in art, history, economics, geography, politics, and other disciplines. Some of the more interesting features of ancient coins are the stories they tell about the time and the people who used them. Ancient coins are unlike modern coins, which are minted by the thousands, put in bags, and transferred to banks to be used in circulation. It is difficult for anyone to imagine that ancient coins were individually created under conditions far from ideal. They were made between a pair of dies. The artist made the engraving into a thick bronze disk, which was placed on a hard surface (usually an anvil). This was the obverse of the coin, or the lower die. Then he engraved the upper die, or the reverse of the coin, at the base of a punch. The finished dies were used to transfer the images on blanks of metal that were either heated or, more often, warm. The moneyer then put the piece of metal upon the obverse die seated in the anvil. He then took the hammer and the punch containing the reverse die and placed the punch upon the blank. With a swift blow from his hammer, often more than one blow, the coin was made. This process of striking ancient coins changed a little in the first century AD by placing several metal blanks in round sockets connected by channels already engraved by the artist. The moneyer then struck several coins at a time connected by metal strips. Those metal strips were removed after the coin cooled down. An example of this process can be seen heavily in Judaean coins, as portions of the strips still can be seen on most of their coins. The process discussed here was not fully applied in early Greek coins. These early coins had only an obverse image, and the reverse showed only punch marks.

By understanding the process of striking ancient coins, we may realize why we see so many ancient coins that were struck weakly, double struck, and off center. The ancients did not replace the striking dies as often as we do in modern days. Most ancient coins were struck from worn dies, and this was one of the reasons for the weakness of the strike. Other reasons—such as the strength of the moneyer, the temperature of the blank, and maybe the day of the week—had something to do with it, especially if the moneyer was slowly coming to work on Monday morning after a rough weekend, or if he was in a hurry for an exciting weekend on Friday afternoon. We need to remember that very few moneyers in ancient time (an exception to Syracuse and Athens in the fourth to third centuries BC) were concerned with creating works of art and especially not worrying about coin collectors for grading. They did their job the best way they knew how as long as the coins met the standard weight. It was not important if only two-thirds of the image was shown or the coin was double struck from hitting the blank many, many times. Some of these coins were made 2,650 years ago and were probably hoarded, buried, or hidden for the last 2,500 years and now have been unearthed and given new life for us to protect. It is my pleasure and hope that this book becomes a meaningful tool to describe the fascination of the ancient coins of biblical times and cultivates the imagination of the ancient rulers by having a piece of what was once their country in our hands. Considering all the circumstances, it is absolutely amazing that so many fine specimens have come down to us from the ancients. We are lucky and ought to be very grateful.

Some of the coins in this book encountered one or more of the common problems ancient coins have, such as incrustation, corrosion, rough surfaces, discoloring, stripped patina, off center, double striking, test cuts, rough edges, and even banker's marks and irregular shapes. Most of the coins in my collection are grades VF or better, except for some coins that were so rare that I was willing to accept them in any grade that I could find and considered myself fortunate just to own one specimen of them.

For our surprise, many of the ancient coins in this book are dated. Not the common dating that we know in modern time. Generally, the Greek coinage prior to the Roman Empire divided up into three major periods: the Archaic period; the Classical period ; and the Hellenistic period, which lasted 300 years. In the Archaic and the Classical periods, coin dating was mainly by the name of the annual magistrate, which was well-known at the time the coins were in circulation. This was not very precise information to the numismatists. Greek coins were not dated in their year of issue until the late period of the Hellenistic kingdoms, which commenced in 312 BC when Seleukus I took possession of Babylon after defeating Demetrius. This dating according to a known era enabled numismatists to assign the time of striking the coins with high accuracy. This practice continued through the Roman Imperial times, and the Parthian kings dated their coins by the Seleukid era, which lasted until the third century AD. The Ptolemies, kings of Egypt, used the regnal year of the king. This system was rather confusing to numismatists because the dynasty lasted 300 years and all their kings bore the same name: Ptolemy. Dating of Judaean coins was first introduced in the reign of Alexander Jannaeus (103–76 BC), king of Israel and the second high priest after Simon Maccabee, founder of the Hasmonean dynasty. The regnal-year dating system was used on these Jewish coins (known as widow's mites) and also on Herod the Great coins. The first Jewish war (66–70 AD) coins were dated year one to year five, and the ones from the second Jewish war (132–135 AD), known as the Bar Kochba War, were dated year one and year two. Roman and Byzantine coins also used the regnal-year system for their dating.

Collecting ancient coins can connect you with the ancient civilizations and knowledge about the history, geography, religions, and the way of life of the ancient people. Above all, it is a lot of *fun*. Trust me, when you find a particular coin that you have been in search of for years, it can be as thrilling as landing on the moon and returning back to earth alive.

PART I
THE OLD TESTAMENT

Abraham's Journey to Canaan

God created the earth and the heavens in six days. By the seventh day, he rested from all the work of his creations. As God made the first humans, he named them Adam and Eve. He put them into the garden of Eden. Four branches of rivers flowed into the garden: the Tigris, the Euphrates, the Pishon, and the Gihon. The Euphrates and the Tigris are well known from the cuneiform tablet found in the Babylonian palace of Nippur in modern-day Iraq. Most scholars believe that it was in ancient Mesopotamia. Regardless of the actual location of the garden, the biblical description of Eden is that is was lush and green—nothing like Iraq today.

> The Lord God took the man and put him in the Garden of Eden to work it and take care of it. The Lord God commanded man, you are free to eat from any trees in the garden, but you must not eat from the tree of knowledge of good and evil, for when you eat of it you will surely die.
>
> Genesis 2:15–17 (NIV)

Eve ate the fruit of the tree of knowledge and offered some of it to Adam. He ate it, and that was the beginning of the fall of man.

Adam and Eve were the parents of many nations of this earth. Man became sinful, and every thought in their hearts was evil, and God saw how great man's wickedness on the earth had become.

> So the Lord said I will wipe mankind, whom I have created, from the face of the earth, men and animals, and creatures that move along the ground and birds of the air for I am grieved that I have made them, but Noah found favor in the eyes of the Lord.
>
> Genesis 6:7, 8 (NIV)

In the eyes of the Lord, Noah was a good and righteous man, and he walked with God. The earth was full of violence and badly corrupted. God told Noah to make an ark for him and his family and two of every creature that moved on the ground, for the Lord God was going to flood the earth. Noah finished building the ark as per God's specifications. The water flooded the earth for 150 days. Every living thing on the face of the earth was wiped out. Only Noah and those around him survived in the ark. The ark landed on Mount Ararat, the highest mountain in the area, standing 16,872 feet above sea level. The Lord made a covenant with Noah that he would never flood the earth again and destroy all life. God set the rainbow in the clouds for all generations to come to be the sign of God's covenant between him and the earth.

Noah and his sons and daughters were very fruitful, and they multiplied and became many nations (as said in the Bible). When Nahor was twenty-nine years old (Nahor was the descendent of Noah's sons), he became the father of Terah, and when Terah was seventy years old, he became the father of Abram (Abraham). Terah decided to move to Haran from the city of Ur of the Chaldeans and ultimately to continue from there to Canaan. So he took Abraham and his family with him. Assumedly, they followed the Euphrates River from Ur to Babylon, and then to Mari, and then to the Balikh River, which led them straight to the city of Haran. Terah died in Haran, and his trip to Canaan never was accomplished. Now Abraham had great responsibility after his father died. He had to rule over the fate of the family, the servants, and the slaves. He became the patriarch, and he had to choose where to live, build a house, or pitch a tent. He had to deal with all the merchants and traders and keep good relations with his nomadic neighbors. This anxiety did not last very long before God called on Abraham: "The Lord had said to Abraham, leave your country, your people and your father's household and go to the land I will show you" (Genesis 12:1, NIV). Abraham did what the Lord told him to do. He moved from Haran to Canaan—the promised land. They arrived to Shechem, and he built the first altar to the Lord.

The Bible does not specify how Abraham arrived to Canaan from Haran, except that they arrived to the City of Shechem. Scholars assume that a nomadic traveler like Abraham would have taken the main caravan road later known as the kings highway from Haran which led them to Aleppo, Hamath/ Emesa, and Damascus across the Transjordan plateau to Shechem.

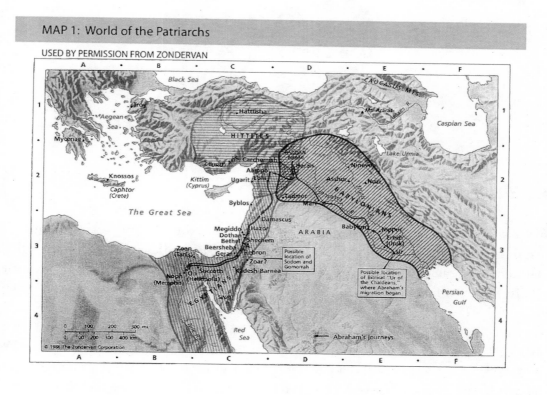

MAP 1: World of the Patriarchs

USED BY PERMISSION FROM ZONDERVAN

Here, I would like to present coins for the cities that Abraham traveled en route to the promised land, including the trip he made with his father (Terah) through Babylon from his birth place, the city of Ur.

Babylon, Greek Babylonia. 295-280 BC.
AR Tetradrachm (25 mm, 15.9 gr.), Struck under
Seleukos I. Baal enthroned left/Loin walking left. RARE

Babylon, Greek Babylonia. 311-280 BC.
AR Hemidrachm (12 mm, 2.0 gr.).
Baal seated left/Lion walking left. Rare.

Babylon, Greek kings of Syria. 320-315 BC,
Seleukos I Nikator. AR Tatradrachem (29 mm, 17.13 gr.).
Struck in the name of Philip III of Macedon. Head of
Herakles right, wearing lion skin/Zeus seated left. Scarce.

BABYLON

The city of Babylon was mentioned in the Old Testament as the first center of the kingdom of Nimrod, who was the grandson of Ham, son of Noah, and the original founder of Babel (Babylon). "The first center of his kingdom were Babylon Erech, Akkad and Calneh in Shinar" (Genesis 10:10, NIV).

Babylon was located in ancient Mesopotamia and could be found in present-day Al Hillah, Iraq, about fifty miles south of Baghdad. It was the Holy City of Babylonia by approximately 2300 BC and the seat of the Neo-Babylonian Empire from 612 BC. It has been estimated that Babylon was the largest city in the world from circa 1770 to 1670 BC and again between circa 612 and 320 BC. The city was famous with its Ishtar Gate and the Hanging Gardens of Babylon (one of the Seven Wonders of the World). It is said to have been built by Babylonian King Nebuchadnezzar (604–561 BC) for his homesick wife, Amyitis. They took the lion for strength and confidence, and that was one of the symbolic features—the "Lion of Babylon"—engraved on their coins.

HARAN

Haran, also known as Carrhae, is located in the southeast province of Turkey near the Syrian boarder. Haran was a major city in Mesopotamian commercial, cultural, and religious centers.

> Terah took his son, Abram, his grandson, and his daughter-in-law and together they set out from the city of Ur of the Chaldeans to go to Canaan, but when they came to Haran, they settled there.
>
> Genesis 11:31 (NIV)

Terah died there, and Abraham lived there after his father's death before heading to Canaan. Haran controlled the caravan traffic from Damascus and joined the road between Nineveh and Carchemish.

Haran. Roman Mesopotamia, Carrhae. Caracalla, 198-217 AD. AE (15 mm, 2.5 gr.) Laureate head right/Turreted and veiled head of Tyche right. Scarce.

Haran. Roman Mesopotamia, Carrhae. 217-218 AD, Diadumenian. AR Tetradrachem (24 mm, 12.99 gr.). Laureate bust right/Eagle standing right on bull's head. Scarce.

Just like any important ancient city, it was invaded by the Assyrians, Babylonians, Meds, Persians, Greeks, and Romans. Even the crusaders had battles in Haran in AD 1104.

The city of Carrhae was well known for the battle of Carrhae in AD 53, in which the Parthians, commanded by General Surena, defeated three Roman legions, under the command of Crassus, and captured them. It was, according to legend, the worst battle/disaster ever suffered by Roman arms—about 20,000 Romans were killed and 10,000 were taken prisoner.

BEROEA

Beroea, known as Aleppo in modern-day, is located in the northern part of Syria. Aleppo is one of the oldest inhabited cities in the world. It had human settlement since the eleventh millennium (11,000 BC). It occupies a strategic trading point midway between the Mediterranean Sea and the Euphrates.

The Arabic name for the city is Halab, which means "milked." This came from the ancient tradition that Abraham, on his way to the promised land, milked his cow and gave the milk to travelers throughout the region. The color of his cow was ashen (*shahbah,* in Arabic); therefore, the official name for the city today is Halab Ash-Shahbah (He milked the ashen cow).

Beroea. Roman Syria, Cyrrhetica. Trajan, 98-117 AD.
AE (26.9 mm, 12.84 gr.) Laureate head
of Trajan right/BEROI/AIWN.

Beroea. Roman Syria, Cyrrhetica. Macrinus,
217-218 AD. AR Tetradrachem (25 mm, 12.8 gr.)
Laureate bust right/Eagle standing facing. Scarce

The city passed through the hands of the Assyrians, Persians, Greeks, Romans, and Byzantine empires. The crusaders besieged the city twice, but it was not conquered. The city came under the control of Saladin in AD 1183.

EMESA

Emesa is located about one hundred miles north of Damascus on the Orontes River. The city was a good resting stop for Abraham before he continued his travel to Damascus. It was the capital of a kingdom ruled by the Emesani dynasty, which gave the city its name. It was originally a pagan center of worshiping El-Gabal, the Sun god. Based on recent excavation at the citadel of Emesa, it suggests that the area had settlement dates back to around 2400 BC. Biblical scholars have related the city with Kadesh, as mentioned in the Bible. There was a war between the Egyptian Empire under Ramesses II and the Hittite Empire under Muwatall II at the city of Kadesh (now ruins in the vicinity of Emesa) in 1274 BC. Emesa did not emerge in the light of civilization until the time of Seleucus I Nicator upon the death of Alexander the Great in 323 BC. The inhabitants of the city of Emesa became vassals to the Romans by helping their troops in various wars. The Emesani dynasty showed their support once more when they aided Julius Caesar in the siege of Alexandria, Egypt, in 41 BC. Emesa was involved in the Roman Civil War between Mark Antony and the pro-Caesar Octavian.

The Emesani dynasty reached its golden age under the reign of Roman Emperor Augustus from 29 BC to AD 14. The city of Emesa grew in rank with the important cities of Damascus, Sidon, and Tyre because of its location on the caravan road between Palmyra and Egypt. However, Roman Emperor Aurelian conquered Queen Zenobia of Palmyra, which caused the city's downfall when Palmyra sank to insignificance in AD 273. Under the Byzantine Empire, the city became an important center for Eastern Christianity and was given high status after the discovery of John the Baptist's head around the city of Emesa in AD 453. Emesa was conquered by the Muslim forces in the seventh century AD. At present, Emesa is known as Hims, is the third largest city in Syria, and has a population of about one million inhabitants.

Emesa. Roman Syria, Seleucis and Pieria. 198-217 AD,
Caracalla. AR Tetradrachem (26 mm, 13.72 gr.)
Laureate head right/Eagle standing
facing, radiate bust of Shamash.

Emesa. Roman Syria, Seleucis and Pieria. 217-218 AD,
Macrinus. AR Tatradrachem (23 mm, 13.73 gr.)
Laureate head right/Eagle standing
facing, radiate bust of Shamash.

Emesa. Roman Syria, Seleucis and Pieria. 218-222 AD,
Elagabalus. AE (23 mm, 8.45 gr.)
Laureate bust right/Agonistic flanked by palms

DAMASCUS

Damascus is the oldest continuously inhabited city in the world. The city is called Dimashq or Ash-Sham, which means "land of Shem" (son of Noah) in Arabic. The city was inhabited as early as 6000–5000 BC. It is known that the Aramaeans first established the water distribution system by constructing canals and tunnels, which maximized the efficiency of the Barada River. It was improved later by the Romans but still forms the basis of watering systems of the old section of Damascus today.

When Abraham rescued his nephew, Lot, he gathered 318 trained men to fight the king of Sodom and Gomorrah. He won and brought back Lot and all his possessions. "During the night Abram divided his men to attack them and routed them, pursuing them as far as Hobah north of Damascus" (Genesis 14:15, NIV). The name of Abraham is famous, even now, in the country of Damascus, and there is a village named after him: the Habitation of Abraham.

In 1100 BC, the city became the center of a powerful Aramaean nation called Aram Damascus. The kings of Aram Damascus, such as Ben-Haddad, were involved in many wars against the Assyrians and the Israelites. "When the Arameans of Damascus came to help Hadadezer, King of Zobah, David struck down twenty two thousand of them" (2 Samuel 8:5, NIV).

Damascus. Greek kings of Syria. 121-97 BC,
Antiochos VIII Epiphanes (Grypos). AR Tetradrachm
(28 mm, 16.01 gr.) Dated SE 197 (116/115 BC).
Diademed head right/Zeus standing left.

Damascus. Roman Syria, Coele-Syria. 30-29 BC,
Octovian. AE (21 mm, 6.46 gr.). Dated SE 283
(30/29 BC). Draped bust of Artemis/
Athena standing facing. Rare

Damascus. Roman Syria, Coele-Syria. 198-217 AD,
Caracalla. AE (22 mm, 11.34 gr.)
Laureate bust right/Turreted bust of Tyche.

The city fell to the Babylonian Empire of Nebuchadnezzar in 572 BC, and the Persians captured it in 528 BC under Cyrus and made it the capital of the Persian province of Syria. The giant western control of Damascus came when Alexander the Great swept through the Near East in 327 BC. Damascus became the site of struggle between the Seleucid and Ptolemaic empires after Alexander's death in 323 BC. The Roman and Byzantine empires took hold of the city during the first seven centuries AD. At the birth of Islam, Damascus became the capital of the Umayyad Empire from 661 to 770 AD. Damascus is one of the most fascinating cities in the Middle East due to antiquity and the tremendous amounts of history that lie around it.

SHECHEM

Shechem is also called Neapolis, or modern Tell Balatah, Israel. It is located at the edge of the city of Nablus. The city was the final destination of Abraham when God made the covenant with him in Haran regarding the possession of the land of Canaan. "Abraham traveled through the land as far as the site of the Great Tree of Moreh at Shechem" (Genesis 12:6, NIV). The Lord appeared to Abraham there and confirmed the covenant by giving this land to Abraham and to his offspring. So Abraham built an altar there to the Lord.

Shechem. Roman Judaea, Neapolis. Domitian,
81-96 AD. AE (25 mm, 13.52 gr.).
Dated CY 11 (82/83 AD). Laureate head right/
legend and date within laurel wreath. Scarce

Shechem. Roman Judaea, Neapolis. 81-96 AD,
Domitian. AE (20 mm, 7.74 gr.).
Dated CY 11 (82/83 AD). Laureate head right/
Palm tree, L-AI (date). Scarce

Shechem. Roman Judaea, Neapolis. 161-180 AD,
Marcus Aurelius. AE (24.6 mm, 8.69 gr.). Bare head
right/simulacrum of Zeus Heliopolites. Scarce

Shechem. Roman Judaea, Neapolis.161-180 AD,
Faustina Jr., wife of Marcus Aurelius.
AE (25.5 mm, 11.23 gr.). Bust of Faustina Jr. right/
Tyche with cornucopia and rudder. Scarce.

Shechem. Roman Judaea, Neapolis. 251-253 AD,
Volusian. AE (26 mm, 12.82 gr.)
Laureate bust right/Eagle standing with open wings,
supporting mount Gerizim. RARE

Shechem dates back an estimated 4,000 years. It has been destroyed and rebuilt twenty-two times by many empires during its history. The city was completely destroyed during the first Jewish revolt (AD 66–70). Roman Emperor Vespasian (AD 72) built another city on its site. He gave the city the name Neapolis.

Shechem became a very important part in the history of Israel. God gave the land to Abraham and Jacob, who dug a well there that can still be seen today, and the bones of Joseph were buried in his tomb there.

> And Joseph's bones, which the Israelites had brought up from Egypt were buried at Shechem in the trace of land that Jacob bought for a hundred pieces of silver from the sons of Hamor, the father of Shechem. This became the inheritance of Joseph's descendants.
>
> Joshua 24:32 (NIV)

When the kings of Israel moved the capital to Samaria, Shechem lost it strategic importance, and we do not hear of it until the fall of Jerusalem in 587 BC.

Abraham's Journey to Egypt

A severe famine was in the land of Canaan, so Abraham, just like any nomadic herder, went to Egypt and eventually to the Nile Delta, where there was plenty of water and pasture. Abraham left the city of Shechem and traveled south on Kings' Highway, passing through Raphia, which was the last city in Judaea and a resting stop for Abraham before arriving to Egypt. The Bible did not specify what nearby town Abraham was in, but recent discoveries, as well as many scholars, indicate that Abraham was, along with many herdsmen, in the plains around the city of Memphis. The city of Memphis was the Egyptian capital at that time. The Bible tells the story about how beautiful Abraham's wife, Sarah, was, and he was afraid the Egyptian men would kill him just to have her. Before they entered Egypt, he told her to say that she was his sister so his life would be spared. The news reached Pharaoh's palace, where the pharaoh asked his guards to bring her to his palace. Pharaoh was taken with Sarah's beauty. Abraham was then very well compensated, receiving slaves, gold, silver, and livestock because of Sarah's beauty. When Pharaoh discovered later that Sarah was Abraham's wife, he was angry. Abraham and Sarah were then allowed to leave the country, and Pharaoh permitted Abraham to keep all the treasures, gifts, and livestock that he had given him, including one young Egyptian female slave who later played an important role in Abraham's life. So Abraham left the Nile Delta to go to Canaan without knowing that his grandson, Joseph, would come back to Memphis and become the second most powerful man in Egypt.

RAPHIA

Raphia is the southernmost city in Judaea, situated about twenty miles south of Gaza. Raphia was first recorded in an inscription of Egyptian Pharaoh Seti I in 1303 BC. The city is located on the Egyptian border and was a rest stop between Egypt and the Levant.

Raphia. Roman Judaea, Raphia.193-211 AD,
Septimius Severus. AE (17 mm, 5.42 gr.)
Dated year 258 (198/199 AD).
Laureate bust right/Dionysos nude. Very Rare.

Raphia was the site of a battle where Assyrian King Sargon II defeated the Egyptian army in 720 BC. Another famous battle was the battle of Raphia, where Ptolemy IV defeated Antiochus III, and it was said to be the largest battle ever fought in the Levant, with about 100,000 men and hundreds of war elephants. The Jewish community settled in this city from the ninth through twelfth centuries AD, and most of them moved to Ashkelon about 200 years later. Raphia fell to Islamic rule and was a postal station for Saladin on the road to Egypt. Napoleon Bonaparte, commander of the Revolutionary army in France, passed through Raphia during the invasion of Egypt and Syria. In modern day, Raphia is the site of the border crossing (the only crossing) between Gaza Strip and Egypt.

MEMPHIS

Memphis was founded around 3000 BC and was the capital of Egypt, and the ruins of it are located about twelve miles south of modern Cairo. It was the legendary city of Menes, the king who united Upper and Lower Egypt. The city was more likely a fortress from which Menes controlled the land and water routes between Upper Egypt and the Delta. By the third dynasty, Memphis became a big city. It became a cosmopolitan community and was probably one of the largest and most important cities in the ancient world. According to Herodotus, in the fifth century BC, the city contained many nationalities—such as Greeks, Jews, Phoenicians, and Libyans—among the population. Many Egyptian kings (pharaohs) established their palaces in Memphis and built the Great Pyramids as a burial site.

Memphis. Greek kings of Egypt. 323-305 BC, Ptolemy I Sorter. AR Tetradrachem (26 mm, 16.95 gr.) struck in the name of Alexander the Great. Head of Herakles right wearing lion skin/ Zeus Aetophoros seated left. Very Rare.

Memphis. Greek kings of Egypt. 323-305 BC, Ptolemy I Sorter. AR Tetradrachem (29 mm, 16.88 gr.) struck in the name of Alexander the Great. Head of Herakles right wearing lion skin/ Zeus Aetophoros seated left. Very Rare

The cemeteries of the Memphite lie around Memphis in Abu Rawash, Giza, and Saqqara. The most prominent monument is the Great Pyramid of Kheops, which was considered one of the Seven Wonders of the World. The Great Pyramids, the Sphinx, and many of the great monuments can still be seen today and, some 4,500 years after they were built, still inspire the millions of tourists with wonder and awe.

The Patriarchs

God spared Noah and his family when he decided to flood the earth, because God's creation had been marred by man's persistent wickedness. Then God gradually separated one family line and eventually chose one man, Abraham, promising that he and his clan would have a historical destiny and would aid in bringing divine blessings upon all the scattered families of mankind.

When God told Abraham to leave his country, his people, and his father's household and go to the promised land that he would show him, he also said to him, "I will make you into a great nation and I will bless you, I will make your name great, and you will be a blessing. I will bless those who bless you, and whoever curses you I will curse, and all people on earth will be blessed through you" (Genesis 12:2–3, NIV). Abraham left Egypt to settle back in the land of Canaan in the vicinity of Hebron and Jerusalem. The Bible tells us that the pharaoh's gifts had made Abraham very wealthy. His family and his herds had increased and multiplied beyond the capacity of any typical nomadic tribe in his area. Abraham and his wife, Sarah, were childless. Abraham was troubled. If he died, who would take his great wealth? Also he wondered how the great nation that God had promised him would come about. As Mesopotamian chieftain, Abraham had the option to take one of his wife's female slaves and designate her as a "surrogate mother," which was a widely acceptable practice in Babylonia. The Bible tells us in Genesis 16 that Sarah made this arrangement to her husband. The name of the maid was Hagar, whom Pharaoh gave to Abraham when he left Egypt after the famine. Abraham accepted the arrangement, and Hagar bore him a child named Ishmael, which means "God hear me," after the Canaanite God Most High (El) and the Hebrew word for hear (shama). Genesis 21 says that Ishmael grew up in the wilderness of Paran in the northeastern region of the Sinai Peninsula. When Ishmael reached maturity, Hagar found a wife for him from the land of Egypt. Ishmael had many sons and daughters. He had a big nation, and his clan was called Ishmaelites.

Nabataean. Greek Nabataean kingdom, Petra. 9 BC-40 AD, Aretas IV, AE (20 mm, 4.7 gr.) Jugate bust right of King Aretas and Queen Shuqailat/two crossed cornucopias.

Nabataean. Greek Nabataean kingdom, Petra. 9 BC- 40 AD, Aretas with Shuqailat. AR drachm, (15 mm, 3.94 gr.) Dated RY 37(28/29 AD).

The Ishmaelites caravan, mentioned later in the Bible story, carried Isaac's grandson, Joseph, to Egypt when his brothers sold him as a slave. Ishmael's firstborn was named Nebaioth and was the founder of—as the Greeks and Romans called it—the Nabataeans Kingdom. The city of Petra was the kingdom's capital.

PETRA

According to many historians, Petra was the capital of the Nabataeans, had Aramaic-speaking Semites, and was the center of their caravan trade that controlled the main commercial routes. These routes passed through Gaza in the west, Bostra and Damascus in the north, and the Gulf of Aqaba in the Red Sea and across the Arabian Desert to the Persian Gulf.

Petra. Roman Syria, Decapolis, Petra. Hadrian 117-138 AD. AE (27 mm, 12.4 gr.). Laureate bust right/Tyche seated left. Scarce

Petra. Roman Syria, Decapolis, Petra.198-217 AD, Caracalla. AE (24 mm, 7.0 gr.) Laureate bust right/Tyche seated left. Scarce.

Petra. Roman Syria, Decapolis, Petra.193-211 AD, Septimius Severus. AE (22 mm, 8.3 gr.) Laureate bust right/Tyche, holding stele and trophy, seated left in distyle temple. Scarce

Petra. Roman Syria, Decapolis, Petra.198-217 AD. Caracalla. AE (18 mm, 3.9 gr.) Laureate head right/Tyche seated left. Scarce

It is believed by many scholars that many stations of the exodus, when the Israelites left Egypt under the leadership of Moses, were associated with Petra. According to Arab tradition, Petra is the place where Moses struck the rock with his staff and water came forth from the rock. Moses's brother, Aaron, was buried there at Mount Hor, which is still known to this day as Mount Aaron. The narrow valley at the head where Petra is sited is called Wadi Musa, or Valley of Moses. The shrine of Moses's sister, Miriam, on the mountaintop was still shown to pilgrims during St. Jerome's time in the fourth century AD. Petra is famous for its rose beds, rock cut architecture, and water conduits system, which was established around the sixth century BC. Petra was chosen as one of the Seven Wonders of the World in 2007, and the BBC chose Petra as one of "the ten places you have to see before you die." You may be surprised to learn that the Petra site was featured in some classic films, such as *Indiana Jones and the Last Crusade, Sinbad and the Eye of the Tiger,* and *Arabian Nights.*

When Ishmael was thirteen years old, the Bible tells us, that God promised Abraham and Sarah a son, and when Abraham heard this, he fell on his face, laughing. True enough, the Bible says, "Sarah conceives and presents Abraham with a son." Abraham called him Isaac, which means "he who laughs."

God put Abraham to the painful test. "Then God said, take your son, your only son, Isaac, whom you love and go to the region of Moriah. Sacrifice him there as a burnt offering on one of the mountains I will tell you about" (Genesis 22:2, NIV). The Bible did not give any detail about where the region of Moriah was, but the author of Chronicles identifies the area as the site of the temple in Jerusalem (2 Chronicles 3:1, NIV). Abraham built an altar and placed Isaac on top of the altar on top of the wood he collected, ready to offer his son as a burnt offering to the Lord. Then the angel of the Lord came down and asked Abraham not to hurt Isaac and gave Abraham a ram instead for the burnt offering. Abraham sacrificed the ram as a burnt offering instead of his son. Since Abraham proved to be obedient and to fear God, the angel of the Lord called Abraham from heaven and said, "I will surely bless you and make your descendants as numerous as the stars in the sky and the sand of the seashore. Your descendants will take possession of the cities of their enemies" (Genesis 22:17, NIV).

Abraham lived 175 years and died at a good old age. His sons, Isaac and Ishmael, buried him in the cave of Machpelah in the field of Ephron, son of Zohar the Hittite. Isaac grew up to be a young man and married Rebekah, who was barren. Isaac prayed to God on behalf of his wife. Isaac's wife conceived and presented Isaac with twins. They called them Jacob and Esau. They grew up together with conflicts for their father's attention.

Later in history, the Muslims erected a very impressive structure in AD 691 called the Dome of the Rock over Mount Moriah in Salem (Jerusalem). A large outcropping of rock inside the building is still pointed to the traditional site of the intended sacrifice of Isaac.

SALEM

The Old Testament name for Jerusalem was Salem, as mentioned several times in the Bible. Jerusalem was renamed to Aelia Capitolina by the Romans. The city of Jerusalem has a history that goes back to the fourth millennium BC, making it one of the oldest cities on earth. Jerusalem is the capital of Israel and has been the holiest city in Judaism and the spiritual center of the Jewish people since the tenth century BC.

Salem. Roman Judaea, Aelia Capitolina. 138-161 AD,
Antoninus Pius. AE (22 mm, 7.53 gr.)
Laureate bust right/draped bust of Tyche right. Scarce

It contains a number of significant ancient Christian sites and is considered the third holiest city in Islam. The old city is home to sites of key religious importance, among them the temple of Mount Moriah, the Western Wall, the Church of the Holy Sepulchre, the Dome of the Rock, and Al-Aqsa Mosque. The city is located in the Judaean mountains, between the Mediterranean Sea and the northern tip of the Dead Sea. According to Hebrew scripture, King David reigned there until 970 BC, and he was succeeded by his son, Solomon, who built the holy temple on Mount Moriah.

Jacob's Trip to Haran

The Bible tells us that Isaac was very old and his eyes were so weak that he could no longer see. Rebekah and Jacob tricked his brother, Esau, by making the meat stew before Esau returned from his hunting trip. Rebekah covered Jacob's hands and neck with goat skin and dressed Jacob in one of Esau's sweatshirts for his father to think he was Esau. Jacob then carried the meal to his father. Isaac believed he could feel the hair on Esau's hands and even smell Esau's masculine scent. Isaac asked Jacob, "'Are you really my son Esau?' he asked. 'I am,' he replied" (Genesis 27:24, NIV). The meat stew was delicious, and then Isaac blessed Jacob. When Esau came back from his hunting trip and heard that Jacob was blessed by his father, he was very angry. Isaac was very shocked when he realized he had been deceived, but what happened had happened, and the transfer of birthright could not be withdrawn. "Esau held a grudge against Jacob because of the blessing his father had given him. He said to himself, the days of mourning for my father are near, then I will kill my brother Jacob" (Genesis 27:41, NIV).

Isaac and Rebekah sent Jacob off to Haran to escape his brother and find a wife. He went to see Laban, his mother's brother. According to the Bible, Jacob followed the "road of Aram," which is very similar to the route Jacob's grandfather, Abraham, took many years earlier.

Jerusalem. Roman Judaea, Aelia Capitolina.138-161 AD, Antoninus Pius. AE (19.5 mm, 8.39 gr.) Laureate bust of Pius right/Bust of Marcus Aurelius with CAC at top.

Shechem. Roman Judaea, Neapolis. 147-175 AD, Faustina Junior. AE (26 mm, 10.6 gr.) Dated CY 89 (160/161 AD).Draped bust right/ Tyche standing left. Scarce

Shechem. Roman Judaea, Neapolis 218-222 AD, Elagabalus. AE (22 mm, 9.16 gr.) Laureate bust right/Tyche standing left. Scarce

Shechem. Roman Judaea, Neapolis. 251-253 AD, Trebonianus Gallus. AE (27 mm, 12.14 gr.) Laureate bust right/legend in five lines. Rare

He left Beersheba and went north to Jerusalem and to Shechem through the Valley of Jezreel—the most fertile valley around. On the way, he stopped in a little community called Luz, just north of Jerusalem and around the city of Gaba. Jacob had a dream there in which he saw a stairway extending up into heaven, and the angels were going up and down it, and God was standing above it. God blessed Jacob and promised him the land he was lying on. From there, he continued his trip north through Damascus, Emisa, Aleppo, and ultimately to Haran.

Damascus. Roman Syria, Coele Syria. 251-253 AD,
Trebonianus Gallus. AE (25 mm, 10.33
gr.) Laureate bust right/Agonistic urn
containing a cypress, ram's head below. Rare

Emesa. Roman Seleucis and Pieria. caracalla,
198-217 AD. AR Tetradrachem (24 mm, 12.34 gr.)
Laureate head Right/Eagle standing facing
bust of sun-god Shamash under. Scarce

Emesa. Roman Seleucis and Pieria. Macrinus,
217-218 AD. AR Tetradrachem (26 mm, 12.82 gr.)
Laureate head Right/Eagle standing facing
bust of sun-god Shamash under. Scarce

Emesa. Roman Seleucis and Pieria. Elagabalus,
218-222 AD. AE (22 mm, 8.6 gr.)
Radiate head right/Agonistic urn flanked by palms.

Beroea. Roman Syria, cyrrhestica, Beroea. 138-161 AD,
Antonninus Pius. AE (23 mm, 9.6 gr.)
Laureate head right/Beroi. Scarce

Beroea. Roman Syria, cyrrhestica, Beroea. 98-117 AD,
Trajan. AE (23 mm13.18gr.).
Laureate head right/Beroi. Scarce

Haran. Roman Mesopotamia, Carrhae. 198-217 AD,
Caracalla. AE (18 mm, 3.22 gr.)
Laureate head right/Turreted bust of Tyche.

GABA

The city of Gaba was located in the Valley of Jezreel. Very little is known about the city, but the valley is the most fertile in the area. Since ancient times, many wars and battles have taken place on this valley because it was the largest fertile agriculture plain in Palestine. The Bible says, " Some time later there was an incident involving a vineyard belonging to Naboth the Jezeerlite. The vineyard was in Jezreel, close to the palace of Ahab king of Samaria" (1 Kings 21:1, NIV). The Jezreel Valley is located between the mountains of Samaria in the south and the Galilee Heights in the north.

Gaba. Roman Judaea, Gaba.117-138 AD,
Hadrian. AE (23 mm, 9.11 gr.)
Laureate head right/Nike advancing left. Rare

Gaba. Roman Judaea, Gaba. 117-138 AD,
Hadrian. AE (23.5 mm, 12.36 gr.).
Laureate bust right/Victory with trophy left. Rare

Gaba. Roman Judaea, Gaba. 117-138 AD.
Hadrian, AE (29 mm 24.89gr.)
Dated CY185 (124/125 AD)
Laureate bust right/Tyche standing left. Rare

Gaba. Roman Judaea, Gaba. 138-161 AD.
Antoninus Pius. AE (23 mm, 9.43 gr.)
Dated CY 217 (156/157 AD) Laureate head
right/Men standing facing, head left. Rare

Gaba. Roman Judaea, Gaba. 117-138 AD.
Hadrian, AE (24 mm, 9.77 gr.)
Dated CY 177 (116/117 AD).
Laureate head right/Nike advancing left. Rare.

Most of the wars that took place in this valley were after Moses died, and it was in the Israelites' hands by the time of Solomon, who then fortified the ancient fortress of Megiddo to guard the valley. In Megiddo, King Josiah was killed in a fateful attempt to block the Egyptian armies from using the valley to march north to lend aid to the Assyrian armies trapped by the Babylonians. First and Second Kings describe all the battles in detail over this valley. The city of Gaba was destroyed back in ancient time, and the most probable location for the city is the ruins shown on the hill near Kibbutz in the Jezreel Valley.

The Israelites Moved to Egypt

The Bible tells us that Laban had two daughters: the oldest was named Leah, and the youngest was named Rachel. The Bible says, "Jacob was in love with Rachel and said I will work for you seven years in return for your younger daughter Rachel" (Genesis 29:18, NIV). On the wedding night, Laban took Leah and put her in bed to lie with Jacob. When Jacob realized what his father-in-law did, he angrily went and asked Laban about this. Laban told him that in the customs of Mesopotamia, the older daughter gets married first, and then the younger daughter is next. Laban then told Jacob that if he wanted his younger daughter, then he would give her to him as a wife—but he had to work for seven more years in return. Jacob did not have a choice, so he worked for Laban seven more years in return for Rachel.

Jacob had twelve sons altogether from Leah, Rachel, and from the maidservants. These twelve children became the twelve tribes of Israel later on in history. Jacob loved his son Joseph more than any of his other children, because he had been born to Israel in his old age and he was the son of Rachel, his first love. Jacob's father, Isaac, died at the age of 180 years old. He decided to move back to Canaan, his father's country. Jacob took his wives, maidservants, his children, and all he owned in Haran and set out to go to Canaan. On the way, God appeared to Jacob and blessed him and told him, "God said to him, your name is Jacob, but you will no longer be called Jacob; your name will be Israel. So he named him Israel" (Genesis 35:10, NIV).

All Israel's (Jacob) children were very jealous of Joseph because he was his favorite son; therefore, one day, when his brothers were grazing their flocks near Shechem, Joseph went to check on them as per his father's request. His brothers threw him into a cistern, and he had no food or water. They decided later to sell him to the Ishmaelites' (Midianites, the descendants of Ishmael) caravan. They sold their brother Joseph for twenty shekels of silver, and they took him to Egypt. His brothers came back home and told their father, Israel, that some ferocious animal devoured Joseph and tore him to pieces. Israel wept and mourned for a long time, and he refused to be comforted, as the Bible says, "Meanwhile, the Midianites sold Joseph in Egypt to Potiphar, one of the Pharaoh's officials, the captain of the guard" (Genesis 37:36, NIV).

The captain of the guard made Joseph the overseer of the house and put him in charge of everything he owned. Potiphar's wife tried to seduce Joseph to sleep with her because he was a very handsome young man, but he pushed her away and ran out of the house, leaving her standing with his garment in her hand. As mentioned in Genesis, his master's wife called out to her servants and said loudly that the "Hebrew" came in wanted to lie with her. When her husband heard this, he put him in prison. During his imprisonment, Joseph became known for dream interpretation. The pharaoh of Egypt had a dream after a couple of years of Joseph's imprisonment. Joseph interpreted the dream, and the pharaoh was very pleased with Joseph's interpretation and his future recommendations on how to go about it. The pharaoh appointed Joseph to be the overseer of the land and made him the second highest officer in Egypt.

The Bible says, "And all the countries came to Egypt to buy grain from Joseph, because the famine was severe in all of the world" (Genesis 41:57, NIV). Jacob asked his children to go to Egypt to buy grain. All of Jacob's children went to Egypt, except one, Benjamin—Jacob's other son by his beloved Rachel. They did not recognize Joseph, but Joseph noticed them, and he formed plans for his brothers in his mind. Joseph accused his brothers of being spies, but they told Joseph that they were twelve brothers and the youngest, Benjamin, had stayed with their father in Canaan. Joseph told his brothers one of you shall remain here as a hostage until you bring back the youngest son, Benjamin. Joseph pointed to Simeon. So the brothers went home with their grain, and they told Jacob the bad news that his son Simeon would be killed unless they all returned with Benjamin. The famine continued to be very severe, and Jacob had no choice but to send all his sons—including Benjamin—back to Egypt.

Jacob sent all his children, including Benjamin, and when they arrived for the second time to Egypt. Joseph treated them with a great hospitality in the palace and sent them back to Canaan, but he put the silver that they bought the grain with back in their sacks, along with Joseph's personal silver goblet in one of Benjamin's sacks. When they arrived to the border, they were stopped by Joseph's guards, who claimed that one of Joseph's precious goblets was missing. They searched the sacks, and sure enough, Benjamin's bag contained the missing goblet. All of the brothers went back to the palace, and they asked to speak to Joseph personally. When Joseph saw the fear in his brothers' eyes, he could not restrain himself any longer. He turned to his brothers and cried out, "I am your brother Joseph, the one you sold into Egypt, and now, do not be distressed, and do not be angry with yourselves for selling me here. Because it was to save lives that God sent ahead of you" (Genesis 45:5, NIV). The Bible also says, "You shall live in the region of Goshen and be near me, you, your children and grandchildren, your flocks and herds and all you have" (Genesis 45:10, NIV). Thus the clan of Abraham, Isaac, and Jacob moved down to Egypt. Jacob died and was buried in the cave in the field of Machpelah, which Abraham bought as a burial place from Ephron the Hittite. Joseph stayed in Egypt with all the Israelites. He lived 110 years, and when he died, they embalmed him, and he was placed in a coffin in Egypt.

The Twelve Tribes of Israel Out of Egypt

God told Moses to say to the Israelites, "I am the Lord, and I will bring you out from under the yoke of the Egyptians. I will free you from being slaves to them, and I will redeem you with outstretched arm and with mighty acts of judgment. I will take you as my own people, and I will be your God" (Exodus 6:6, NIV). The twelve tribes of Israel (Hebrew nation) lived happily and peacefully in the land of Egypt for about one hundred years. Invaders from the south (the Hyksos) came to unify Egypt to make Upper and Lower Egypt into one kingdom. The Israelites, which were chosen by God, were severely affected by the invasion and the war. They were put in slavery because they were foreigners in Egypt. The pharaoh decided to build a new capital, and the authorities put all the Israelites to work as slaves, and according to Exodus 1:14, the Egyptians made their lives a bitter, hard service in mortar and brick. The Israelites grew in great numbers more than the Egyptians. The pharaoh decided to make the Israelites a smaller nation by killing all firstborn males. One of the couples from the tribe of Levi placed their baby in a papyrus basket, and they made the basket watertight. The pharaoh's daughter found the basket. She felt sorry for the baby and brought him to the palace, and she raised him as her son. She named him Moses.

Moses grew to be a young man. Here again, God talked to Moses from the burning bush and asked him to take the Israelites out of Egypt, out of slavery, and to Canaan, the land that God promised Abraham many hundreds of years ago. By the miracle of God, Moses received the power to stretch his arms and split the Red Sea with his staff and got the Israelites out of Egypt and closed the sea on the pharaoh's army, which was chasing them from behind. The Israelites were able to continue their journey out of bondage in Egypt, and Moses would guide his people to the promised land.

According to the Bible, the number of men that Moses brought out of Egypt were 603,550 men over twenty years of age. Assuming that each man had one wife and an average of two children each, that would total at least 2.5 million people, including women and children. In addition to that, all their animals and their tents and households. Let's imagine a nation and logistics of this size roaming around the desert of Sinai under the leadership of Moses. That alone put a tremendous amount of burden on the shoulders of Moses.

Moses performed many miracles in the desert of Sinai. By the power of the lord, he was able to ask for rain and provide food and water for the Israelites. Moses brought the Israelites to the place where his mission began. He brought the twelve tribes of Israel to the shadow of the great mountain called Mount Sinai and pitched his camp there. According to the Bible, Moses talked with God face-to-face and received the Ten Commandments there. The Ten Commandments outlined moral codes, a formal covenant between God and man, and a code of human behavior that would inspire, Jews, Christians, and Muslims up to today. God instructed Moses to build the ark of the covenant, the table, the lampstand, and the tabernacle exactly like God told him. According to the Bible, the materials used for building all that were: 29 talents and 730 shekels of gold; 100 talents and 1,775 shekels of silver; and 70 talents and 2,400 shekels of bronze. That will calculate to 35,000 ounces of gold; 121,000 ounces of silver; and 86,000 ounces of bronze. Obviously, the Israelites were not just a nomadic tribe, but they were very wealthy as well when they left Egypt. As the Bible described, the ark of the covenant is the physical link between the Israelites and God—"the footstool of God's throne." It became the holiest shrine of the Hebrews. When the ark and all the furnishings were finished, God covered the tent of the meeting with a cloud. As the Bible says:

> In all the travels of the Israelites, whenever the cloud lifted from above the tabernacle, they would set out, but if the cloud did not lift, they did not set out until the day it lifted. So the cloud of the Lord was over the tabernacle by day, and fire was in the cloud at night, in the sight of all the house of Israel during their travels.
>
> Exodus 40:36–38 (NIV)

During the wandering in the desert, priests carried the ark in advance of the people. The ark was kept in a variety of shrines and often carried into battle but was ultimately enshrined in Jerusalem in Solomon's temple. The ark was presumably lost when Babylonian King Nebuchadnezzar captured Jerusalem in 587 BC, and it was hidden in a secret location, which remains to be discovered. Moses wandered in the desert of Sinai for forty years, leading the Hebrew nation from one place to the other. Finally, he arrived at Mount Nebo in Moab. Moses spoke to the Israelites from Nebo and told them that what they saw in front of them was the land that God made and promised on oath to give to Abraham, Isaac, and Jacob's descendants. He also told them, "I am no longer able to lead you, because the Lord said to me 'you shall not cross the Jordan,' but Joshua will succeed me and cross over." Moses had led the Israelites out of Egypt and brought them to the promised land, but he did not set his feet on it. "And Moses the servant of the Lord died there in Moab. As the Lord had said, he buried him in Moab, in the valley opposite Beth Peor, but to this day no one knows where his grave is" (Deuteronomy 34:5–6, NIV). The Israelites grieved and wept for Moses in the plain of Moab for thirty days. The Bible tells us:

> Since then, no prophet has risen in Israel like Moses, whom the Lord knew face to face, who did all those miraculous signs and wonders the Lord sent him to do in Egypt, To Pharaoh and to all his officials and to his whole land. For no one has ever shown the mighty power or performed the awesome deeds that Moses did in the sight of all Israel.
>
> Deuteronomy 34:9–12 (NIV)

From Joshua to Solomon

The Israelite tribes approached Canaan after forty years of desert traveling. Joshua decided to invade Canaan with the new Israelite army he gathered. Within a few years, all the highland territory of Canaan was in the hands of the Israelites. They conquered north and south of the Canaanites' territories, and they went west to the Mediterranean Sea, as well as east to the Dead Sea.

Philistia. Greek Palestine. 5th century-333 BC. AR
Drachm (12x7 mm, 4.3 gr.) Owel standing right,
head facing, AOE to right/Blob. Rare

They totally destroyed the five cites of the Philistines, among them the key cities of Ashkelon and Gaza. The Philistines were the people who occupied the southern coast of Canaan, and their territory was called Philistia.

COURTESY OF CNG (WWW.CNGCOINS.COM)

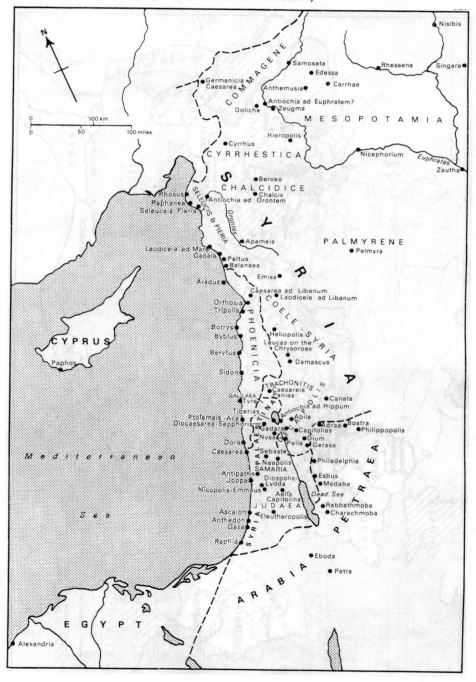

ASHKELON

Ashkelon is a coastal city in the southern portion of Israel. "The men of Judah also took Gaza, Ashkelon and Ekorn—each city with its territory" (Judges 1:18, NIV). The ancient city of Ashkelon, modern-day Ascalon, dates back to the Bronze Age (3000 BC). The city was a strategic Mediterranean port for almost 5,000 years and was the largest seaport in Canaan. During the course of history, the city was ruled by the Canaanites, the Philistines, the Babylonians, the Phoenicians, the Romans, the Muslims, and the crusaders. The Philistines conquered Canaanite Ashkelon in about 1150 BC. Ashkelon became one of the five Philistine cities that were always in war with the Israelites and the kingdom of Judah. Babylonian King Nebuchadnezzar destroyed Ashkelon after a long siege in 604 BC, and all the people were taken into exile to Babylon. The city was rebuilt by Alexander the Great around 320 BC and became an important Hellenistic seaport.

Ashkelon. Roman Judaea, Ascalon. 14-37 AD, Tiberius.
AE (22 mm, 10.21 gr.) Dated CY 135 (31/32 AD)
Bare head right/Astarte-Tyche standing
on prow, holding scepter. Rare

Ashkelon. Roman Judaea, Ascalon. 98-117 AD Trajan.
AE (18 mm, 5.28 gr.) head of Trajan right/
Phanebal, holding palm and shield.

Ashkelon. Roman Judaea, Ascalon. 98-117 AD Trajan,
AE (24 mm, 13.09 gr.) head of Trajan right/
turreted city-Goddess on galley. Scarce

Ashkelon. Roman Judaea, Ascalon. 117-138 AD, Hadrian.
AE (24 mm, 10.56 gr.) Head of Hadrian right/
turreted city-Goddess on galley. Scarce

Ashkelon may have been the birthplace of Herod the Great. The city played a very important roll between the crusaders and the Islamic forces. The city was captured by a crusader army led by King Baldwin III of Jerusalem. In AD 1187, Saladin took Ashkelon as part of the conquest of the crusader states, and he demolished the city because of its strategic importance to the Christians.

ANTHEDON

Anthedon was located just two to three miles north of Gaza on the southern shore of the Philistine territory. The city dates back to the Assyrian time and was an active city in the eighth century BC. Anthedon was used by Alexander the Great to store all his war equipment to carry out the siege of Gaza in 332 BC. During the Roman period, Emperor Augustus gave Anthedon to Herod the Great as a gift because he was very loyal to Rome during the Roman Civil War between Augustus and Mark Antony with Cleopatra the VII.

Anthedon. Roman Judaea, Anthedon.
Severus Alexander 222-235 AD. AE (25 mm, 10.08 gr.)
Dated RY 9 (230 AD) Laureate bust right/
Tyche seated left. Extremely Rare.

The city was destroyed around the Jewish revolts, and now the site is located on a high hill projecting out over the sea. Coins for the ancient city of Anthedon were minted for a short period of time, and they are very rare.

GAZA

Gaza is the largest city in the Palestinian territories. The city is one of the oldest in the world and has been shaped by its strategic location on the Mediterranean coastal route between North Africa and the greener lands of Syria and Turkey.

Gaza. Greek kings of Egypt, Ptolemy II, 285-246 BC.
AR Tetradrachem (23 mm, 13.92 gr.)
Head of Ptolemy left/Eagle standing on
thunderbolt, date and monogram behind.

Gaza. Roman Judaea, Gaza. 27 BC-14 AD, Augustus.
AE (21 mm, 9.46 gr.) Dated Pompeian Era 66 (5/6 AD).
Bare head right/Tyche standing facing,
date to right. Rare

Gaza. Roman Judaea, Gaza. Hadrian, 117-138 AD. AE (19 mm, 6.04 gr.) Dated Epidemia 2 (130/131 AD). Head right/Herakles standing facing, Phoenician "mem" to right. Rare

Gaza. Roman Judaea, Gaza. 138-161 AD, Antoninus Pius. AE (26 mm, 18.03 gr.) Dated CY 217 (156/157 AD) Head right/Tyche. Scarce

Gaza. Roman Judaea, Gaza. 161-180 AD, Marcus Aurelius. AE (29 mm, 22.67 gr.) Bust right/Tyche standing left. Scarce

Gaza. Roman Judaea, Gaza. 177-192 AD, Commodus AE (26 mm, 14.0 gr.) Dated CY 245 (184/185 AD). Bust right/Artemis and Marnas standing in distyle temple. Scarce

Ancient Gaza was a prosperous trade center and a rest stop on the caravan route between Egypt and Syria. The Bible tells us that Samson, who had an awesome God-given physical strength and tore down the temple of the Philistines with his own hands, was imprisoned and met his death in Gaza. "One day Samson went up to Gaza, where he saw a prostitute. He went in to spend the night with her" (Judges 16:1, NIV). Samson certainly possessed the physical strength but definitely lacked the moral strength, which ultimately led to his death. Just like any coastal city in Palestine, it was occupied by Neo-Assyrians, Neo-Babylonians, Persians, Greeks, and Romans. The Ptolemy and Seleucids dominated the city in 300 BC and 198 BC, respectively. In 145 BC, Gaza was conquered by Jonathan Maccabaeus, the Hasmonean (brother of Judah the Maccabee). Herod the Great occupied the city in 30 BC. Later on in history, the city was occupied by the Islamic and crusaders' forces.

As the new Israelite tribes grew, tension with the Canaanites increased, and in many places, there was a renewal of hostilities with the Moabites. Moab encompassed the expensive grain-filled plateau between the Dead Sea and the eastern desert on both sides of the enormous rift of the Arnon River gorge. The main road to go through Moab was the Kings' Highway, a track connecting the cities of Heshbon and Kir Haroshet, going through Aroer and Medeba, which points north and south.

CARACHMOBA

Carachmoba has been inhabited since at least the Iron Age and was an important city of the Moabites (who called it Kir). Later, the city was identified as having been subject to the Assyrian Empire: "The King of Assyria complied by attacking Damascus and capturing it. He deported its inhabitants to Kir and put Rezin to death" (2 Kings 16:9, NIV). Kir was the chief city of Moab, and it dominated the main caravan route, linking Syria to Egypt and Arabia. The city eventually fell under the power of the Nabateans (Ishmail clans), as the Romans conquered it in AD 105.

Carachmoba. Roman Arabia, Carachmoba. 218-222 AD,
Elagabalus. AE (20 mm, 5.78 gr.)
Laureate bust right/Tyche standing. Extremely rare.

The crusaders held the city from AD 1142–1188. In modern day, Al Karak is located in Jordan, and the Christian population is among the highest in the area. Ancient coins were rarely minted in this city, and they are extremely rare.

ESBUS

Number 21:25 (NIV) says, "Israel captured all the cities of the Amorites and occupied them, including Heshbon and all its surrounding settlements." The city of Heshbon was mentioned in many verses throughout the Bible. It is the ancient Heshbon beyond the Jordan. Heshbon, later known as Esbus, was taken by the Israelites on their entry to the promised land and was assigned to the tribe of Reuben. Afterward, it was given to Gad. It was the capital of Amorite King Sihon, and the Bible tells us the story of the Israelites' victory over Sihon during the time of the exodus under Moses.

Esbus. Roman Arabia, Petraea, Esbus. 218-222 AD,
Elagabalus. AE (18 mm,.6.54 gr.)
Radiate bust/Dionysos with panther. Very rare

The town is located about five miles from the site where the events occurred during the time of Moses, who died in the region after viewing the promised land from the top of Mount Nabo. Later in history, the town came under Moabite control. Heshbon was famous for its pools, as it was blessed with an abundant supply of spring water. The ancient town is believed to be located at the ruins called Hisban—about twelve miles south of Amman, modern-day Jordan, and five miles north of the city of Medaba.

MEDABA

First Chronicles 19:7 (NIV) says, "They hired thirty two thousand chariots and charioteers, as well as the king of Maacah with his troops, who came and camped near Medeba, while the Ammonites were mustered from their towns and moved out for battle." Medaba is located about five miles from Mount Nabo, where God buried Moses, about five miles from Esbus, and about ten miles southwest of Amman, the capital of Jordan.

Medaba. Roman Arabia, Medaba. 193-211 AD,
Septimius Severus. AE (29 mm, 16.5 gr.)
Dated CY 105(210-211 AD). Draped bust right/
Helios driving facing quadriga. Very Rare.

The city is famous and known for its Byzantine and Umayyad mosaics. Especially the six-century AD Byzantine mosaic map that was unearthed, detailing a map of Palestine and the Nile Delta and showed Jerusalem's buildings. Medaba has a long history, going back to the Neolithic Period. The city was mentioned in many chapters of the Bible. It was only twelve miles to the south of Medaba, where supposedly the head of John the Baptist was cut off and presented to Salome.

RABBATHMOBA

Deuteronomy 3:12 (NIV) says, "Of the land that we took over at the time, I gave the Reubenites and the Gadites the territory north of Aroer by the Arnon Gorge, including half the hill country of Gilead, together with its towns."

Rabbathmoba. Roman Arabia, Rabbathmoba. 198-217 AD, Caracalla. AE (29 mm, 17.82 gr.) Dated CY 105 (210-211 AD) Draped bust right/Statue of Ares standing. Very rare.

Rabbathmoba. Roman Arabia, Rabbathmoba. 198-217 AD, Caracalla. AE (30 mm, 14.09 gr.) Dated CY 105(210-211 AD) draped bust right/ Statue of Ares standing facing. Very rare.

Aroer, known as Rabbathmoba by the romans, is a town located on the bank of the River Arnon, to the east of the Dead Sea, in present-day Jordan. The city was still standing in the time of Eusebius (the bishop of Caesarea Palastina, AD 314, who is often referred to as the father of church history). It appears first as having been captured by the Amorite from Moab. This is the city mentioned in the Bible in the book of Numbers, with the southern towns as having been built by the children of God. According to the book of Jeremiah, the Moabites ultimately recovered it from the Israelites.

As the Bible tells us, the tribes of Israel elected temporary leaders called judges, each of whom is given temporary jurisdiction over tribal territories. The land was divided between the twelve tribes, and each tribe had towns and surrounding settlements. Some of the people of Judah lived in the town of Jarmuth, which was called Beit Gurvin or Beit Jibrin in the Talmud. Jarmuth is about a few miles from the city of Eleutheropolis.

ELEUTHEROPOLIS

Eleutheropolis, City of the Free, was the Greek name of a Roman city in Palestine. The biblical name for the city was Jarmuth. Its remains still straddle the ancient road to Gaza near Jarmuth. "In En Rimmon, in Zorah, in Jarmuth" (Nehemiah 11:29, NIV). The city is famous for its cage caves.

Eleutheropolis. Roman Judaea, Eleutheropolis.
193-211 AD, Septimius Severus. AE (26 mm, 12.35 gr.)
Dated CY 8(206-207 AD). Draped bust right/
Tyche in tetrastyle temple. Very rare

Eleutheropolis. Roman Judaea, Eleutheropolis.
198-217 AD, Caracalla,.AE (23.7 mm, 7.74 gr.)
Laureate bust/cult figure flanked by bulls. Rare

According to the Midrash, Eleutheropolis was the biblical "Mount Sur of the Horites." It is only three miles from the Valley of Elah, where David slew Goliath, and only two miles from Marisah, where the Lord smote thousands of Ethiopian invaders. In the first Jewish revolt of AD 68, Roman General Vespasian slaughtered and enslaved its inhabitants. The settlement was demolished once again during Bar Kochba's revolt—the second Jewish revolt—in AD 132. Eleutheropolis is called Beit Gurvin in modern-day.

ANTIPATRIS

The Israelites were in constant conflicts with their neighbors. One of the battles was very important when the Israelites, under the leadership of Ahab, fought Ben-Hadad, king of Aram, defeated him. "The rest of them escaped to the city of Aphek, where the wall collapsed on twenty-seven thousand of them, and Ben-Hadad fled to the city and hid in an inner room" (1 Kings 20:30, NIV).

Many scholars belief Aphek is Cannanite royal town of Antipatris, located on the coast of Palestine. It is mentioned in Egyptian documents dating from the nineteenth century BC and was one of the cities mentioned in a list of Canaanite cities captured by Tuthmosis III (1504–1450 BC).

Antipatris. Roman Judaea, Antipatris. 218-222 AD,
Elagabalus. AE (16 mm, 4.73 gr.)
draped bust right/Tyche standing. Very Rare

Also, it was at Aphek that the Philistines gathered their forces in preparation to do battle with Israel. The Philistines captured the ark of the covenant in this city. In 132 BC, the city was conquered by John Hyrcanus I. The city was destroyed and rebuilt by Herod the Great and named Antipatris after his father, Antipater. Apostle Paul was brought to this town on his way to Caeserea for trial before the Roman governor. "So the soldiers, carrying out their orders, took Paul with them during the night and brought him as far as Antipatris " (Acts 23:31, NIV).

By now the Israelites had become established in the promised land, and many of the covenant promises God had given to the patriarchs in Canaan and to the fathers in the desert had now been fulfilled. King David had expanded the Hebrew nation by pushing the Philistines out of the thin coastal strip of Philistia itself. King David and his son, King Solomon, after him had restored the promised land, as God promised. During their expansion, they had conquered and occupied four important cities—Nysa-Scythopolis, Hippo, Dor, and Rabbah of the Ammonites—and King Solomon had built the city of Tadmor in Palmyra.

NYSA-SCYTHOPOLIS

Nysa-Scythopolis, biblically known as Beth Shan, is located about eighteen miles northeast of Shechem and is known as the key to western Palestine. It has been a strategic city from the ancient times, for it lies on major caravan routes that linked Egypt and Mesopotamia. The city is first listed among Thutmosis III conquests in the fifteenth century BC.

Nysa- Scythopolis. Roman Syria, Decapolis. 57-55 BC, Aulus Gabinius. AE (20 mm, 5.74 gr.) Female bust/Nike advancing. Very Rare

Nysa- Scythopolis. Roman Syria, Decapolis. 238-244 AD, Gordian III. AE (25 mm, 10.18 gr.) Laureate bust/Tyche-Nysa seated. Very Rare

Nysa- Scythopolis. Roman Syria, Decapolis. 238-244 AD, Gordian III. AE (24 mm, 14.02 gr.) Laureate bust/legend in five lines. Very Rare

The Philistines occupied this city, and they found Saul, the king of Israel, dead with his three sons. They cut off his head and hung his body on the city wall. "They put his armor in the Temple of the Ashtoreths and fastened his body to the wall of Beth Shan" (1 Samuel 31:10, NIV). King David retook this city in reprisal.

The Greeks under Alexander the Great reoccupied the city and drove the Persians, and it was renamed Scythopolis, probably named after the Scythian mercenaries who settled there as veterans. Based on Greek mythology, the city was founded by Dionysus, and his nursemaid, Nysa, was buried there—thus it was known as Nysa-Scythopolis. Some of the coins presented here are showing the city-goddess Nysa enthroned and nursing infant Dionysus. John Hyrcanus I captured the city in 63 BC, and it was taken by Pompey the Great and was made the capital city of the Roman Decapolis.

HIPPOS

Hippos is located in Israel on a hill overlooking the Sea of Galilee. In ancient time, it was called Tob. "When the Ammonites realized that they had become a stench in David's nostrils, they hired twelve thousand men from Tob" (2 Samuel 10:6, NIV). During the Greek-Roman times, the city's name was changed from Tob to Hippos, the Greek word for horse, because from above, the plateau on which Hippos was built very vaguely resembles the head and neck of a horse. Also, the Israelites called it Susita, because the Hebrew word *sus* means horse. In the Greek occupation of the Ptolemy and the Seleucid dynasties, the city was called Antiochia ad Hippum.

Hippos. Roman Syria, Decapolis. 161-169
AD, Lucius Verus. AE (25 mm, 10.06 gr.)
Diademed bust/Tyche stands alongside horse. Rare

Hippos. Roman Syria, Decapolis. 161-180 AD,
Marcus Aurelius. AE (23 mm, 10.40 gr.)
Laureate bust/Tyche holding horse by bridle. Rare.

The Maccabean revolt in 142 BC resulted in an independent Jewish kingdom under the Hasmonean family. The city was destroyed by Alexander Jannaeus and was later was captured and rebuilt by Pompey the Great. Jesus Christ performed many miracles in Hippos's surrounding areas east of the Sea of Galilee. In modern days, the area around Hippos is called the Golan Heights.

DOR

Dor is located in the most southern settlement of the Phoenicians on the coast of Syria. It is located about ten miles north of Caesarea on the Mediterranean coast of Israel. The Bible tells us that when King Solomon ruled over all Israel, he presented all his chief officials as who they were and where they lived. "Ben-Abinadab in Naphoth Dor, he was married to Taphath daughter of Solomon " (1 Kings 4: 11, NIV).

Dora. Roman Phoenicia, Dora. 67-68 AD, time of Nero. AE (21 mm, 10.11 gr.) Head of Dora right/Astarte standing facing. Scarce

Dora. Roman Phoenicia, Dora. 98-117 AD, Trajan. AE (26 mm, 13.87 gr.) Laureate head star before/head of Doros. Scarce

Dor was an ancient royal city of the Canaanites commanding the heights of Dor, whose king became an ally of Jabin of Hazor in the conflict with Joshua. In the book of Judges, we are told that Dor was incorporated into David's Israelite kingdom. In the tenth century BC, it became the capital of the heights of Dor under Solomon and was governed by his son-in-law, Ben Abinadab, as one of Solomon's commissariat districts. Alexander Jannaeus annexed the city through negotiation, and Pompey the Great later conquered the city and returned it to its former owners.

PHILADELPHIA

Philadelphia (Rabbah) referred to in the Bible as the place where "children of Ammon" or Ammonites were living east of the Jordan River. The origin of these people in the old testament traces to an illegitimate son of lot, the nephew of the Patriarch Abraham. "So David mustered the entire army and went to Rabbah, and attacked and captured it" (2 Samuel 12:29, NIV).

Philadelphia. Roman Arabia, Philadelphia. 2nd century AD. AE (16 mm, 3.08 gr.) Helmeted head of Athena/legend in three lines. Rare

Philadelphia. Roman Arabia, Philadelphia. 117-138 AD, Hadrian. AE (24 mm, 11.20 gr.) Laureate bust/head of Herakles, lion skin tied around neck. Scarce

Philadelphia. Roman Arabia, Philadelphia.
138-161 AD, Antoninus Pius. AE (18 mm, 3.35 gr.)
Laureate Bust/Tyche standing. Scarce

Philadelphia. Roman Arabia, Philadelphia. 161-169 AD,
Lucius Verus. AE (25 mm, 12.64 gr.)
draped head/veiled but of Asteria. Rare

Philadelphia. Roman Arabia, Philadelphia. 198-217 AD,
Caracalla. AE (20 mm, 7.58 gr.)
Laureate head/Shrine in quadriga. Rare

The city was mentioned many times throughout the Old Testament. When the Israelites invaded Canaan, they passed by the frontier of the Ammonites.

Rabbah changed names many times during ancient history. The city's name was Rabbah-Ammon, Ammon, later called Philadelphia by Ptolemy II Philadelphus, and now it is known as Amman. It is the capital of modern-day Jordan. When the Israelites of the exodus, under the leadership of Moses, paused before their territory, the Ammonites prohibited them from passing through their lands. The capital, Rabbah, was captured, and the Bible tells us that David slaughtered the Ammonites, and numerous captives were taken from all the cities of the children of Ammon. Just like any ancient city in the area, it was conquered by the Assyrians, Babylonians, Greeks, Romans, and Islamic forces.

Rabbah-Ammon was part of the Arabian Peninsula back in ancient times. There were three kingdoms in the Arabian Peninsula: the Minaean, the Sabaean, and the Himyarite. Most of these kingdoms flourished partly because of their controlling positions on the caravan routes linking the seaports of the Mediterranean with the frankincense-growing region of Hadhramaut. The Sabaean kingdom was widely referred to Saba, and it has been widely believed that the queen of Sheba mentioned in the Bible and, as well as in the Quran, who visited King Solomon in Jerusalem in around 950 BC was Sabaean. Both the Bible and the Quran mentioned that the Israelites included the territories of the Arabian Peninsula east of the Jordan in their kingdom under King Solomon's rule. The Sabaean kingdom lasted almost 800 years, from around 950–115 BC.

Himyarites, Arabia. circa 50-150 AD. AR half Denarius (14 mm, 1.5 gr.) Male head/smaller male head, name and mint in Sabaean. Scarce

Himyarites, Arabia. circa 50-150 AD. AR half Denarius (14 mm, 1.4 gr.) Male head/smaller male head, name and mint in Sabaean. Scarce

The Himyarites followed the Sabaeans as the leaders in Arabia, and they lasted from around 115 BC to AD 525. The Himyarites prospered in the frankincense, myrrh, and spices trade until the Romans opened the sea routes through the Red Sea.

PALMYRA

Palmyra (Tadmor) was a very important city in ancient times. It is located in central Syria, about 130 miles northeast of Damascus. Solomon, son of King David, built this city. "He also built up Tadmor in the desert and all the store cities he had built in Hamath" (2 Chronicles 8:4, NIV). The city had long been a vital caravan city for travelers crossing the Syrian Desert and was known as the "Bride of the Desert." Palmyra was a very wealthy and elegant city located along the caravan route linking Persia with the Mediterranean ports of Roman Syria and Phoenicia.

The Seleucids took control of Syria in 323 BC, and Palmyra was left to itself and became an independent state.

Palmyra. Roman Palmyrene. 2nd-early 3rd centuries AD. AE (13 mm, 1.04 gr.) draped bust of Astargatis/radiate bust of uncertain solar deity left. Extremely Rare.

Palmyra was made part of the Roman province of Syria during the reign of Tiberius (AD 14–37). It steadily grew in importance as a trade route linking Persia, India, China, and the Roman Empire. The city trade diminished as the Sasanids occupied the mouth of the Tigris and the Euphrates rivers. When Roman Governor Odaenathus of Palmyra was assassinated by his nephew, Maconius, his wife, Septimia Zenobia, took power and proclaimed herself Augusta in AD 271, ruling Palmyra on behalf of her son. Queen Zenobia tried to expand her territory; she occupied Bostra and all the cities as far as Egypt. Next, she attempted to take Antioch to the north. In AD 272, Roman Emperor Aurelian finally retaliated, captured her, and brought her back to Rome in historical golden chains. The emperor allowed her to live in a villa in Tibur, where she spent the rest of her life. Palmyra was occupied by the Byzantine Empire, and they built few churches. And later, the Islamic dynasties took over the city. At the present time, the remaining palaces, the Temple of Baal, the theaters, and some of the Roman columns still stand. Ancient coins were minted in Palmyra, but they are extremely rare, especially in good condition.

PHOENICIA

On the west region of Canaan, there was a narrow strip of land sandwiched between the Israelites land in Canaan and the Mediterranean Sea called Phoenicia. The Phoenicians were merchants, craftsmen, seafarers of the eastern Mediterranean, and descendants of earlier Canaanites. They settled along the coast in about 1200 BC. The Phoenicians performed their trading by means of a galley, and they are credited with the invention of the bireme (a second row of oars above the first). The Phoenician civilization was organized in city-states similar to ancient Greece. Each city-state was politically independent; although, they could have conflict, be occupied by another city-states, or unite in leagues of alliances. They had many cities on the coast of the Mediterranean Sea, such as Acco, Tyre, Sidon, Berytus, Byblus, Tripolis, and Aradus (see map number two). Tyre and Sidon were the most powerful states. King Solomon used cedars of Lebanon, provided by King Hiram of Tyre, in the building of his temple. All the Phoenician cities started making their own coins during the occupation by the Greek and Roman empires.

The Phoenicians were skilled artisans, famous for their fine work in metal and manufacturing glass. They were credited with the invention of glass blowing. Their major contribution to humanity seems to have been the development of the alphabet. Although they continued to use cuneiform, the Phoenicians had an alphabetic script as early as the fifteenth century BC consisting of twenty-two consonants. It was the basis for Hebrew, Arabic, Syriac, and various other Near Eastern alphabetic scripts. Their alphabet was adopted by the Greeks, spread throughout western civilization, and is believed to be the foundation of the English alphabet.

Phoenicia reached its zenith with the colonization of Mediterranean lands early in the first millennium BC. By 900 BC, it had expanded into Cyprus, Sicily, Sardinia, Africa, and Spain, and by 814 BC, the Phoenicians conquered the city of Carthage. Unfortunately, this magnificent civilization ended with the Assyrian conquest.

PTOLEMAIS-ACE

Ptolemais-Ace (Acco) is a city in the western Galilee region of northern Israel. Historically, Acco has been regarded as the key of the Levant due to its strategic coastal location. "Nor did Asher drive out those living in Acco or Sidon…" (Judges 1:31, NIV).

Acco. Roman Phoenicia, Ace Ptolemais. 54-68 AD, time of Nero. AE (18 mm, 2.62 gr.) Nike left/ Caduceus between crossed cornucopias. Rare

Acco. Roman Phoenicia, Ace Ptolemais. Trajan, 98-117 AD. AE (24 mm, 9.06 gr.) Head right/Tyche seated on rocks. Scarce

The city has been in continuous existence for more than 2,500 years and appeared on the tribute lists of Thutmos III, circa 1500 BC. Around 725 BC, Acco joined Sidon and Tyre in a revolt against Shalmaneser V. Greek historians refer to the city as Ake, meaning "cure." According to the Greek myth, Hercules found curative herbs here to heal his wounds. The name was changed to Antiochia Ptolemais shortly after the Alexander the Great conquest and then to Ptolemais. The city was captured by Alexander Janneus, Cleopatra VII of Egypt, and Tigranes II of Arminia. After the permanent division of the Roman Empire in AD 395, Acco belonged to the Byzantine Empire. The city fell to the Islamic forces under Saladin, and the crusaders recaptured it, and then it became the capital of the remnant of the kingdom of Jerusalem. History tells us that 80,000 crusaders died taking this city in a two-year siege from AD 1189–1191.

TYRE

Second Samuel 5:11 (NIV) says, "Now Hiram King of Tyre sent messengers to David along with cedar logs and carpenters and stone masons, and they built a palace for David."

Tyre. Roman Phoenicia, Tyre. 98-117 AD, Trajan. AR Tetradrachem (24 mm, 13.86 gr.) Head of Trajan, eagle/bust of Melkart-Herakles

Tyre. Roman Phoenicia, Tyre. 98-117 AD, Trajan. AR Tetradrachem (26 mm, 14.80 gr.) Head of Trajan, eagle/bust of Melkart-Herakles

Tyre. Roman Phoenicia, Tyre. 198-217 AD, Caracalla.
AE (31 mm, 23.57 gr.) Laureate bust/Astarte-Tyche
standing, Murex and Nike on each side. Very Rare

Tyre is located about fifty miles south of Beirut, Lebanon, and originally consisted of two distinct urban centers: one on an island and the other on the adjacent coast. Alexander the Great connected the island to the mainland during his siege of the city. Tyre was founded around 2750 BC, according to Herodotus, and it appeared on monuments as early as 1300 BC. The commerce of the ancient world was gathered into the warehouses of Tyre. Tyrian merchants were the first to navigate the Mediterranean waters, and they founded their colonies on the coasts and neighboring islands of the Aegean Sea, in Greece; on the northern coast of Africa, at Carthage; and other places in Sicily, Corsica, and Spain. In the time of King David (circa 1000 BC), the Israelites struck a friendly alliance between the kingdoms of Israel and Tyre, which was ruled by Hirami. The city of Tyre was famous for the production of a rare and expensive sort of purple dye that was produced from the murex shellfish, known as "Tyrian purple." This color was reserved for the use of royalty or at least nobility. The city was conquered by the Assyrians, Babyloninas, Persians, Greeks, the Romans, and later the crusaders but continued to maintain much of its commercial importance.

SIDON
Ezekiel 27:8 (NIV) says, "Men of Sidon and Arvad were your oarsmen, your skilled men, O Tyre were aboard as your seamen." Sidon is another Phoenician city located about twenty-five miles north of the city of Tyre in modern-day Lebanon.

Sidon has been inhabited since around 4000 BC. From this city, the colonizing progress of the Phoenicians found the city of Tyre. Sidon was just like Tyre, known for its craftsmen and particularly producing glass and purple dye. Both cities were in competition, claiming to be the Metropolis (mother city) of Phoenicia. Like any other Phoenician city-states, Sidon suffered from a succession of conquerors. Under the successors of Alexander the Great, the city enjoyed relative freedom and organized games and competitions in which the greatest athletes of the region participated.

Sidon. Greek Phoenicia, Sidon. 365-352 BC,
Abdashtarti. 1/16 shekel (10 mm, 0.68 gr.)
Dated RY 3 (362-361 BC). Phoenician pentekonter left
on waves/Persian king standing, fighting lion. Very Rare

Sidon. Roman Phoenicia, Sidon. 222-235 AD,
Severus Alexander. AE (18 mm, 3.91 gr.)
draped bust/Kadmos standing on prow.

Sidon fell under Roman domination, and the Romans built a theater and other major monuments in the city. During the Byzantine period, when the great earthquake of AD 551 destroyed most of the cities of Phoenicia, Beirut's school of law took refuge in Sidon. The town continued quietly for the next century until it was occupied by the Arabs in AD 636. Sidon was sacked in the First Crusade by King Baldwin of Jerusalem and became the center of the "Lordship of Sidon." It was destroyed many times by the crusaders and again by the Mongols. The remains of the original walls are still visible today.

BERYTUS

Berytus, called Beirut in modern-day, is the capital and largest city of modern Lebanon, with a population over 2.5 million. It serves as the country's largest and main seaport.

Berytus. Roman Phoenicia, Berytus. Augustus,
27 BC-14 AD. AE (26 mm, 8.78 gr.) bare head
right/pontiff driving yoke of oxen. Scarce

Berytus. Roman Phoenicia, Berytus. Augustus,
27 BC-14 AD. AE (21 mm, 10.09 gr.) Bare
head right/priest driving yoke of oxen. Scarce

Berytus. Roman Phoenicia, Berytus.
Claudius, 41-54 AD. AE (20 mm, 7.87 gr.)
Laureate head left/two aquilae. Scarce

Berytus. Roman Phoenicia, Berytus.
Hadrian, 117-138 AD. AE (19 mm, 5.78 gr.)
Laureate head/legionary aquilae in wreath.

The city is the focal point of the region's cultural life and is renowned for its press, theaters, and cultural activities. Some people called it "the Paris of the East." The city's history goes back more than 5,000 years. Excavations in the downtown area have unearthed layers of Phoenician, Hellenistic, Roman, Arab, and Ottoman remains. Berytus was not as prosperous as the other Phoenicians cities, like Sidon and Tyre. The city was destroyed in 140 BC by Diodotus Tryphon in his contest with Antiochus VII for the throne of the Seleucid monarchy. Berytus was soon rebuilt on a more regularized Hellenistic plan and was renamed Laodicea ad Phoenicia, in honor of Seleucid Laodice. Under the Romans, it was enriched by the dynasty of Herod the Great and was made a colony. It was passed to the Arabs in AD 635 and was in the hands of the crusaders in AD 1290. The crusaders built a cathedral and dedicated it to St. John the Baptist. It is now the principal mosque of this prosperous trade center.

BYBLUS

Ezekiel 27:9 (NIV) says, "Veteran craftsmen of Gebal were on board as shipwrights to caulk your seams, all the ship of the sea and their sailors came alongside to trade for your wares." The Phoenician city of Gebal was named Byblus by the Greeks. It is located on the coast of the Mediterranean of present-day Lebanon, about twenty-five miles north of Beirut. It is very attractive to archaeologists because of the successive layers of debris resulting from centuries of human habitation.

Byblos. Greek Phoenicia. 336-323 BC, Alexander
the Great. AR Tetradrachm (28 mm, 16.60 gr.)
Herakles wearing lion skin/Zeus seated. Rare

Byblos. Roman Phoenicia, Byblos. Caracalla,
198-217 AD. AR Tetradrachm (26 mm, 13.06 gr.)
draped bust/eagle, alter between legs. Rare

The first of the city was about 3,000 years ago, with the remains of well-built houses of uniform size. This was the period when the Phoenician civilization began to develop. Archaeological evidence at Byblus, dating back to around 1200 BC, shows existence of a Phoenician alphabetic script of twenty-two characters. The use of the alphabet was spread by Phoenician merchants through their maritime trade into parts of North Africa and Europe.

The city struck and made their own coins as early as around the time of Alexander the Great. Egyptian vessels traded with this city from the dawn of history. The port of Byblus shipped the famed cedars of Lebanon used by ancient monarchs in palace construction, which includes the temples of David and Solomon. Just like any Phoenician city, Byblus was invaded by the Assyrians, Persians,

Greeks, and Romans. In the Assyrian period, Sibittibaal of Byblus became tributary to Tiglath-Pileser III in 738 BC. In the Persian period (538–332 BC), Byblus was the fourth Phoenician vassal kingdom established by the Persians, with the first there being Sidon, Tyre, and Arvad. Hellenistic rule came with the arrival of Alexander the Great in the area in 332 BC. The city fell to the crusaders and eventually was taken by Saladin.

TRIPOLIS

Tripolis was another Phoenician city located about fifty miles north of Beirut, Lebanon.

Tripolis. Roman Phoenicia. 117-138 AD, Hadrian. AE (24 mm, 10.52 gr.) Dated CY 428 (117 AD). Laureate bust/ jugate draped bust of the Dioskouroi. Scarce

Tripolis. Roman Phoenicia. 117-138 AD, Hadrian. AE (25 mm, 11.84 gr.) Dated 117 AD. Laureate bust/Astarte, HKY(date) left. Scarce

Tripolis. Roman Phoenicia. 27 BC-14 AD, time of Augustus. AE (23 mm, 7.23 gr.) Conjoined Laureate heads of the Dioskouroi/Nike standing on prow. Scarce

In ancient times, it was the center of a Phoenician confederation, which included Tyre, Sidon, and Arvad. There is evidence of an early settlement in Tripolis that dates back as early as 1400 BC. In the ninth century BC, the Phoenicians established a trading station in Tripolis. Under the Hellenistic rule (the Greek), Tripolis was used a naval shipyard, and the city enjoyed a period of autonomy. The city came under the Roman rule around 64 BC, and that is when the city began to be prosperous. Tripolis is similar to Beirut in respect of fame, where both cities were not as famous as the rest of Phoenician cities. During the Crusades, the city became the capital of the county of Tripolis.

ARVAD

Ezekiel 27:11 (NIV) says, "Men of Arvad and Helech manned your walls on every side..." Arvad is an island off the coast of modern-day Syria.

Arvad. Greek Phoenicia, Arados. 348-339 BC, AR Stater.(21x18 mm, 10.41 gr.) Dated year 5 (343-342 BC). Baalarwad/Gally sailing. Rare

Arvad. Greek Phoenicia, Arados 138-44 BC, AR Tetradrachm. (28 mm, 15.26 gr.) Dated CY 168 (92/91 BC). Turreted head of Tyche Nike advancing. Scarce

Arvad. Greek Phoenicia, Arados. 120-119 BC, AR Drachm. (18 mm, 3.70 gr.) Bee, MP (date) /Stag, palm tree. Rare

Arvad. Greek Phoenicia, Arados. 62-61 BC, AR Tetradrachm. (28 mm, 15.3 gr.). Dated year 198 (62/61 BC). Turreted Bust of Tyche/ Nike walking left. Scarce

Arvad. Greek Phoenicia, Arados. 62-61 BC, AR Tetradrachm. (28 mm, 14.9 gr.). Dated year 198 (62/61 BC). Turreted Bust of Tyche/ Nike walking left. Scarce

Arvad. Greek Phoenicia, Arados. 61-60 BC, AR Tetradrachm. (29 mm, 15.3 gr.). Dated year 199 (61/60 BC). Turreted Bust of Tyche/ Nike walking left. Scarce

Arvad. Greek Phoenicia, Arados. 94-93 BC, AE (20 mm, 6.64 gr.) veiled bust of Astarte/humped bull.

It is the only island in Syria, called Arwad in modern-day, and is located about two miles off the shore of the city of Tartus on the Mediterranean Sea. The island was settled by the Phoenicians in about 2000 BC. Under Phoenician control, it became an independent kingdom called Arvad and has been cited as one of the first-known examples of a republic in the world in which the people, rather than a monarchy, are described as sovereign. The island was important as a base for commercial venture into the Orontes Valley.

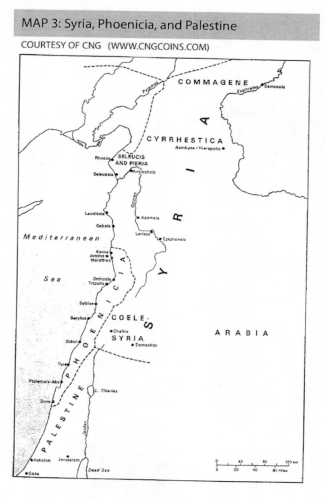

MAP 3: Syria, Phoenicia, and Palestine

COURTESY OF CNG (WWW.CNGCOINS.COM)

Arvad was developed as a trading city in early times, as were most of the Phoenician cities on this coast.

It had a powerful navy, and its ships are mentioned in the monuments of Egypt and Assyria. The city had its own local dynasty and coinage, and some of the names of the kings have been recovered. The city brought under its authority some of the neighboring cities on the mainland, such as the city of Marathus. Under the Persian rule, Arvad was allowed to unite in a confederation with Sidon and Tyre, with a common council at Tripolis. When Alexander the Great invaded Syria in 332 BC, Arvad submitted without a struggle under her king, Strato, who sent his navy to aid Alexander in the reduction of Tyre. As mentioned earlier, Arvad added Marathus to its kingdom.

MARATHUS

Marathus was known as Amrit in ancient times and was located near present-day Tartus in Syria. It was founded during the Ammorite period, around 2000 BC. During the time of Alexander the Great, the city was known as Marathus. It was one of the largest cities in the east.

Marathus. Greek Phoenicia, Marathus. 199-169 BC.
AE (20 mm, 7.4 gr.) draped bust of Ptolemy VI
as Hermes/marathus. Scarce

Marathus. Greek Phoenicia, Marathus.198-168 BC.
AE (19 mm, 6.08 gr.) draped bust of Ptolemy VI
as Hermes/Marathus. Scarce

Marathus. Greek Phoenicia, Marathus. 2nd century BC.
AE (17 mm, 3.63gr.) Turreted head
of Tyche/marathus. Scarce

It was in confederation with the city of Arvad and enjoyed the same economic prosperity. Coins were minted in this city for the Greek Empire around 200 BC.

HELIOPOLIS

Heliopolis is a town in the Bekaa Valley of Lebanon, built at an altitude of 3,850 feet, situated east of the Litani River. It is famous for its exquisitely detailed yet monumentally scaled temple ruins of the Roman period. The town was called Heliopolis during this period and was one of the largest sanctuaries in the empire. The city is located about fifty miles north of Damascus, Syria, fifty miles northeast of Beirut, Lebanon, and is called Baalbek in modern-day.

Heliopolis. Roman Coele-Syria. 193-211 AD,
Septimius Severus. AE (16 mm, 3.29 gr.)
draped bust/caduceus within wreath. Scarce.

Heliopolis. Roman Coele-Syria. 193-211 AD,
Septimius Severus. AE (20 mm, 7.19gr.)
Laureate bust/Legend, two eagles. Scarce.

Heliopolis. Roman Coele-Syria. 244-249 AD,
Philip I. AE (28 mm, 15.39 gr.) draped bust/
Tyche between two female figures. Rare.

The Phoenicians settled in Heliopolis as early as 2000 BC and built their first temple dedicated to the god Baal, the Sun god, from which the city got its name. The city retained its religious function during Roman time when the sanctuary of the Heliopolitan Jupiter-Baal was a pilgrimage site. Roman Emperor Trajan consulted the oracle there about whether he would return alive from his wars against the Parthians. The Romans had built a temple complex in Heliopolis consisting of three temples: Jupiter, Bacchus, and Venus, and on a nearby hill, they built a fourth temple dedicated to Mercury.

The city, then known as Heliopolis, was made a Roman colony in 15 BC, and a legion was stationed there. This city is absolutely amazing with its Corinthian columns, which can reach sixty to seventy feet high. The original number of Jupiter columns was fifty-four in total. The sloping terrain necessitated the building of retaining walls on the northwest and south of the complex. The lowest stone on these walls are estimated to weigh 300 to 400 tons each. These stones represent one of the largest cut stones from the ancient world.

Just like any east Mediterranean city, it was invaded and came under the Persians, Greeks, Romans, and Byzantine and Islamic rules. The city now stands near the mountain of Lebanon, where David and Solomon got most of their cedar to build the temple of Jerusalem. Baalbek is one of the very fascinating tourist spots in the Middle East.

It is widely believed that Phoenicia controlled the southern portion of Coele-Syria (Empty Syria) for a short period of time, where two very important cities were located. The two cities are Laodicia ad Libanum and Leucas ad Chrysoroas. The southern region of Coele-Syria is known today as the Beqaa and Ghouta valleys. These valleys were the major agricultural source and remain Lebanon's most important farming region today. The valleys are situated between Mount Lebanon to the west and Anti-Lebanon ranges to the east, and it is about seventy-five miles long and fifteen miles wide. Because of the importance of these valleys, many wars and conflicts took place in the area since the Israelites invaded Canaan in about 1500 BC. The largest conflict was between the Ptolemaic kingdom of Egypt and the Seleucid Empire of Syria, which lasted about 200 years in a series of six wars from 318–168 BC. These wars drained the strength of both parties involved and led to their eventual destruction at the hands of the Romans and the Parthians.

LAODICIA AD LIBANUM

Laodicia ad Libanum (Kedesh) is located on the Orontes River in present-day Syria, about fifteen miles southwest of Hims, thirty miles northeast of Baalbeck, and fifteen miles southeast of Tel Kalach. According to the Bible, the Israelites did evil in the eyes of the Lord again and again. So the Lord sold them into the hands of Jabin, king of Canaan.

Laodicea ad Libanum. Roman Coele- Syria. 193-217 AD,
Julia Domma. AE (21 mm, 5.54 gr.)
draped bust/veiled bust of Tyche. Scarce.

Laodicea ad Libanum. Roman. Coele- Syria 198-217 AD.
Caracalla, AE (23 mm, 8.76 gr.)
Laureate bust/Men standing, bridle horse. Rare

Since the Israelites had no leader then, Deborah, a prophetess, led Israel at that time, and all the Israelites came to her to decide their disputes. "She sent Barak son of Abinoam from Kedesh…" (Judges 4:6, NIV). The city of Kedesh was under the Hittites in 1300 BC. The famous battle of Kadesh was between the forces of the Egyptian kingdom, under Ramesses II, and the Hittite kingdom, under Muwatalli II, in 1274 BC. According to scholars, the battle was probably one of the largest ever fought in the area. Both armies were about 70,000 men and 5,000 to 6,000 chariots, and the casualties are still unknown. The site of Laodicia ad Libanum can still be seen roughly two miles southwest of Lake Homs, Syria.

LEUCAS AD CHRYSOROAS

Leucas ad Chrysoroas's location is still under debate; however, according to *Barrington Atlas of the Greek and Roman World,* as well as most scholars, the city was the site of modern Az-Zabadani in Syria. The town is located in the Ghouta Valley on the Barada River, about sixteen miles northwest of Damascus.

Leucas ad Chrysoroas. Roman Coele-Syria. 238-244 AD,
Gordian III. AE (21 mm, 5.90 gr.)
draped bust/Herakles holding club. Very Rare.

The Barada River descends through a steep, narrow gorge, named Rabwe, before it arrives near Damascus and splits into seven branches that supply water to the oasis of Ghouta. The ancient name for Barada River is Abana or Amanah, and the classic Greek name is Chrysorrhoas. The Barada River was mentioned in the Bible in the book of Kings when Naaman, the commander of the army of the king of Aram, developed leprosy. He went to the Prophet Elisha to cure him, and the prophet told him to go to the Jordan River and dip himself seven times, and then he would be cured from leprosy. But Naaman told the prophet Elisha, "Are not Abana and Pharpar, the rivers of Damascus, better than any of the water of Israel? Could not I wash in them and be cleansed? So he turned and went off in a rage" (2 Kings 5:12, NIV).

From Solomon to the Exile

King David and his son, Solomon, ruled over seventy years and made Israel an independent nation, which extended north to Aram, east to the Syrian Desert, south to Egypt, and west to the Great Sea. They combined all the twelve tribes of Israel into one land called the "United Kingdom of Israel."

After the death of Solomon, the Israelites did not remember all the promises of God, who had created them and established them in the land. As a result, they lost their unique identity as God's chosen people and army of loyal citizens of his emerging kingdom. They got too comfortable and attached themselves to Canaan's people's religious beliefs and gods and practiced Canaan's social life. God's kingship over the Israelites had been established by the covenant at Sinai and again by Moses on the plains of Moab and lastly by Joshua at Shechem. Israel had rejected the kingship of the Lord again and again, and they turned to the gods of Canaan to obtain the blessings of family and flocks, and they forgot God's law for daily living.

King Solomon's reign was full of forced labor, and he worshiped Milcom, the god of the Ammonites; Astarte, the goddess of the Sidonians; and Chemosh, the god of Moab, which provoked God's wrath. This and many resentments against Solomon's conduct caused the kingdom of Solomon to split into the northern kingdom (Israel) and the southern kingdom (Judah). According to biblical narrative, each kingdom claimed to be the rightful heir to God's covenant with the Israelites.

Solomon's kingdom became very weak and started to break away. The king of Damascus in Syria, Ammon, Moab in Transjordan, and the Philistines in the west became independent kingdoms. The great wealth of Solomon's kingdom came to an end by losing income from the trade routes, the way of the sea, and the Kings' Highway. The trading with Egypt, Sheba, and Africa diminished after Solomon's death.

The two kingdoms had many wars with each other, coups and assassinations being the rule in the northern kingdom of Israel. Both kingdoms were seriously weakened by religious quarrels at home and by decades of warfare with Syria and the kingdom of Transjordan.

Finally, Assyrian King Sargon II conquered the northern kingdom of Israel and took its capital, Samaria, in 721 BC. Two hundred years after king Solomon's death, the northern kingdom of Israel had come to an end. The Assyrians took tens of thousands of Israelites captive into exile in eastern Mesopotamia.

In 605 BC, Babylonian King Nebuchadnezzar defeated the Assyrians and their allies, Neco, at the battle of Carchemish, and in the following year, he advanced southward to the coastal plain of Philistia. The Assyrians were disappearing from history, killed, or absorbed by their conquerors. Nebuchadnezzar moved south and invaded both the northern and southern kingdoms of Israel and put a siege on Jerusalem, the capital of Judah. After a long period of siege, the Babylonians were finally successful in breaking the walls of Jerusalem, and they burned it without any mercy in 587 BC. The kingdom of Israel, some 400 years after David's kingship, was no more.

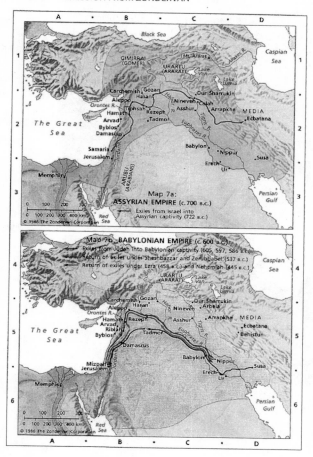

The inhabitants of Jerusalem were either slaughtered or carried off into captivity. In the meantime, the Jewish captives set out on the road to Babylon. Many of them were taken south into exile in Egypt. The Babylonians destroyed Jerusalem and looted King Solomon's temple of all the gold, silver, antiquity, and artifacts that the Jewish nation accumulated the previous 500 years. From the Bible's point of view, this act was the result of God's anger because of the neglect of covenant obligations to the Lord. The Lord warned the Jewish nation of this act many times in the past. Jerusalem lay in ruins, and Samaria was captured by the Babylonians. The Israelites lost the promised land that God gave their forefathers. The Jews were a scattered nation and were taken into exile in Egypt, Babylonia, and Assyrian lands.

During the time of the Babylonians, from the seventh century to the sixth century BC, coins were minted and circulated in Asia Minor in the provinces of Lydia and Ionia (modern-day western Turkey).

The coins minted at this time frame are considered to be the earliest coins on earth. The coins were made of electrum, an alloy of gold and silver that occurs naturally, but can also be fabricated. Electrum's obvious flaw is that its main composition, gold and silver, have significantly different values. Their relative worth depends on time and place, but gold usually is ten to fifteen times more valuable than silver, with the typical ratio being about thirteen. Since the gold content of electrum coins ranged from about 20 to 80 percent, their alloy greatly affected their color and value.

By around 550 BC, near the end of the archaic period, only a few mints were striking electrum. The large denomination electrum coins were struck for trade, and all of them were archaic in appearance. These coins usually bore no inscriptions, unlike most other classical period coins that identified the issuing authority and sometimes the magistrates of engravers.

Earliest coins on Earth. 650-600 BC, EL 1/48 stater.
(6 mm, 0.28 gr.) lion's head left/
quadripartite incuse square. Extremely Rare.

Earliest coins on Earth. 650-600 BC, EL 1/12 stater.
(6.5 mm, 1.12 gr.) lion's head right/
cross, pellets within incuse. Extremely Rare.

Earliest coins on Earth. Greek Troas 650-600 BC,
EL 1/24 stater.(6.5 mm, 0.59 gr Eagle standing left/
circular incuse. Extremely Rare.

Mysia. Greek Mysia, Kyzlkos. 500-475 BC, EL Hekte.
(8.5 mm, 2.37 gr.) dog walking left/
quadripartite incuse square. Extremely Rare.

Phokaia. Greek Phokaia. 477-388 BC, EL Hekte,
(10 mm, 2.5 gr.) head of Dionysos/
quadripartite incuse. Very Rare.

The transportation of the Israelite captives by the Assyrians in 721 BC and the Babylonians in 587 BC took different routes to arrive to their destinations. The Assyrians took their captives from Samaria north to Damascus, Aleppo, Haran, and then followed the old northern caravan route along the Tigris River to arrive to their capital, Nineveh. The Babylonians took their captives from Jerusalem north to Damascus, Aleppo, Haran, and then east through northern Syria along the Euphrates River to arrive to their capital, Babylon. This route was roughly the same when Abraham and his father moved from the city of Ur to Babylon, Haran, and later on to Aleppo, Damascus, and ultimately to Shechem. By the time of the exiles, 1,500 years later, many communities, towns, and even cities were built around the ancient routes along the Tigris and Euphrates rivers.

The Bible did not give detailed transportation routes of the Israelites from the promised land to Mesopotamia. Since archeologists found pottery and proof of human settlements in northern Syria and eastern Mesopotamia around the seventh century BC, it is widely believed that the Israelites stopped in many of these towns during their long journey of captivity. Those towns or cities (see map number two) that were located on or around the trade routes are: Cyrrhus, Hieropolis, and Doliche in northern Syria, and Zeugma, Edessa, Samosata, Rhesaena, Singara, Nisibis, Antiochia ad Euphratem, and Hatra in Mesopotamia. These towns are described below, along with their coinage.

CYRRHUS

Cyrrhus is located in northern Syria and on the western edge of Mesopotamia near the modern town of Kilis on the border between modern Syria and Turkey. The city played an important role as a base of the tenth legion Fretensis.

Cyrrhus. Roman Syria, Cyrrhestica. 98-117 AD
Trajan. AE (25 mm, 13.48 gr.) Laureate head/
legend in two lines. Scarce.

Cyrrhus. Roman Syria, Cyrrhestica. Philip I,
244-249 AD. AE (29 mm, 14.91 gr.)
Laureate head/Zeus in hexastyle temple. Scarce.

Cyrrhus. Roman Syria, Cyrrhestica. Philip Sr.
244-249 AD. AE (29.6 mm, 16.83 gr.)
Laureate head/Zeus in hexastyle temple. Scarce.

This legion was found in 41 BC by Julius Caesar, who needed to put an end to Sextus Pompey's occupation of Sicily, which put the grain supply of Rome into peril. The city of Cyrrhus prospered since the Seleucid kingdom occupied it in the third century BC. It was situated at the place where the road from Antioch to Zeugma or Hierapolis crossed the Sabun River. The city remained in Seleucid hands for almost 200 years but became part of Armenia during the reign of King Tigranes II (the Great). Finally, he was defeated by Roman General Pompey the Great, and the city of Cyrrhus was added to the Roman Empire.

HIEROPOLIS

Hieropolis is located about fifty miles northeast of the city of Aleppo in northern, modern-day Syria. It was the ancient holy city on top of the famous Pamukkale hot springs located in the general area. The city called Manbij in modern-day. The hot springs have been used as a spa since the second century BC, where people come to soothe their ailing.

Hieropolis. Roman Syria, cyrrhestica. 138-161 AD, Antoninus Pius. AE (22 mm, 9.2 gr.) Laureate head/legend in two lines. Scarce.

Hieropolis. Roman Syria, cyrrhestica. 138-161 AD, Antoninus Pius, AE (24 mm, 9.85 gr.) Laureate head/legend in two lines. Scarce.

However, it was customary to build a temple on the site of such a natural phenomenon. The Phrygians built a temple dedicated to Hieron around the first half of the third century BC. This temple was used by nearby towns, like Laodiceia ad Mare, around 225 BC

The city was named after the existing temple or possibly to honor Hiera, wife of Telephus, son of Heracles by Mysian princess Auge. The city began issuing bronze coins in the second century BC. These coins gave the name Hieropolis (town of the temple Hieron) and later changed to Hierapolis (holy city). Earthquakes destroyed the city during the reign of Emperor Tiberius and Nero in AD 17 and AD 60, respectively. The golden age of the city was under the reign of Septimus Severus. He rebuilt the city with Roman baths, gymnasiums, several temples, main streets, and fountains at the hot springs. Hieropolis was one of the most prominent cities in the field of the arts, philosophy, and trade in the Roman Empire and grew to about 100,000 inhabitants. The Israelites grew on their own congregation in Hieropolis, and it was estimated that the Jewish population in the region was as high as 50,000 in 62 BC. Philip the apostle spent the last years of his life there with his three daughters.

In AD 80, he was martyred by crucifixion and was buried there. His daughters remained active as prophetesses in the region, and the martyrium was built on the spot where the apostle was crucified. Many churches were later built in the city during the Byzantine Empire.

DOLICHE

Doliche was known by the ancient Greeks and Romans as Doliche and by the Arab, Seljuks, and Ottomans as Aintab and was officially named Gaziantep.

Doliche. Roman Commagene. 161-169 AD,
Marcus Aurelius and Lucius Verus.
AE (23 mm10.32 gr.) confronted heads of both/legend

Doliche is considered to be among the oldest continually inhabited cities in the world, its history reaching as far back as the Hittites. The city is located in southeast modern-day Turkey and about forty miles from the ancient caravan city of Carchemish, where one of the great battles in history took place. As described in the Bible, the Babylonians defeated the Assyrians, along with their Egyptian allies, in 605 BC. The Assyrians were no more after this battle. The city is known as the center of Pistachio cultivation in Turkey and is known for its extensive olive groves and vineyards. Most Christians in this city are Armenian Christians. There was a sizable Armenian population in the city before World War I, but after the Franco-Turkish war between 1919 and 1921, there were almost no Armenians left.

ZEUGMA

Zeugma is located about thirty miles north of the city of Doliche. The ancient city was originally occupied by Seleucus I Nicater, one of Alexander the Great's generals, in 300 BC. The city was conquered and ruled by the Roman Empire, and with this shift, the name of the city was changed to Zeugma, meaning "bridge passage" or "bridge of boats." Many boats anchored together to form a bridge over the Euphrates River. Zeugma became one of the attractions in the region due to its commercial potential, because the city was on the Silk Road connecting China to Antioch.

Recent excavations uncovered a Roman villa and magnificent mosaic pavements.

Zeugma. Roman Commagene. 218-222 AD,
Elagabalus. AE (34 mm, 16.33 gr.)
Laureate head/tetrastyle temple. Scarce.

Zeugma. Roman Commagene. 247-249 AD,
Philip II. AE (24 mm, 10.36 gr.)
Laureate head/tetrastyle temple. Scarce.

The mosaic, which adorned the villa's gallery, depicted the marriage of Dionysus, god of wine and grapes, to Ariadne. On the clay quarry area, a large Bronze Age cemetery was discovered and excavated. Nearly 8,000 pottery vessels were found in 320 graves going back to the early Bronze Age. Zeugma was fully destroyed by Sasanian King Shapur I. The invasion was so dramatic that Zeugma was not able to recover for many centuries. To make the situation even worse, a violent earthquake buried the city beneath rubble. Indeed, the city never regained the prosperity once achieved during the Greek and Roman times.

EDESSA

Edessa is located about thirty miles north of the city of Carrhae on the Syrian-Turkish border. The ancient city of Edessa was rediscovered by Seleucus I Nicator, and he made it a military colony in 303 BC.

Edessa. Roman Mesopotamia. 242-244 AD,
Gordian III. AE (24 mm, 6.4 gr.)
draped bust/draped bust of Abgar. Scarce.

Edessa. Roman Mesopotamia. 218-222 AD,
Elagabalus. AE (25 mm, 8.37 gr.)
radiate bust/Tyche seated on rocks. Scarce.

The city went through a series of invasions from the Greeks, Romans, Byzantines, and Kurds. Edessa became the capital of the kingdom of Edessa. This kingdom was established by Nabetaean, or northern Arab tribes, and lasted nearly 400 years under twenty-eight rulers who called themselves "king" on their coinage. Following its capture, and sacked by Trajan, the Romans even occupied Edessa from AD 116–118. From AD 212–214, the kingdom of Edessa became a Roman province. Roman Emperor Caracalla was assassinated in Edessa in AD 217 AD on his way to Carrhae. Byzantine Emperor Justin rebuilt the city and called it Justinopolis. This city was taken by the Sasanians and Persians but was lost to the Muslim army under Rashidun Calphate.

Christianity had spread vigorously within Edessa and its surroundings, and the royal house joined the church. According to legend first reported by Eusebius in the fourth century AD, King Abgar was converted to Christianity by Addai, who was one of the seventy-two disciples sent to him by "Judas, who is also called Thomas." Yet many sources confirm that Abgar embraced the Christian faith and made it the official religion of the kingdom. Edessa was the earliest center of Syriac-speaking Christians.

SAMOSATA

Samosata is located in northeast Mesopotamia, modern-day Turkey, about twenty-five miles north of Edessa. The city was the capital of the Hellenistic kingdom of Commagene, circa 323 BC, until it was surrendered to Rome in AD 72.

Samosata. Roman Syria, Commagene. 117-138 AD,
Hadrian. AE (19 mm, 5.67 gr.)
Laureate head/legend in four lines. Scarce.

Samosata. Roman Syria, Commagene. 138-161 AD,
Antoninua Pius. AE (23.7 mm, 10.02 gr.)
Laureate head/Tyche seated left, river god. Scarce.

Samosata.Roman Syria, Commagene. 193-211 AD,
Septimius Severus. AE (25 mm, 10.62 gr.)
Laureate head/two confronted busts of Tyche. Scarce.

Samosata. Roman Syria, Commagene. 244-249 AD,
Philip II. AE (31 mm, 15.90 gr.)
Laureate bust/Tyche seated left on rocks. Scarce.

Samosata.Roman Syria, Commagene. 244-249 AD,
Philip I. AE (35 mm, 20.22 gr.)
draped bust/Tyche seated left on rocks. Rare.

Samosata was the birthplace of Lucian (AD 120–192), a famous comic writer of antiquity, whose trips to the moon are sometimes called the first space novel, as well as eighty works that have survived to this day. Samosata was also the birthplace of "Paul of Samosata," the third leader of the Elkasites, an order of Essene Gnostics, who lived in the mid-third century AD. In the Christian martyrology, seven Christian martyrs were crucified in AD 297 in Samosata for refusing to perform a pagan worship in celebration of the victory of Roman Emperor Maximian over the Persians.

RHESAENA

Rhesaena appeared in many ancient literatures and was mentioned by many authors as an important town at the northern extremity of Mesopotamia near the sources of the Chaboras River (now Khabour) on the way from Carrhae to Nicephorium.

Rhesaena. Roman Mesopotamia. 249-251 AD,
Trajan Decius. AE (26 mm, 12.07 gr.)
radiate bust/Tyche standing beside altar. Rare.

The city is located approximately eighty miles from Nisibis and fifty miles east of Carrhae. Roman Emperor Gordian III fought the Persians in AD 243 around this city. The coins minted in this city showed it was a Roman colony from the time of Septimus Severus. In 393, the city was nearly destroyed by Tamerlane's troops.

NISIBIS

Nisibis (Al Qamishli) is located approximately seventy miles east of Rhesaena.

Nisibis. Roman Mesopotamia. 222-235 AD,
severus Alexander. AE (26 mm, 11.50 gr.)
radiate head/turreted bust of Tyche. Scarce.

Nisibis. Roman Mesopotamia. 244-249 AD,
Philip Sr. AE (25 mm, 8.68 gr.) radiate head/
city goddess, ram leaping, tetrastyle temple. Scarce.

Nisibis. Roman Mesopotamia. 244-249 AD,
Philip I. AE (26 mm, 10.49 gr.) Laureate head/
city goddess, ram leaping, tetrastyle temple. Scarce.

The city appeared in the Assyrian eponym list as the seat of an Assyrian provincial governor, named Shamash-Abua, as early as 852 BC. Nisibis is the ancient Mesopotamian city that Alexander the Great successors re-founded as Antiochia Mygdonia. Nisibis is located on the Silk Road, and from 149 BC to AD 14, the city was the residence of the kings of Armenia, and there, King Tigranes had his treasure houses. Nisibis was taken and retaken many times in ancient history by the Greek, Roman, Armenian, and Sasanian forces. Finally, it was acquired by the Roman Empire and became a Roman colony during the reign of Septimus Severus.

The first theological school of Nisibis, founded at the introduction of Christianity into the city, was closed when the province was ceded to the Persians. The school of Nisibis was above all the schools of theology. This school began to decline after the foundation of the school of Baghdad in AD 832.

SINGARA

Singara is located about sixty miles southeast of Nisibis in modern-day Iraq.

Singara. Roman Mesopotamia. 238-244 AD,
Gordian III. AE (29 mm, 12.72 gr.)
radiate head/Turreted bust of Tyche. Scarce.

The city was a strongly fortified post at the northern extremity of Mesopotamia, which, for a while, was occupied by the Romans as an advanced colony against the Persians. It was called "the city of Arabia" by Ptolemy in the third century BC.

Singara was first taken by the Romans during Trajan's eastern campaigns when General Lusius Quietus captured the city without a fight in the winter of AD 114. It was taken by the Persians, and the Romans took it back in AD 197 by Emperor Septimius Severus, who raised it to the status of a Roman colony, as attested by the legends found on some of the coins minted there during the reign of Gordian III.

HATRA

The ruins of ancient Hatra (Al Hadr) lie about fifty-five miles southwest of the city of Nineveh in Mesopotamia, modern-day Iraq. It is believed that the city was built by the Assyrians in the seventh century BC and was grown to a fortified city in the first century BC. The site of the city of Hatra is a gentle depression in the semi-desert land between the ancient rivers Tigris and Euphrates known as Al-Jazirah. The fortress of Hatra guarded the main caravan routes connecting Mesopotamia with Syria and Asia Minor.

Hatra. Roman Mesopotamia. 3rd cetury AD,
AE (26 mm, 11.12 gr.)
Radiate head of Shamash/large SC. Rare.

Hatra. Roman Mesopotamia. 2nd cetury AD,
AE (25 mm, 13.17 gr.)
Radiate head of Shamash/large SC. Rare.

Recent excavations resulted in the discovery of at least twelve temples built from limestone and gypsum and a mixture of Assyrian, Hellenistic, Parthian, and Roman styles. The temple complex was dedicated to several gods, the chief of which was the sun god, Shamash. Sculptures of Apollo, Poseidon, Eros, Hermes, Tyche (the guardian goddess of Hatra), and Fortuna have been discovered in Hatra. In AD 240, the Sasanids, under Shapur I, captured the city, and it was later occupied by the Arabs that dominated upper Mesopotamia. At some point, the city was finally destroyed and fell into ruins.

ANTIOCHIA AD EUPHRATEM

Antiochia ad Euphratem was located in northern Syria in the Commagene province.

Antiochia ad Euphratem. Roman Syria, Commegene.
161-180 AD, Marcus Aurelius. AE (23 mm, 11.62 gr.)
draped bust/helmeted Athena. Rare

The city was first mentioned in Assyrian texts as an ally of Assyria but eventually was annexed as a province in 708 BC under Sargon II. The Persian Empire then conquered Commagene in the sixth century BC, and Alexander the Great conquered the whole territory in the fourth century BC. After the break up of Alexander's empire, Commagene became a state and a province in the Greco-Syrian Seleucid Empire.

From the Exile to the Greek Empire

After the Babylonians' victory over Judah in 587 BC, Judah suffered many deportations at the hand of Nebuchadnezzar. The Babylonians killed a number of the prominent political, military, and religious figures and subsequently deported to Babylonia most of the remaining leaders, along with their families. Among the important figures deported to Babylon were Daniel, King Jehoiachin, Ezekiel, and King Zedekiah.

During the exile, the Jews were allowed to live together in communities, and they farmed, built houses, and engaged in other useful work. Jeremiah instructed the exiles in Babylonia to take the best of the situations. He encouraged them to take wives and have families, multiply there, and to not decrease in numbers. He assured the Jewish nation in Babylonia that the exile was the punishment God had been threatening the Israelites with for centuries, but nonetheless, the exiles should maintain hope for the coming day of redemption.

The Bible tells us that while the Jews were in exile in Babylon, King Nebuchadnezzar told his court officials to bring in some of the Israelites from royal families and nobility to serve in his palace. They brought four men from Judah, Daniel, Hananiah, Mishael, and Azariah. God gave Daniel the wisdom to understand visions and all kinds of dreams. Daniel became well known in the palace, and Nebuchadnezzar made him the official dream interpreter for the king and where all wise men and astrologers could not reveal the mysteries of dreams.

The Bible tells us (in Daniel, chapter 2) that king Nebuchadnezzar had a dream of a large dazzling statue standing before him. The statue was made of a pure-gold head, silver chest and arms, bronze belly and thighs, iron legs, and feet made of iron and clay. Also, Daniel had a vision of four beasts coming up out of the sea, as mentioned in chapter 7:

> The first was like a lion, and it had the wings of an eagle. I watched until its wings were torn off and it was lifted from the ground so that it stood on two feet like a man, and the heart of a man was given to it. And there before me was a second beast, which looked like a bear. It was raised up on one of its sides, and it had three ribs in its mouth between its teeth, it was told, get up and eat your fill of flesh. After that, I looked and there before me was another beast, one that looked like a leopard, and on its back it had four wings like those of a bird. This beast had four heads, and it was given authority to rule. After that in my vision at night I looked, and there before me was a fourth beast, terrifying and frightening and very powerful. It had large iron teeth, it crushed and devoured its victims and trampled underfoot whatever was left. It was different from all the former beasts, and it had ten horns.
>
> Daniel 7:4–7 (NIV)

It is widely believed by biblical scholars and historians that in Nebuchadnezzar's dream of the dazzling statue, the gold head represents the Babylonian Empire, the silver chest and arms represent the Persian Empire established by Cyrus the Great, the bronze belly and thighs represent the Greek Empire established by Alexander the Great, and the iron legs and feet represent the Roman Empire.

As mentioned in the biblical narrative explained by scholars, as well as mentioned in Daniel, chapter 8, the interpretation of Daniel's vision is as follows: the lion with an eagle's wings is a cherub, symbolizing the Babylonian Empire, where they took the lion as their symbol. The bear raised up on one of its sides refers to the superior status of the Persians in the Medo-Persian federation. The three ribs may represent the three principal conquests: Lydia (546 BC), Babylon (539 BC) and Egypt (525 BC). The leopard with four wings represents the speedy conquest of Alexander the Great, and the four heads correspond to the four main divisions into which his empire fell after his unexpected death in 323 BC: Macedon and Greece under Antipater and Cassander, Thrace and Asia Minor under Lysimachus, Syria under Seleucus I, and Palestine and Egypt under Ptolemy I. The fourth unnamed terrifying and frightening beast—with its irresistible power, surpassing all its predecessors—points to the Roman Empire, while the ten horns correspond to the later confederation of states occupying the territory formerly controlled by the Roman Empire.

USED BY PERMISSION FROM ZONDERVAN

Daniel, along with biblical scholars, historians, and archeologists, were not far off at all from the truth. In 553 BC, King Cyrus II (559–523 BC), also known as Cyrus the Great, fought the Meds and defeated them. It is widely believed that King Cyrus was the descendant of a legendary figure named Achaemenes. Later, the dynasty was called the Archaemenid dynasty. He allowed religious freedom and respected the native customs of those he occupied.

King Cyrus mobilized his forces and destroyed the Babylonian army in a bloody battle at Opis on the Tigris River in 539 BC. The mighty Babylonian Empire was no more.

King Cyrus commanded his invading army to respect the cities' inhabitants and their properties. An anonymous Jewish prophet in exile saw Cyrus as the anointed one sent to redeem God's chosen people. As the Bible tells us: "Who says of Cyrus, he is my shepherd and will accomplish all that I please, he will say to Jerusalem, let it be rebuilt and of the temple, let its foundation be laid" (Isaiah 44:28, NIV). This prophecy is fulfilled when King Cyrus abandoned the Assyrian and Babylonian rules of deportation of conquered peoples for a program of restoration.

Persian Empire. Greek Lydia, time of kroisos, 561-546 BC. AR half stater (16x12 mm, 5.23 gr. confronted foreparts of roaring lion and a bull/ double incuse punch. Very Rare.

Persian Empire. Time of Darius I to Xerxes I circa 485 BC. AR Siglos (15 mm, 5.52 gr.) Persian king kneeling/incuse punch. Scarce.

Persian Empire. Time of Artaxerxes to Darius III, 450-330 BC. AR Siglos (13 mm, 5.47 gr.) Persian king kneeling/incuse punch. Scarce.

Persian Empire. Time of Artaxerxes to Darius III, 450-330 BC. AR Siglos (13 mm, 5.47 gr.) Persian king kneeling/incuse punch. Scarce.

Persian Empire. Time of Artaxerxes to Darius III, 450-330 BC. AR Siglos (15 mm, 5.50 gr.) Persian king kneeling/incuse punch. Scarce.

In 538 BC, King Cyrus issued an edict allowing Jews to return to Judah and rebuild the temple of Jerusalem, as mentioned twice in the book of Ezra, from his royal treasury. Also, he commanded that all the holy objects taken from the temple by Nebuchadnezzar were to be returned. The return of the Jews to Jerusalem was over three different periods. It began in 538 BC under king Cyrus, and then in 458 BC under Ezra, and the third group returned under Nehemiah in 432 BC. The temple continued to be built under new Persian King Darius I (522–486 BC), son of Cyrus, and his son after him, Xerxes I (486–465 BC). After the death of Xerxes I in Susa, his son, Artaxerxes I (465–425 BC), the ruling Persian monarch, authorized Ezra to go to Jerusalem and also permitted him to return any temple treasures still held by the Babylonians. Ezra came to Jerusalem, bringing back the covenant law, one of the most significant events in the history of Judaism.

SUSA

Susa is one of the oldest cities in the world. Scholars believe it could have been founded around 4200 BC. Evidence of painted pottery suggested that civilization in Susa is dated to 5000 BC. Susa was the capital of the Elamite Empire and later the Persian Empire.

Susa. Greek kings of Syria, Seleukos I Nikator,
312-281 BC. AR Tetradrachm (25 mm, 17.11 gr.)
struck in the name of Alexander the Great.
Head of Herakles wearing lion skin/Zeus seated. Scarce.

Susa was mentioned in the Hebrew Bible. Both Daniel and Nehemiah lived in Susa during the Babylonian captivity of Judah in the sixth century BC. Also, an orphan girl named Esther was in exile after her father and mother died. Esther 1:2 (NIV) says, "At the time King Xerxes reigned from his royal throne in the citadel of Susa." She was very beautiful in form and features. Esther 2:17 (NIV) says, "Now the King was attracted to Esther more than to any of other women, and she won his favor and approval more than any of the other virgins. So he set a royal crown on her head and made her queen instead of vashti." Esther became the queen of Persia in Susa, and later, she saved all the Jews in the exile from genocide. The Code of Hammurabi, one of the greatest ancient systems of law, was also found in Susa. Hammurabi ruled around 1700 BC.

The Assyrians leveled the city during a war in 647 BC. The city was rebuilt and was conquered again by Persian King Cyrus the Great in 538 BC, and he made it his capital. The city of Susa is famous for having the winged sphinx in the palace of Darius, son of Cyrus. The city lost some of its importance when Alexander the Great conquered it in 331 BC and destroyed the first Persian Empire. After Alexander, Susa fell to the Seleucid Empire and was renamed Seleukia. Parthia gained its independence from the Seleucid Empire, and Susa became its capital again, and later, the Sasanians made the city their capital after they became independent. Roman Emperor Trajan captured Susa in AD 116, but he had to withdraw due to revolts to his rear. Some legends mentioned that Alexander the Great, his generals, and thousands of his soldiers took Persian brides in a ceremony, which symbolized the marriage of Greece and Asia.

PART II
THE TIME BETWEEN
THE TESTAMENTS

Finally, Ezra and Nehemiah finished rebuilding the temple, and the community in Judah was safe for the moment, and Judaism had the law, the great monument by which Israelites maintained themselves for the last 1,100 years. With the reforms of these two men in the second half of the fifth century BC (432 BC), the historical narrative of the Old Testament came to an end. We know almost nothing from the Bible about the Israelites and Jewish history until shortly before the outbreak of the Maccabean revolt in the second century BC. However, with the rise and fall of new empires—especially those of Greece and Rome—the land bridge between Asia and Africa continued to be the battleground of the mighty.

The Greek Empire

As mentioned earlier, the scholars identified the four beasts in Daniel's vision. The lion represents the Babylonians, the bear refers to the Persians, the leopard refers to the Greeks, and the terrifying unnamed points to the Romans. Almost half of Daniel's vision has been fulfilled up to this point: the Babylonians defeated the Assyrians and the Persians wiped out the Babylonians. To our surprise, the NIV Bible did not mention very much, if any, about the Greek Empire. However, many Bibles mention the Greek Empire in detail. An empire that lasted more than 300 years who gave a facelift to the entire civilized world and helped shape the world we live in today. An empire cannot be ignored, especially from the numismatic point of view, where the most fascinating ancient coins ever minted in the world were produced during the Greek Empire period. In the following pages, I would like to discuss briefly what happened to the ancient world and the Israelites during the time between the Testaments. Also present, the third beast of Daniel's vision and its four wings—the Greek Empire.

Greece was never a single nation but was a series of states and was often in wars. The Greeks existed from about 8000–30 BC when the Ptolemaic Egypt (the last major Hellenistic kingdom) came under Roman rule. This will be discussed in little more detail later on in the book. The Greeks went through four periods during their ancient history: (1) The Dark Age, which most historians date from 1050–750 BC, where the Dorians had settled much of the Peloponnese, Crete, and southwest Asia Minor. (2) The Archaic period, from 750–479 BC, when the Persian invasions ended and the cities of Chalcis and Euboea emerged as the leading settlements in Greece. From 800 BC, the Greeks began to work on their ambitions by colonizing many parts of Europe and Asia Minor. (3) The Classical period, from 479–336 BC. This represents the period from the end of the Persian invasions to the accession of Alexander the Great. From 479 BC, Athens rose in power and replaced Sparta as leader of the Greeks. (4) The Hellenistic period, from 336–30 BC. This represents the period from the accession of Alexander the Great in 336 BC to the final conquest of the Greek world by Rome in 30 BC. During this time, there was an enormous expansion in Greek territory as far as India and many monarchies were established. Also, during this period, many Greek cities were found, and a shift of the culture centered to Alexandria in Egypt. The Greeks always had proud deep-cultured roots. They considered themselves leaders of philosophy, literature, music, mathematics, and science. The best-known school at the time was the school at Athens, such as Plato's Academy, founded in 385 BC, and Aristotle's Academy founded in 335 BC. Alexandria in Egypt, founded during Alexander the Great's reign, became the center of culture with a university, an astronomical observatory, a botanical garden, and, above all, a magnificent library containing more than 400,000 volumes and texts. It was considered to be the greatest center of learning in the ancient world.

Early civilizations undertook trade by barter or exchange based on units of value, such as weighed silver. As mentioned in the Bible, Abraham weighed thirty shekels of silver to buy the cave for him and his family's burial ground. Coins were a development from the use of objects and were minted with a regulated weight. The first coins were minted in Lydia from the mid-seventh century BC and were flat, pebble-shaped staters or fractions of electrum (gold and silver alloy). The first coins had a grooved surface on one side and an incuse punch mark on the other, and later coins were of pure gold and pure silver. They were struck by hand using two dies or a die and punch. Aegina was probably the first Greek state to mint coins in the early sixth century BC with the badge of a sea turtle (the city's emblem) on one side and an incuse punch mark on the other.

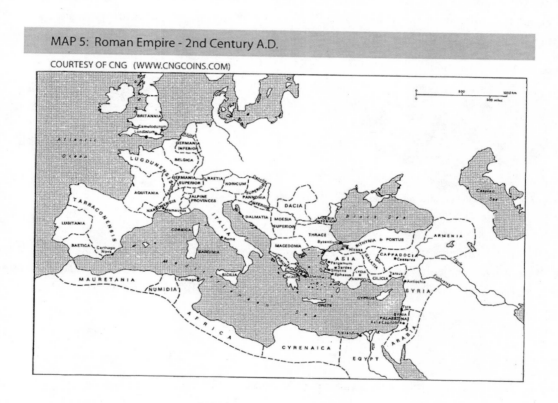

MAP 5: Roman Empire - 2nd Century A.D.

COURTESY OF CNG (WWW.CNGCOINS.COM)

This was followed by coins from Athens, where the first Athenian coins used a diverse series of Heraldic devices relating to Athena. In the late sixth century BC, Athens minted new double-sided coins termed "owls." On the obverse was the helmeted head of Athena, and on the reverse was the sacred owl of Athena, the city's name, and an olive branch. Minting spread rapidly throughout the Greek world, including the city-states of Italy, Thrace, Aeolis, Paeonia, Thessaly, Phokis, and many other places. Also, the Greek-minted coins were in some of their colonies in Asia Minor, such as Mysia, Lycia, Pisidia, Pamphylia, and Cilicia, and along east Mediterranean coast. The following are some coins representing these city-states, and one can easily notice the variation of changes in coin design over the centuries. The Greek coins described in the following pages represent only a fraction (a very, very small fraction) of the coins minted by the Greeks. However, the majority of the Greek coins are beyond the scope of this book.

AIGINA

Aigina (Aegina) is one of the Greek islands in the Saronic Gulf, about sixteen miles southwest of Athens. The mother of Aeacus was born on and ruled the island during the ancient times and was a rival to Athens, the great sea power of the sea. The island is roughly about nine miles from east to west and about ten miles from north to south. The history of Aigina goes back to its earliest inhabitants coming from Asia Minor, circa 2000 BC.

Aegina. Greek Attica. 550-525 BC, AR Stater
(19 mm, 12.1 gr.) collard sea turtle/
rough incuse square. Scarce.

Aegina. Greek Attica. 480-457 BC. AR Stater
(18 mm, 12.17 gr.) collard sea turtle/
incuse skew pattern. Scarce.

It was the Aeginetes who, within thirty to forty years of the invention of coinage by the Lydians (650 BC), introduced coinage to the Western world. Aigina was probably the first place to be trading coins around European Greece. Their coins featured a smooth-shelled turtle with a single row of dots on its back.

ATTICA

Attica (Athens) refers to the eastern-most part of central Greece. Its original name was possibly Acte. It is an arid and hilly region divided by four mountain ranges into three interconnecting plains. The area's natural resources include its famous marbles and lead and silver from Laurium. Laurium formed one of the largest mining districts in the Greek world, particularly for silver from the ore Galena. Athens became the main city in Attica, both in terms of politics and religion. "So when we could stand it no longer, we thought it best to be left by ourselves in Athens" (1 Thessalonians 3:1, NIV).

Athens struck coins with Athenian silver bearing an owl and symbols of Athena, goddess of wisdom. The archaic coin of the head of Athena (obverse) and owl (reverse) had changed a little in design and size over 200 years and lasted to the Roman period. The coins of Athena were used in trading around the Mediterranean coast for almost 250 years.

Attica. Greek Attica. AR Tetradrachm, 449-413 BC.
(25 mm, 16.84 gr.) helmeted head of
Athena, monogram/owl standing right.

Attica. Greek Attica. AR Tetradrachm, 339-350 BC.
(21 mm, 16.85 gr.) helmeted head
of Athena/owl standing right.

Attica. Greek Attica. AR Tetradrachm, 393-300 BC.
(24 mm, 17.1 gr.) helmeted head of Athena,
monogram/owl standing right.

Attica. Greek Attica. AR Tetradrachm, 393-300 BC.
(24 mm, 16.2 gr.) helmeted head of Athena/
owl standing right.

Attica. Greek Attica. AR Tetradrachm, 137-136 BC.
(28 mm, 17.5 gr.) helmeted head of Athena/
owl standing right on amphora.

THRACE

Thrace was originally the area in the northern Balkans as far as the Danube River.

It was later regarded as the region of southeastern modern Bulgaria and European Turkey. The inhabitants were Indo-Europeans but not Greek in origin. From the eighth century BC, the Aegean coastal areas were extensively colonized by the Greeks forming independent city-states, but the interior was untouched. In 513 BC, a large part of Thrace became a Persian satrapy until Xerxes retreated in 480 BC. In 342 BC, Philip II of Macedonia took over Thrace and established Greek and Macedonian colonies. Lysimachus, a successor of Alexander the Great, re-conquered the country in 308 BC, and later, the Gauls invaded Thrace in 297 BC. Finally, Thrace became a Roman province in AD 48.

Thrace. Greek Thrace, Maroneia. 398-385 BC,
AR Tetrobol (14 mm, 2.75 gr.)
forepart of horse/grape bunch and vine.

Thrace. Greek Thrace, Maroneia. 365-348 BC,
AR Tetrobol. (16 mm, 2.48 gr.) forepart of
horse/grape cluster within dotted square.

Thrace. Greek Thrace, Chersonesos. 386-338 BC,
AR Hemidrachm. (14 mm, 2.50 gr.) forepart of
lion/quadripartite incuse, pellet, grape bunch

Thrace. Greek Thrace, Maroneia. 189-49 BC,
AR Tetradrachm. (33 mm, 15.81 gr.)
head of young Dionysos/Dionysos standing.

Thrace. Greek Thrace, Apollonia pontica. 4th
century BC, AR Drachm. (15 mm, 2.53 gr.)
facing gorgonian/upright anchor.

AEOLIS

Aeolis was an area that comprised the west and northwestern region of Asia Minor, mostly along the coast, and also several offshore islands (particularly Lesbos), where the Aeolian Greek city-states were located.

Aeolis incorporated the southern parts of Mysia, which bounded it to the north, Ionia to the south, and Lydia to the east. In early times, by the eighth century BC, the Aeolians' twelve most important cities were independent, and they formed a league. The most celebrated of the cities was Smyrna (modern Izmir, Turkey), but in about 700 BC, Smyrna became part of an Ionian confederacy. In 133 BC, Aeolis was made part of the Roman province of Asia Minor.

Aeolis. Greek Aeolis, Myrina. Circa 165 BC,
AR Teteradrachm. (35 mm, 16.75 gr.)
Grynion/Apollo Grynion standing. Scarce.

PAEONIA

In the time of classical Greece, Paionia originally included the whole Axius River Valley and the surrounding area in what is now the northern part of the Greek region of Macedonia, most of the republic of Macedonia, and a small part of western Bulgaria.

Paeonia. Greek kings of Paeonia, Patraos. 335-315 BC,
AR Tetradrachm. (24 mm, 12.64 gr.)
head of Apollo/horseman riding down foe.

Paeonia. Greek kings of Paeonia, Patraos. 335-315 BC,
AR Tetradrachm. (25 mm, 12.36 gr.)
head of Apollo/horseman riding down foe.

The Paionians seem to have been Thracian tribes, though they were considered to be of mixed Thraco-Illyrian origin, and the ancient writer, Herodotus, even compared them to the Thracians as a rude and barbaric people. The Paionians are sometimes regarded as ancestors of the Phrygians of Asia Minor from Europe.

In 180 BC, the Gallic invaders under Brennus ravaged the land of the Paionians who, being hard pressed by the Dardani, had no alternative but to join the Macedonians. In 146 BC, the Roman legions ended the history of Macedon, and Paionia formed the third district of the Roman province of Macedonia.

PHOKIS

Phokis is a territory in central Greece that was organized as a confederation of small towns.

Phokis. Greek Phokis, central Greece. 480-460 BC,
AR Triobol. (13 mm, 2.4 gr.)
head of Artemis/bull head. Scarce.

In the Persian wars, Phokis was forced to take the side of the Persians but later fought against them at the battle of Plataea. In 356 BC, Phokis seized the temple at Delphi, leading to the outbreak of the Third Sacred War. Philip II of Macedonia defeated Phokis, which was surrendered in 346 BC and considerably weakened. In 196 BC, it belonged to the Aetolian confederacy, and after its dissolution by the Romans in 189 BC, they formed a Phocian confederacy that lasted into the Roman period.

THESSALY

Thessaly is a region of northern Greece south of Macedonia, east of Epirus, and bordering the Aegean Sea.

Thessaly. Greek Thessaly, Perrhaiboi. 470-400 BC,
AR Obol. (12 mm, 0.84 gr.) horse/Athena. Scarce.

Thessaly. Greek Theaasly, Larissa. 460-440 BC,
AR Hemidrachm (15 mm, 2.93 gr.)
forepart of horse/youth restraining forepart of bull.

Thessaly. Greek Thessaly, Larissa. 460-440
BC, AR Hemidrachm. (15 mm, 2.87 gr.)
forepart of horse/youth restraining forepart of bull.

Thessaly. Greek Thessaly, Larissa. 356-342 BC,
AR Drachm. (20 mm, 5.20 gr.)
head of Nymph Larissa/horse grazing.

From the seventh century BC, there was a Thessalian confederacy under an elected military leader. During the sixth century BC, Thessaly became the major power in northern Greece. During the fifth century BC, a powerful unified state was created by the rulers of the city-state of Pherae. However, Thessaly was defeated by Philip II of Macedonia in 352 BC. In 196 BC, the Romans created a new Thessalian confederacy detached from Macedonia and later becoming part of the Roman province of Macedonia.

LUCANIA, CALABRIA, AND BRUTTIUM
These three districts comprised the entire southern part of Italy.

Lucania. Greek Lucania, Thourioi. 443-425 BC, AR Nomos. (20 mm, 7.8 gr.) helmeted head of Athena/bull. Scarce.

Lucania. Greek Lucania, Thourioi. Circa 380 BC, AR Nomos. (19 mm, 7.76 gr.) helmeted head of Athena/bull. Scarce.

Lucania. Greek Lucania, Velia. 300-280 BC, AR Nomos. (20 mm, 7.21 gr.) helmeted head of Athena/lion. Scarce.

Bruttium. Greek Bruttium, Kroton. 420 340 BC, AR Nomos. (22 mm, 7.6 gr.) eagle with spread wings/tripod. Scarce.

Calabria. Greek Calabria, Tarentom. 380-345 BC, AR Nomos. (20 mm, 7.7gr.) naked horsman/ Taras seated on dolphin. Scarce.

The district of Lucania was named for the Lucanias, who conquered the area near the middle of the fifth century BC. The Lucanians gradually conquered the whole country (with the exception of the Greek towns on the coast) from the border of Campania to the southern extremity of Italy.

Subsequently, the inhabitants of the peninsula, now known as Calabria, broke into insurrection and, under the name of Bruttians (from Bruttium), established their independence, after which the Lucanians became confined within the limits already described. They were engaged in many hostilities from their neighbors, mainly Tarentum, and they had the first Punic War in 281 BC. All three territories were invaded by Hannibal's army in 216 BC. These three districts never recovered from these disasters, and under the Roman government, the districts fell into decay. For administrating purposes under the Roman Empire, Lucania was united with Bruttium.

MYSIA

Acts 16:7 (NIV) says, "When they came to the border of Mysia, they tried to enter Bithynia, but the spirit of Jesus would not allow them to."

Mysia. Greek Mysia, Lampsako. 390-330 BC, AR Trihemibol. (11.5 mm, 1.96 gr.) janiform male and female/quadripartite incuse. Rare.

Mysia. Greek Mysia, Parion. 350-300 BC, AR Hemidrachm. (14 mm, 2.4 gr.) Gorgoneion/bull.

Mysia was a district in northwest Asia Minor, with Lydia to the south, Phrygia to the east, and Propontis to the north. The road to the west was sometimes regarded as part of its territory. It came under the control of King Croesus of Lydia and then fell to the Persians. It was taken by Alexander the Great and became part of the Seleucid Empire. When Antiochus III was defeated by the Romans in 189 BC, Mysia was incorporated with the Roman kingdom of Pergamum.

PISIDIA

Acts 14:24 (NIV) says, "After going through Pisidia, they came into Pamphylia." The area of Pisidia has been inhabited since the Paleolithic Age with some settlements known from historical times ranging in age from 7000–2000 BC. The ancestors of the classical Pisidians were likely present in the region before the fourteenth century BC. Herodotus mentioned the Pisidic people in the text where they were called Lakuna, and this was the name given to Pisidic tribes that occupied a little mountainous region north of the Antalya Bay.

Pisidia. Greek Pisidia, Selge. 300-190 BC, AR Stater.
(25 mm, 7.4 gr.) two wrestlers/slinger. Scarce.

Pisidians are known to be among the nations that helped the Persians in their war against the Greeks. After Alexander the Great died, the region became part of the territories of Lysimachus of Thrace. The cities of Pisidia were among the last in western Anatolia to fully adopt Greek culture and to coin their own money. The Pisidians cast their lot with Pirate-dominated Cilicia and Pamphylia until Roman rule was restored in 102 BC.

LYCIA

Ancient Egyptian records describe the Lycians as allies of the Hittites. Lycia may have been a member state of the Assuwa league, circa 1250 BC. According to Herodotus, Lycia was named after Lycus, the son of Pandion II of Athens. The region was never unified into a single territory in antiquity but remained a tight-knit confederation of fiercely independent city-states. The Lycians fell under Persian domination, and by 412 BC, Lycia is documented as fighting on the winning side of Persia.

Lycia. Greek Lycia, Dynasty of Lycia. 500-470 BC,
AR Stater. (17 mm, 9.28 gr.)
Pegasos flying/roaring lion's head. Rare.

After the death of Alexander the Great, Lycia became part of the Ptolemaic and then the Seleucid empires. Antiochus III defeated the region in 197 BC, but the territory was granted to Rhodes by Rome after his defeat at the battle of Magnesia in 189 BC. In AD 43, Roman Emperor Claudius annexed it to the Roman Empire and united it with Pamphylia as a Roman province.

ACHAEA

Act 18:12 (NIV) says, "While Gallio was proconsul of Achaia, the Jews made a united attack on Paul and brought him into court." The ancient province of Achaea (Achaia) is located on the northern end of the Peloponnesos on the Gulf of Corinth.

Achaia. Greek Achaia, Achaian League. 188-180 BC, AR Hemidrachm. (13 mm, 2.32 gr.) Laureate head of Zeus/monogram across field. Scarce.

Achaia. Greek Achaia, Patari. Circa 31 BC, AR Hemidrachm. (16 mm, 2.3 gr.) Zeus/legend.

Achaia. Greek Achaia, Patrae. Augustus, 29 BC-14 AD. AE (25 mm, 8.4 gr.) radiate head/ togate male, two yoked oxen. Scarce.

According to the Hittite texts and Greek writer Homer, the Achaeans were driven to this region by the Dorian invaders of the Peloponnese in the thirteenth century BC. It was conquered and incorporated into the Roman Empire in 146 BC. Roman Emperor Augustus made Achaea a senatorial province in 29 BC. Augustus did this because Achaea was geographically closer to Rome than other provinces. That gives political advantage and superior status in order to maintain a political equilibrium within the Roman Empire. Achaea fell to the Ottoman Empire in the mid-fifteenth century AD, was later invaded by the Venetians in the seventeenth century AD, and later was invaded by the Ottomans again.

PAMPHYLIA

Acts 13:13 (NIV) says, "From Paphos, Paul and his companions sailed to Perga in Pamphylia, where John left them to return to Jerusalem." Pamphylia is the region in the southern portion of Asia Minor, between Lycia and Cilicia, extending from the Mediterranean Sea to the Taurus Mountains.

Pamphylia. Greek pamphylia, Aspendos. 380-330 BC,
AR Stater. (22 mm, 10.76 gr.)
Two wrestlers/slinger. Scarce.

Pamphylia. Greek Pamphylia, Aspendos. 370-325 BC,
AR Stater. (25 mm, 11.0 gr.)
Two wrestlers/slinger. Scarce.

There was Greek colonization along the coast, but the area came under the control of Lydia and then Persia until its surrender to Alexander the Great in 333 BC. Subsequently, it became part of the Ptolemaic and then the Seleucid empires. Antiochus III ceded the region to Rome in 189 BC.

BITHYNIA

The ancient province of Bithynia is located on the fertile shores of the Black Sea in the north and the Sea of Marmara in the west in Asia Minor (modern-day Turkey). The city of Nicaea is located in Bithynia, and it is noted for being the birthplace of the Nicene Creed.

Bithynia. Greek Bithynia, kios. 350-300 BC,
AR hemidrachm. (14 mm, 2.5 gr.) Apollo/Galley.

Bithynia. Greek Bithynia, kios. 350-300 BC,
AR 1/4 drachm. (10 mm, 1.3 gr.) Apollo/Galley.

The province was conquered by the Persians in 546 BC and was included in the satrapy of Phrygia. Bithynia was conquered by the Greeks and the Romans and appeared to have attracted so much attention because of its roads and strategic position between the frontiers of the Danube in the north and the Euphrates in the southeast. Bithynia's most important cities in early Christianity were Nicomedia and Nicaea.

CILICIA

Cilicia extends inland from the southeastern coast of Asia Minor, due north and northeast of the island of Cyprus, and comprises about a third of the land area of modern Anatolia.

Cilicia. Greek Cilicia, Triptolemos. 360-345 BC,
AR Obol. (10 mm, 0.72 gr.) youthful head/
eagle standing on back of a lion. Rare.

Cilicia. Greek Cilicia, Tarsos. 361-334 BC,
AR Stater. (22 mm, 10.77 gr.)
lion bringing down bull/Baal of Tarsos seated.

Cilicia. Greek Cilicia, Tarsos. 164-27 BC,
AE (22 mm, 5.33 GR.)
head of Tyche/Sanadan standing.

Cilicia. Greek Cilicia, Tarsos. 164-27 BC,
AE (25 mm, 13.64 gr.)
Tyche seated/Zeus seated left.

Cilicia. Greek Cilicia, Korykos. 1st century BC,
AE (21 mm. 6.01gr.)
turreted head of Tyche/Hermes.

Cilicia. Greek Cilicia, Soloi. 100-30 BC,
AE (23 mm, 14.08 gr.)
bust of Artemis/Athena standing.

The land became subject to the Persians, but was liberated unopposed by Alexander the Great. Cilicia became part of the Seleucid Empire but was long disputed between the Ptolemies and Seleucids. In the late second century BC, pirates were based in Cilicia, which led to it being occupied by the Romans.

The Legacy of Alexander the Great

The conflicts between the Persians and the Greeks went on and on for centuries. Philip II (382–336 BC) of Macedon, Alexander III's (the Great) father, tried to defeat the Persian Empire, but he did not live long enough to achieve this goal due to his assassination in 336 BC.

Philip II. Greek Kings of Macedon. 359-336 BC,
Philip II. AR Tetradrachm. (25 mm, 14.44gr.)
head of Zeus/youth holding palm on horseback. Scarce.

After Philip II's death, Alexander III became the king and ruler of Macedonia. He was twenty years old and was born in Pella, the capital of Macedonia, in 356 BC.

Pella. Greek Macedonia. 187-31 BC,
AE (23 mm, 13.18 gr.) head of Apollo/tripod.

Pella. Greek Macedonia, Demetrios I, 306-283 BC.
AE (15 mm, 4.24 Gr.) Macedonian shield/helmet.

The NIV Bible narratives describe briefly this part of the history of Alexander the Great and the four empires after his death. However, the New Revised Standard Version Bible (NRSV) described the same period of history in great detail, even down to each individual ruler.

The first book of Maccabees in the NRSV Bible sums up the brief dramatic story of Alexander the Great.

> He advanced to the ends of the Earth, and plundered many nations. When the Earth became quiet for him, he was exalted, and his heart was lifted up. He gathered a very strong army and ruled over countries, nations and princes, and they became tributary to him.
>
> 1 Maccabees 1:1–3 (NRSV)

Alexander the Great is one of the most famous conquerors in the history of mankind. The Greek historians credited Alexander as being the son of the Greek supreme god, Zeus Ammon. Three hundred years later, many Romans emperors promoted him as their model and honored him as a true descendant of Heracles.

Alexander the Great gathered his army of approximately 40,000 soldiers and crossed the strip of water that separate Asia from Greece called the Hellespont in 334 BC, fully determined to send the Persians back to Babylon. At Issus, he crushed the Persian army of Darius III in 333 BC, even though he was by far outnumbered. From Issus, he went south to destroy the Persian naval control of the eastern Mediterranean. After seven months of siege, the city of Tyre was leveled, and according to legend, about 8,000 Persians were killed, and Alexander had 2,000 prisoners put to death. This action ended the Persian fleet base in the east Mediterranean.

Alexander the Great. Greek Macedonia, 336-323 BC.
AR drachm (17 mm, 4.32 gr.) Herakles/Zeus.

Alexander the Great. Greek Macedonia, 336-323 BC.
AR drachm (17 mm, 4.28 gr.) Herakles/Zeus.

Alexander went into Egypt, and the Persians had no choice but to give up this important outpost of their empire without a fight. Many historians believe that Alexander personally chose the site, laid out the plans, and built the city of Alexandria, Egypt, in 331 BC. Alexandria was named after him and became one of the great centers of the Greek Empire and of Hellenistic culture and indeed one of the greatest cities of the ancient world.

Alexandria. Greek kings of Egypt,
Ptolemy II, 285-246 BC. AE Hemidrachm.
(33 mm, 32.96 gr.) Zeus/eagle.

Alexandria. Greek kings of Egypt,
Ptolemy II, 285-246 BC. AE Hemidrachm.
(36 mm, 45.41 gr.) Zeus/eagle.

Alexandria. Greek kings of Egypt, Ptolemy II, 285-246 BC.
AE Tetradrachm. (25.5 mm, 13.9 gr.)
diademed head of Ptolemy/eagle standing.

Alexandria. Roman Egypt, Nero and Tiberius, 54-68 AD.
BI Tetradrachm. (25 mm, 13.8gr.)
Nero left/Tiberius right.

Alexandria. Roman Egypt, Tacitus, 275-276 AD.
BI Tetradrachm. (20 mm, 6.7gr.)
Laureate bust/Nike advancing.

Alexandria. Roman Egypt, Carus, 282-283 AD.
BI Tetradrachm. (19 mm, 7.6gr.)
Laureate bust/Dikaiosyne standing.

Alexandria. Roman Egypt, Diocletian, 284-305 AD.
BI Tetradrachm. (19 mm, 6.8gr.)
Laureate bust/Zeus standing.

Alexandria. Roman Egypt, Diocletian, 284-305 AD.
BI Tetradrachm. (20 mm, 6.4gr.)
Laureate bust/Zeus sitting.

Alexander's army went back north through Syria and east through Mesopotamia. To reinforce his victory over the Persians, he went on and conquered Darius's capital at Babylon, where he took the gold and silver from the immense Persian treasury and burned Darius's great palace.

Babylon. Greek kings of Syria, Seteukos I Nikator,
312-281 BC. AR Tetradrachm
(25 mm, 16.6 gr.) Herakles/Zeus.

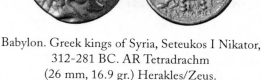

Babylon. Greek kings of Syria, Seteukos I Nikator,
312-281 BC. AR Tetradrachm
(26 mm, 16.9 gr.) Herakles/Zeus.

After Babylon, Alexander continued his eastern campaign, going to the end of the earth. Alexander was remembered for his loyalty of the local people. He worshiped at their temples to win the locals and bring them over to his side. The young Alexander championed Hellenism and founded many cities based on the Greek model.

Alexander the Great reached the Indus River in India, where he stopped his campaign because he was pressured by his war-weary army and they refused to go any farther.

Alexander the Great. Greek Macedonia, 336-323 BC.
AR drachm (17 mm, 4.21 gr.) Herakles/Zeus.

Alexander the Great. Greek Macedonia, 336-323 BC.
AR Tetradrachm (25 mm, 17.11 gr.) Herakles/Zeus.

Alexander the Great.Greek Macedonia, 336-323 BC.
AR Tetradrachm (30 mm, 16.85 gr.) Herakles/Zeus.

Alexander the Great. Greek Macedonia, 336-323 BC.
AR Tetradrachm (32 mm, 16.27 gr.) Herakles/Zeus.

Alexander the Great. Greek Macedonia, 336-323 BC.
AR drachm (16 mm, 4.24 gr.) Herakles/Zeus.

Alexander the Great ended his dream and went back to Babylon, having laid claim to Asia Minor, Egypt, all east Mediterranean, Mesopotamia, and east to Afghanistan. Alexander never returned to his homeland and did not live long enough to enjoy his massive empire. At Babylon, Alexander died of a fever in 323 BC brought on by an ailment that has never been fully explained to this day. Alexander the Great was only thirty-two years old, and he occupied almost the entire civilized world in twelve years. With him died his soaring ambition of world conquest.

Alexander's sudden death at age thirty-two caused confusion and disorder within his empire. After his death, a power struggle occurred between his generals. The empire was agreed between his generals to be divided as follows:

1. Macedon and Greece under Antipater and Cassander.

2. Thrace and Asia Minor under Lysimachus.

3. Judaea, Palestine, and Egypt under Ptolemy I.

4. Syria and Mesopotamia under Seleucus I.

The Bible narratives tell us in Daniel's vision 300 years earlier that the third beast was a leopard with four heads. This prophecy had been fulfilled. The speedy leopard was Alexander the Great, and the four heads were the four dynasties created by his generals after his death. The Bible says, "And after Alexander had reigned twelve years, he died. Then his officers began to rule, each in his own place. They all put on crowns after his death, and so did their descendants after them for many years, and they caused many evils on the earth" (1 Maccabees 1:7–9, NRSV).

MACEDONIA AND GREEK KINGDOMS

Antipater was born in 399 BC and served as a soldier and a diplomat under King Philip II, Alexander the Great's father. After the assassination of Philip II in 336 BC, Antipater made sure that Alexander III succeeded his father's wish. In the following year (335 BC), Alexander rewarded him. He appointed many relatives of him as commanders in the Macedonian army and made Antipater supreme commander of the forces in Europe. Disagreements had broken out between Antipater and Alexander's mother, Olympias. She kept sending letters to Alexander when he was fighting in the east about Antipater's misbehavior. Alexander then sent about 11,000 veterans under his trusted general, Craterus, to go to Macedonia and succeed Antipater as a supreme commander. Alexander asked Antipater to come to Babylon while Alexander was residing there. Antipater refused to go to. He sent his son, Cassander, to Babylon instead in 323 BC. Alexander the Great died on June 11, 323 BC, at the very young age of thirty-two. The cause of death was that the young king developed a fever, but most literature believed that Cassander was responsible for the death of Alexander the Great. It is widely believed that Cassander killed Alexander the Great's mother, Olympias, and her son Philip III in 315 BC. Also, he was accused of killing Alexander the Great's wife, Roxane, and her son, Alexander IV, in 311 BC. Alexander the Great's bloodline had been wiped out from the face of this earth.

Philip III. Greeek kings of Macedon. Philip III, 323-317 BC.
AR Drachm (17 mm, 4.29 gr.) Herakles/Zeus.

Philip III. Greeek kings of Macedon. Philip III, 323-317 BC.
AR Drachm (17 mm, 4.27 gr.) Herakles/Zeus.

Kassander. Greek Macedonian kings. 319-297 BC.
AE (17 mm, 3.49 gr.) Herakles/lion.

Kassander. Greek Macedonian kings. 319-297 BC.
AR Tetradrachm (27 mm, 16.90 gr.)
Herakles wearing lion skin/Zeus.

Antigonos Gonatas. Greek Macedonian
kings. 277-239 BC. AE (13 mm, 1.80 gr.)
helmeted Athena/Pan erecting a trophy.

Antigonos Gonatas. Greek Macedonian
kings. 237-239 BC. AE (22 mm, 7.66 gr.)
helmeted Athena/Pan erecting a trophy.

Philip V. Greek Kings of Macedon. 221-179 BC.
AE (24 mm, 10.78 gr.)
radiate head of Helios/winged thunderbelt.

Perseus. Greek Kings of Mecedon. 178-168 BC.
AE (19 mm, 5.44 gr.)
head of Perseus/eagle with spread wings.

Antipar and his son, Cassander, gained control of Macedonia and formed a coalition in 301 BC with Ptolemy I, Lysimachus, and Seleucus I against Antigonus Gonatas. They defeated Antigonus and killed him in the battle of Ipsus. After Cassander's death in 297 BC, the kingdom slid into civil war and was ruled by Demetrius I from 294 to 288 BC. The kingdom was ruled very shortly by King Philip V, and Perseus was the last king to rule Macedonia and Greece before the Romans conquered it in 168 BC.

THRACE AND ASIA MINOR KINGDOMS

Lysimachus became the governor of Thrace and northwest Asia Minor after Alexander the Great's death in 323 BC. Lysimachus was born in 362 BC and was educated in Pella, just like the young Alexander. During Alexander's Persian campaign, he was one of his immediate bodyguards. In 315 BC, he joined Cassander, Ptolemy, and Seleucus against Antigonus, and they defeated Antigonus I and Demetrius I at the battle of Ipsus in 301 BC.

Seleucus I became dangerous in thinking of going west to occupy Thrace, and then Lysimachus allied himself with Ptolemy by marrying his daughter, Arsinoe II of Egypt, in 299 BC. Eventually, Seleucus I defeated and killed him at the battle of Corupedium in 281 BC. According to legend, after some days, Lysimachus's body was found on the battleground protected from birds of prey by his faithful dog. Thrace and Asia Minor kingdoms became the property of the Seleucid Empire in 281 BC.

Lysimachos. Greek Kings of Thrace. 323-281 BC.
AR Tetradrachm (28 mm, 16.26 gr.)
head of deified Alexander/Athena seated.

Lysimachos. Greek Kings of Thrace. 323-281 BC.
AR Teteradrachm (34 mm, 16.60 gr.)
Head of deified Alexander/Athena seated

JUDAEA AND EGYPT (THE PTOLEMAIC KINGDOM)

Following Alexander the Great's death in 323 BC, Ptolemy I Soter, one of Alexander's ablest generals, ruled Egypt from 323 BC in the name of the joint kings Philip III and Alexander's infant son, Alexander IV, who had not been born at the time of his father's death.

Ptolemy I. Greek Kings of Egypt. 323-285 BC.
AR Tetradrachm (30 mm, 15.6 gr.)
head of Alexander/Athena walking

Ptolemy took the title of king. As Ptolemy I Soter (Saviour), he founded the Ptolmaic dynasty that was to rule Egypt for the next 300 years.

During the reign of Ptolemy II, thousands of Greeks were given farmlands, and Greeks settled throughout the country. They established a prosperous kingdom, but the native population enjoyed only a few benefits. The problems of nationalism reached a peak in the reign of Ptolemy IV Philopator (221–205 BC). The kingdom began to weaken when others gained control over some districts and ruled as a line of native "pharaohs." Ptolemy V Epiphanes (205–181 BC) succeeded in subduing them, but the underlying anger continued, and many riots broke out later in the dynasty. Also, family conflicts affected the dynasty in later years when Ptolemy VIII fought his brother, Ptolemy VI Philometor, and briefly seized the throne. The conflict was continued by his sister and niece (who both became his wives) until they issued an amnesty decree in 118 BC.

Ptolemy II. Greek Kings of Egypt. 285 246 BC.
AE (21 mm, 6.45 gr.)
Alexander wearing lion's skin/eagle standing left.

Ptolemy II. Greek Kings of Egypt. 285-246 BC.
AR Tetradrachm (28 mm, 13.7 gr.)
head of Ptolemy/eagle.

Ptolemy II. Greek Kings of Egypt. 285-246 BC.
AR Tetradrachm (28 mm, 13.8 gr.)
head of Ptolemy/eagle.

Ptolemy II. Greek Kings of Egypt. 285-246 BC.
AE (41 mm, 73.04 gr.)
head of Zeus/two eagles.

Ptolemy IV. Greek Kings of Egypt. 225-205 BC.
AE (39 mm, 47.35 gr.) head of Zeus/eagle.

Ptolemy IV. Greek Kings of Egypt. 225-205 BC.
AE (41 mm, 71.81 gr.) head of Zeus/eagle.

Ptolemy V. Greek Kings of Egypt. 205-180 BC.
AE (33 mm, 32.14 gr.)
head of Zeus/two eagles.

Ptolemy VI. Greek Kings of Egypt. 180-145 BC.
AE (32 mm, 32.69 gr.)
head of Zeus/two eagles.

During the reign of the Ptolemaic pharaohs, many Jews migrated from Palestine and Judaea by the hundreds of thousands. They welcomed the peace and prosperity in the Egyptian land. There always had been many Jewish communities in Egypt that were made up of exiles, most of whom arrived after the destruction of Jerusalem in 586 BC by Nebuchadnezzar, the Babylonian king. By the time Ptolemy II ruled Egypt, the language of the Egyptians Jews was Greek, and after a few generations, immigrants from Judaea forgot their Semitic speech. They knew their Hebrew Scriptures only in Greek translation. According to legend, the translation of the Hebrew Scriptures (only the first five books of the Old Testament) had been made by the seventy translators under Ptolemy II Philadelphus (285–246 BC). Therefore, the five books of the law were translated by the seventy during the last 300 years before the Christian era.

The Ptolemaic kingdom became very weak, especially at the reign of Ptolemy XII. After the death of Ptolemy XII in 51 BC, his eighteen-year-old daughter, Cleopatra VII, and her brother, twelve-year-old Ptolemy XIII, became joint monarchs. She married her young brother, and she had no intentions of sharing power with him.

Ptolemy XII. Greek Kings of Egypt. 80-51 BC.
AR Tetradrachm (23 mm, 14.3 gr.)
head of Ptolemy/eagle standing left

Cleopatra VII, Thea Neotera, Queen of Egypt.
51-30 BC. AE (21 mm, 9.78 gr.)
diademed, draped bust of Cleopatr/
eagle standing left. Very Rare.

Cleopatra VII, Thea Neotera, Queen of Egypt.
51-30 BC. AE (21 mm, 7.41 gr.) Dated CY
280 (33/32 BC). diademed,draped bust of
Cleopatra/Tyche seated left. VERY RARE.

In 51 BC, Cleopatra dropped her brother's name, and only her face appeared on coins, which went against Ptolemaic tradition of female rulers being subordinate to male co-rulers. Because of this action, Cleopatra was removed from power, and she was forced to leave Egypt with her only surviving sister, Arsinoe, in 51 BC. Julius Caesar went to the Egyptian capital and took it over because of anger after Cleopatra's brother Ptolemy XII ordered the death of Pompey, the consul of Rome.

Gaius Julius Caesar was a Roman military and political leader. He played a critical role in the transformation of the Roman Republic into the Roman Empire. He conquered Gaul, which extended the Roman world to the North Sea, and he also made the first invasion of Britain in 55 BC.

Julius Caesar. Roman Imperatorial. 46 BC.
AR Denarius (18 mm, 3.89 gr.) head of Ceres/
simpulum, sprinkler, capisand lituus. Rare.

Gaul. British Celtic. 55-54 BC. AV Stater.
(17x21 mm, 6.17 gr.) abstracted head of Apollo/
disjointed horse left. Rare.

Gaul. British Celtic. 55-54 BC. AV 1/4 Stater.
(12 mm, 1.46 gr.) abstracted pattern/
geometric pattern. Rare.

After he got control of the government, he proclaimed "dictator in perpetuity" and became the undisputed figure of the Roman Republic.

According to legend, Queen Cleopatra was next to none for her beauty and sexual appeal. To payback Julius Caesar's anger with her brother, she returned to the palace rolled into a Persian carpet and had it presented to Julius Caesar by her servants. When Cleopatra was unrolled, Caesar was charmed by her beauty, and she became his mistress. Nine months later, she gave birth to their child, Ptolemy Caesar (Caesarion).

Brutus. Roman Imperatorial. 54 BC.
AR Denarius (18 mm, 3.73 gr.) head of Libertas/
Brutus walking between two lictors. Rare.

Octavian. Roman Syria. 30-29 BC,
AE (21 mm, 6.46gr.) Dated SE 283(30/29 BC).
bare head of Octavian/Tyche seated left. Scarce.

A group of senators, led by Caesar's former friend, Marcus Junius Brutus, assassinated the dictator on the Ides of March (March 15) in 44 BC, hoping to take the Roman Republic.

However, the result was another Roman civil war, which ultimately led to the establishment of a permanent autocracy by Caesar's adopted heir, Gaius Octavianus (known as Octavian and later as Augustus) in 42 BC

After Julius Caesar's assassination, Cleopatra returned to Egypt, and she had her sister, Arsinoe, killed to safeguard herself and her son, Ptolemy Caesar. She aligned with Mark Antony, with whom she produced three children: Cleopatra Selene II, Alexander Helios, and last son, Ptolemy Philadelphus. Mark Antony was still married to his wife, Octavia Minor, in Rome. Mark Antony's behavior put him in a very bad position with the Romans. Octavian marched into Egypt and conquered it, and as he approached Alexandria, Antony's armies deserted him for Octavian on August 12, 30 BC. When Queen Cleopatra VII lost Egypt, she poisoned herself by inducing an asp to bite her. When Mark Antony's armies deserted him and joined with Octavian, and when he learned that Cleopatra was dead, he stabbed himself in the belly with his sword and died. Cleopatra VII and Mark Antony died the same day on August 12, 30 BC.

Before Mark Antony and Cleopatra's death, Chalkis in Coele-Syria was a complete kingdom and was reigned by Lysanias, son of Ptolemy, as a tetrarch. Mark Antony ordered Lysanias's death and gave the kingdom to Cleopatra VII as gift to renew his relationship with her and to commemorate the enlargement of Cleopatra's power. Antony also gave her a string of coastal cities from Mount Carmel up to Lebanon. This kingdom was called Chalkis ad Libanon. Roman Emperor Augustus later conquered the new kingdom and gave it back to its original owners.

Mark Antony and Cleopatra VII. 36-31 BC. Roman Coele-Syria, Chalkis ad Labanum. AE (20 mm, 5.73 gr.) Bust of Cleopatra/head of Antony. Rare.

Mark Antony and Cleopatra VII. 36-31 BC. Roman Coele-Syria, Chalkis ad Labanum. AE (22 mm, 5.65 gr.) Bust of Cleopatra/head of Antony. Rare.

Chalkis Ad Libanon. Greek Syria, Coele-Syria. 85-40 BC. AE (20 mm, 6.48 gr.) head of Zeus/the Dioskouroi standing facing. Scarce.

Chalkis Ad Libanon. Greek Syria, Coele-Syria. 85-40 BC. AE (20 mm, 6.78 gr.) head of Zeus/the Dioskouroi standing facing. Scarce.

Chalkis Ad Libanon. Greek Syria, Coele-Syria.
40-36 BC. AE (19 mm, 5.16 gr.) head of
Lysanias/Athena Nike-Phoros. Scarce.

Cleopatra's son by Julius Caesar, Caesarion, was proclaimed pharaoh by the Egyptians, but Octavian had already won the country. Caesarion was captured and executed, his fate reportedly sealed by Octavian's famous phrase: "Two Caesars are one too many." The death of Cleopatra ended not just the Hellenistic line of Egyptian pharaohs but also the line of all Egyptian pharaohs. Cleopatra VII was thirty-nine years old when she committed suicide. The three children of Cleopatra and Antony were spared and taken back to Rome, where they were taken care of by Mark Antony's wife, Octavia Minor. The daughter, Cleopatra Selene, was married by arrangement by Octavian to Juba II, king of Mauretania.

Mark Antony and his wife Octavia. summer-autumn
39 BC. AR Cistophoric Tetradrachm (27 mm, 11.61 gr.)
head of Antony/draped bust of Octavia
flanked by coiled snakes. Rare

Juba II. Kings of Mauretania. 25 BC-24 AD.
AR Denarius (16 mm, 3.27 gr.) Juba II with
Cleopatra Selene. head of Juba/star within crescent. Rare.

Juba II. Kings of Mauretania. 25 BC-24 AD.
AR Denarius(18 mm, 2.92 gr.) Juba II with
Cleopatra Selene. head of Juba/star within crescent. Rare.

SYRIA AND MESOPOTAMIA (THE SELEUCID EMPIRE)

After Alexander the Great's death, Seleucus I established himself in Babylon in 312 BC. This date was used as the foundation date of the Seleucid Empire. He ruled over not only Babylonia but also the entire enormous eastern part of Alexander the Great's empire.

Seleukos I. Greek kings of Syria. 312-281 BC.
AR Tetradrachm (27 mm, 17.05 gr.)
head of Herakles/Zeus.

Seleucus I acquired Mesopotamia, Armenia, Seleucid Cappadocia, Persis, Parthia, Arabia, Tapouria, Sogdia, Arachosia, Hyrcania, and other adjacent people that had been conquered by Alexander as far as the river Indus so that the boundaries of his empire were the most extensive in Asia after that of Alexander. Seleucus I Nicator went as far as India, where he made an agreement with Indian King Chandragupta Maurya in exchanging his eastern territories for a considerable force of 500 war elephants, which were to play a vital role at the battle of Ipsus.

Following his and Lysimachus's victory over Antigonus at the battle of Ipsus in 301 BC, Seleucus took control over eastern Anatolia (Asia Minor) and northern Syria. In the latter area, he found a new capital at Antioch ad Orontes (Antioch, Syria), a city he named after his father (Antiochus). An alternative capital was established at Seleucia on the Tigris north of Babylon. He also built Seleucia Pieria as the seaport of the city of Antioch. Apamea, Laodicea ad Mare, Selecuia Pieria, and Antioch formed the Syrian Tetrapolis (map number two and number three).

Tetrapolis. Greek Syria, Seleukis and Pieria.
149-148 BC. AE (24 mm, 15.97 gr.)
conjoined head of the Demoi/Zeus seated. Rare.

Tetrapolis. Greek Syria, Seleukis and Pieria.
149-148 BC. AE (21 mm, 7.47 gr.)
head of Zeus/monogram, winged thunderbolt. Rare.

Tetrapolis. Greek Syria, Seleukis and Pieria.
149-148 BC. AE (21 mm, 7.67 gr.)
head of Zeus/monogram, winged thunderbolt. Rare.

Antioch ad Orontes

Antioch ad Orontes (Antioch) was found by Seleucus I Nicator around 300 BC and was also the seat of a Roman governor after 64 BC. The city is located on the Orontes River near the Syrian border of modern-day Turkey. Its importance is primarily as the capital of the Seleucid Empire. Antioch was one of the largest cities in the ancient world, with a population of about 500,000 by the fourth century AD Alexander the Great is said to have camped in the site of Antioch, where he dedicated an altar that lay northwest of the city to Zeus Bottiaeus. Seleucus founded Antioch on a site chosen through ritual means. An eagle, the bird of Zeus, had been given a piece of sacrificial meat, and the city was founded on the site to which the eagle carried the offering.

Antioch. Greek Kings of Syria, Antiochos III,
223-187 BC. AR Tetradrachm (29 mm, 16.68gr.)
Diademed head/nude Apollo seated.

Antioch. Greek Kings of Syria, Antiochos IV,
175-164 BC. AE (19 mm, 4.51 gr.)
radiate head/Zeus standing.

Antioch. Greek Kings of Syria, Demetrios I,
162-150 BC. AR Drachm (17 mm, 4.16 gr.)
diademed head/Cornucopie.

Antioch. Greek Kings of Syria, Demetrios I,
162-150 BC. AR Tetradrachm (29 mm, 16.36 gr.)
diademed head/Tyche seated.

Antioch. Greek Kings of Syria, Antiochos VII,
138-129 BC. AR Tetradrachm(29 mm, 16.47 gr.)
diademed head/Athena standing.

Antioch. Roman Syria, Seleucis and Pieria.
Caracalla, 198-217 AD. AR Tetradrachm
(26 mm, 12.84 gr.) Laureate head/eagle standing.

Antioch. Roman Syria, Seleucis and Pieria.
Caracalla. 198-217 AD. AR Tetradrachm
(26 mm, 14.21 gr.) Laureate head/eagle standing.

Antioch. Roman Syria, Seleucis and Pieria.
Phipip I, 244-249 AD. AE Assaria (30 mm, 12.83 gr.)
bust of Philip/veiled Tyche.

He did this in the twelfth year of his reign. Antioch soon rose above Seleucia Pieria to become the
Syrian capital. Over the centuries, from the Roman, Byzantine, Arab, and crusader occupations of the
city, Antioch never recovered as a major city, with much of its former role falling to the port city of
Alexandrett (Iskenderun).

Seleucia Pieria

Seleucia Pieria (Suedia) was also built by Seleucus I Nicator around 300 BC. It lay near the mouth of the
Orontes River, not far from Mount Casius, and functioned as the commercial and naval seaport of Antioch.

Seleucia Pieria, Roman Syria, Seleucis and Pieria.
Trajan, 98-117 AD. AE (24 mm, 10.53 gr.)
Laureate head/Shrine of Zeus. Scarce.

As the port of Antioch, it was most notable as the precise point of embarkation from which the Apostle St. Paul set forth on his first missionary journey, as chronicled in the Bible. The city went through many occupations from the Roman period to the crusader time.

Laodicea ad Mare

Laodicea ad Mare (Latakia) was described by Strabo (Greek geographer) as admirably built, with an excellent harbor on the Mediterranean Sea, about forty miles south of Antioch, modern-day Syria. The city is surrounded by rich country, especially fruitful in vines, the wine of which furnished its chief supply to Alexandria. The vineyards were planted on the sides of gently sloping hills, which were cultivated almost to their summits, and extended far to the east, nearly to Apamea.

The city site on the peninsula was occupied by the Phoenicians for a long time under the name of Ramitha. The city was re-founded by Seleucus I and named Laodicea after his mother, Laodice. It was one of the four cities of the Syrian Tetrapolis. It was furnished with an aqueduct by Herod the Great, a large fragment of which is still to be seen. An arch from the time of Septimius Severus has survived until this day.

Leodicea ad Mare. Greek Syria, 41-0 BC.
AE (17 mm, 3.93 gr.)
bust of Tyche/Nike advancing.

Leodicea ad Mare. Greek Syria. 49-48 BC.
AR Tetradrachm (28 mm, 15.02 gr.)
turreted bust of Tyche/Zeus holding Nike. Rare.

Leodicea ad Mare. Roman Syria. 138-161 AD,
Antoninius Pius. AE (25 mm, 11.31 gr.)
Laureate head/turreted bust of Tyche.

Leodicea ad Mare. Roman Syria. 138-161 AD.
Antoninius Pius, AE (25 mm, 8.75 gr.)
Laureate head/turreted bust of Tyche.

Leodicea ad Mare. Roman Syria. 138-161 AD,
Antoninius Pius. AE (30 mm, 14.83 gr.)
Laureate head/turreted bust of Tyche.

Leodicea ad Mare. Roman Syria. 198-217 AD,
Caracalla. AR Tetradrachm(26 mm, 13.34
gr.) Laureate head/ragle standing. Scarce.

Leodicea ad Mare. Roman Syria. 193-211 AD,
Septimius Severus. AE (26 mm, 11.2 gr.)
Laureate head/monogram in four lines.

There seems to have been a sizable Jewish population at Laodicea in the fourth century AD. The heretic Apollinarius was Bishop of Laodicea in the fourth century AD. The city minted coins from the early Roman Empire and became one of the largest cities in the Seleucia and Pieria Roman province.

The city was devastated by earthquakes in AD 494 and 555 and was captured by the Arabs of the Muslim caliphate in AD 638. It was taken by the Byzantine Empire in AD 969 and then by the Seljuks Turks in AD 1084. In AD 1097, it was captured by the crusaders and made part of the principality of Antioch. The Byzantines held it again from AD 1098–1100, and then Saladin took it in AD 1188. From the sixteenth century to World War I, it was part of the Ottoman Empire. All but a few classical buildings have been destroyed, often by earthquakes. Those remaining include a Roman triumphal arch and Corinthian columns, known as the Colonnade of Bacchus. The city of Laodicea is famous in its Latakia tobacco, an especially treated tobacco. It is cured over a stone pinewood fire, which gives it an intense smoky taste and smell. It is an essential ingredient in many pipe tobaccos.

The most historical impressive attraction of Laodicea ad Mare is the site of the ruins of the ancient city of Ugarit. Ugarit, called Ras Shamra in modern-day, is located about three miles from the Laodiciea ad Mare city limits. Excavations began in AD 1929 and have since revealed an important city that takes its place alongside Ur and Eridu as a cradle of urban culture, with a prehistory reaching back to circa 6000 BC. The AD 1929 excavations uncovered a royal palace of ninety rooms laid out around eight enclosed courtyards and many ambitious private dwellings, including two private libraries that contained diplomatic, legal, economic, administrative, scholastic, literary, and religious texts. Crowning the hill where the city was built were two main temples: one to Baal, the "king" son of El, and one to Dagon, the god of fertility and wheat. Several deposits of cuneiform clay tablets were found, and they were written in four languages: Sumerian, Hurrian, Akkadian, and Ugaritic, of which nothing had been known before. The discovery of Ugaritic archives has been a great significance to biblical scholarship, as these archives, for the first time, provided a detailed description of Canaanite and Amorite religious belief during the period directly preceding the Israelite settlement. Genesis 15:16 (NIV) says, "In the fourth generation your Descendants will come back here, for their sin of the Amorites has not yet reached its full measure." It was discovered in Ugarit tablets just how sinful many Canaanite religious practices were, such as their worship was polytheistic and included child sacrifice, religious prostitution, and idolatry. These texts show significant parallels to biblical Hebrew literature, particularly in the areas of divine imagery and poetic form. The discoveries at Ugarit have led to a new appraisal of the Old Testament as literature. Based on clay tablets, the king of Ugarit, Ammurapi, sent a letter to the Hittite king asking for help, because the sea people were invading the city. Unfortunately, no help ever arrived, and Ugarit was burned to the ground around 1200 BC. Ugarit has stayed in ruins until this day.

Apameia and Larissa

The sites of Apamea (Afamia) and Larissa are located about thirty miles to the northwest of Epiphaneia (Hama) on the Orontes River, overlooking the Ghab Valley in modern-day Syria. Apameia and Larissa were twin cities about two miles apart, and they were fortified and enlarged by Seleucus I Nicator in 300 BC. Seleucus named it Apameia after his Bactrian wife, Apama. Seleucus had his commissariat there, with 500 war elephants, 30,000 mares, and 300 stallions.

Apamia. Greek Syria, seleucis and pieria.
20-19 BC. AE (20 mm, 7.52 gr.)
helmeted bust of Athena/Nike advancing. Scarce.

Apamia. Greek Syria, seleucis and pieria.
9-8 BC. AE (20 mm, 7.28 gr.)
head of Dionysos/Thyrsos. Scarce.

Apamia. Roman Syria, seleucis and pieria.
Augustus, 27 BC-14 AD. AE (20 mm, 9.84 gr.)
Laureate head/Nike advancing. Scarce.

Larissa. Greek Syria, Seleucis and Pieria. 86-85 BC.
AE (19 mm, 6.99 gr.) laureate head of Zeus/
monogram around throne of Zeus. Very Rare.

Apameia was one of the four cities that formed the Syrian Tetrapolis. The cities are located at a strategic crossroads for eastern commerce and flourished to the extent that its population eventually numbered half a million. Pompey the Great was marching south from his winter quarters, probably near Antioch or Laodicea, and razed the fortress of Apamea in 64 BC. Hence, both cities were annexed to the Roman Republic. In the revolt of Syria under Q. Caecilius Bassus, the cities were held out against Julius Caesar for three years until the arrival of Cassius in 46 BC.

On the outbreak of the Jewish war against the Romans, the inhabitants of Apamea spared the Jews who lived in their midst and would not suffer them to be murdered or led into captivity. Both cities were destroyed by Chosroes I (Sasanian king) in the seventh century AD and were partially rebuilt and known in Arabic as "Fafia" but were destroyed by an earthquake in AD 1152. The hill is now occupied by the ruins called "Kalat-El-Mudik." The fate of Larissa was the same as Apameia during ancient history. The site of Larissa today corresponds roughly to As-Saqlabiyah in modern Syria.

Seleucia on the Tigris

Seleucia on the Tigris was built as the first capital by Seleucus I Nicator around 305 BC on the bank of the Tigris River just north of Babylon in modern-day Iraq. Although Seleucus soon moved his main capital to Antioch in northern Syria, Seleucia on the Tigris became an important center of trade, Hellenistic culture, and regional government under the Seleucid Empire.

Seleukia on the Tigris. Greek Kings of Syria.
Seleucos I, 312-280 BC. AR Tetradrachm
(28 mm, 16.94 gr.) Herakles/Zeus. Scarce.

The city was populated by Macedonians, Greeks, Syrians, and Jews. Standing at the confluence of the Tigris River with a major canal from the Euphrates, Seleucia was placed to receive traffic from both great waterways along the famous Silk Road. During the third and second centuries BC, It was one of the great Hellenistic cities, comparable to Alexandria in Egypt and greater than Antioch in Syria.

Seleucus was assassinated by Ptolemy Ceraunus in 281 BC. His son and successor, Antiochus I Soter, was left with an enormous empire consisting of nearly all of the Asian portions of the empire, but he proved unable to pick up where his father had left off in conquering the western portions of Alexander's empire. Antiochus I died in 261 BC, and Antiochus II Theos (referred to in the Bible, in the book of Daniel, as the king of the north) reigned from 261 to 246 BC. He was faced with many problems in the west, including repeated wars with Ptolemy II's invasion of the Celtic in Asia Minor. Toward the end of Antiochus II's reign, various provinces simultaneously asserted their independence, such as Bactria, Parthia, and Cappadocia.

Antiochos I. Greek Kings of Syria. 280-261 BC.
AE (14 mm, 2.46 gr.) Bust of Athena/Nike.

Antiochos I. Greek Kings of Syria. 280-261 BC.
AE (18 mm 4.79 gr.) facing Gorgoneion/elaphant.

Antiochos II. Greek Kings of Syria, 261-246 BC.
AE (17 mm 3.2gr.) head of Apollo/tripod.

The governor for the Bactrian territory, modern-day Afghanistan, asserted independence in around 245 BC, although the exact date is far from certain, to form the Greco-Bactrian kingdom.

This kingdom was characterized by a rich Hellenistic culture and was to continue its domination of Bactria until around 125 BC. One of the Greco-Bactrian kings, Demetrius I of Bactria, invaded India around 180 BC to form the Greco-Indian kingdom, which lasted until around AD 20. King Eukratides of Bactria (171–135 BC) was one of the most celebrated of the Indo-Greek monarchs. Eukratides first came to power in revolt against Demetrios I and Euthydemos II. By circa 160 BC, he succeeded in putting his rivals to death, and the following thirty years were probably the most peaceful and prosperous period in the history of the kingdom. Eukratides was murdered by his own son, Heliokles, in 135 BC.

Eukratides. Indo-Greek, Baktria. 171-145 BC.
AR Tetradrachm (36 mm, 16.2 gr.)
helmeted head/the Dioskouroi on horses. Rare.

Eukratides. Indo-Greek, Baktria. 171-145 BC.
AR Tetradrachm (36 mm, 16.4 gr.)
helmeted head/the Dioskouroi on horses. Rare.

Greco-Baktria, Azes. 58-12 BC. AR Tetradrachm
(25 mm, 9.4 gr.) king on horse back/Athena.

Indo- Baktria, India. kushans. Kanishka II,
215-235 AD. AV Dinar(22 mm, 7.76 gr.)
Kanishka standing/Goddess Ardoksho. Scarce.

Indo- Baktria, India. kushans, Vashiska.
235-245 AD. AV Dinar (22 mm, 7.85 gr.)
Vashiska standing/Goddess Ardoksho. Scarce.

Seleucus II Callinicus (246–226 BC) came to the throne after his father Antiochus II's death. Bactria and Parthia seceded from the Seleucid Empire. In Asia Minor too, the Seleucid dynasty seemed to be losing control. Seleucus II died in 226 BC, and his younger son, Antiochus III the Great (223–187 BC), took the throne, and a revival began for the Seleucid Empire. Antiochus III conquered many territories back and placed them under the Seleucid dynasty. He proved himself to be the greatest of the Seleucid rulers after Seleucus I himself. He died in 187 BC during an expedition to the east. The reign of his son Seleucus IV (187–175 BC) was largely spent in attempts to pay the large debt that his father created with the Romans. He was assassinated by his minister. Seleucus IV's younger brother, Antiochus IV (175–164 BC), now seized the throne. He attempted to restore Seleucid power with a war against Egypt, but he was forced to withdraw by Roman Envoy Gaius Popillius Laenas. During his reign, he forced Greek customs and way of life on the Jewish nation. He forced them to worship Greek gods, which led to armed rebellion in Judea—the Maccabean revolt. This revolt will be discussed in the next section. Antiochus IV died during an expedition against the Parthians in 164 BC.

After the death of Antiohus IV, his younger son, Antiochus V (163–162 BC), ruled only one year, and he was overthrown by Demetrius I Soter in 161 BC.

Demetrius I attempted to restore Seleucid power in Judea particularly, but he was overthrown in 150 BC by Alexander Balas (150–145 BC). Alexander Balas reigned until 145 BC when he was overthrown by Demetrius II Nicator (145–139 BC).

Seleukos II. Greek Kings of Syria. 246-225 BC.
AE (19 mm, 8.02 gr.) helmeted Athena/Nike.

Antiochos III. Greek Kings of Syria. 223-187 BC.
AR Tetradrachm (31 mm, 17.16 gr.)
diademed head/Nude Apollo.

Seleukos III. Greek Kings of Syria. 226-223 BC.
AE (17 mm, 3.2 gr.)
diademed head of Artemis/Nude Apollo.

Seleukos III. Greek Kings of Syria. 226-223 BC.
AE (15 mm, 3.8 gr.)
diademed head of Artemis/Nude Apollo.

Seleukos III. Greek Kings of Syria. 226-223 BC.
AE (14 mm, 5.31 gr.)
diademed head of Artemis/Nude Apollo.

Demetrios I. Greek Kings of Syria. 162-150 BC.
AE (22 mm, 8.38 gr.) diademed head/
stern of Phoenician Pentekonter. Scarce.

Demetrios I. Greek Kings of Syria. 162-150 BC.
AR Tetradrachm(29 mm, 16.93 gr.)
diademed head/Tyche seated.

Alexander I Balas. Greek Kings of Syria.
150-145 BC.
AR Drachm (19 mm, 4.0 gr.)
diademed head/Apollo seated.

Alexander I Balas. Greek Kings of Syria. 150-145 BC.
AR Tetrarachm (27 mm, 14.16 gr.)
diademed head/eagle on prow. Scarce.

Demetrios II. Greek Kings of Syria. 146-138 BC.
AE (22 mm, 11.9 gr.)
laureate head/Apollo.

Antiochos VI. Greek Kings of Syria. 144-142 BC.
AE (20 mm, 8.16 gr.) radiate, diademed head/kantharos.

Tryphon. Greek Kings of Syria. 141-138 BC.
AE (18 mm, 3.5gr.)diademed head/helmet.

Antiochos VII. Greek Kings of Syria. 138-129 BC.
AR Tetradrachm (28 mm, 14.18 gr.)
diademed head/eagle on prow. Scarce.

Alexander II. Greek Kings of Syria. 128-123
BC. AE (19 mm, 5.98 gr.) laureate head/Tyche.

Antiochos X. Greek Kings of Syria. 94-92 BC.
AR Tetradrachm (27 mm, 15.4 gr.)
diademed head/Zeus.

Demetrios III. Greek Kings of Syria. 97-87 BC.
AE (21 mm, 6.2 gr.) diademed head/Nike.

Philip I. Greek Kings of Syria. 95-76 BC.
AR Tetradrachm (26 mm,
15.32gr.) diademed head/Zeus.

Philip I. Greek Kings of Syria, 89-83 BC.
AR Tetradrachm (26 mm, 15.61gr.)
diademed head/Zeus.

Antiochos XII. Greek Kings of Syria.
87-83 BC. AE (18 mm, 3.37 gr.)
diademed head/Apollo.

Demetrius II supported Balas's son, the usurping General Tryphon held out in Antioch, but the Seleucid kingdom was deteriorating during the reigns of seven different Seleucid kings from 139–64 BC. The reign on Antiochus VIII Grypus (hooknose) from 125–96 BC played a big role in the fall of the Seleucid dynasty.

Antiochos VIII. Greek Kings of Syria. 120-96 BC.
AR Tetradrachm (29 mm, 16.3 gr.)
diademed head/Zeus.

Antiochos VIII. Greek Kings of Syria. 120-96 BC.
AR Tetradrachm (31 mm, 16.5 gr.)
diademed head/Zeus.

Antiochos VIII. Greek Kings of Syria. 120-96 BC.
AR Tetradrachm (29 mm, 16.26 gr.)
diademed head/Zeus.

Cleopatra Thea and Antiochos VIII. Greek
Kings of Syria. 125-121 BC. AR Tetradrachm
(30 mm, 16.45 gr.) Conjoined head/Zeus. Rare.

He ruled jointly with his mother, Cleopatra Thea, as a teenager in 125 BC. Cleopatra Thea, this extraordinary woman, was the daughter of Ptolemy VI of Egypt. She married, in succession, three of the Seleucid monarchs—Alexander Balas, Demetrios II, and Antiochos VII—and beared a total of eight children by them. Cleopatra Thea reigned alone for a short while after she disposed of her son Seleucus V, Antiochus's elder brother. Cleopatra Thea tried to poison Antichos VIII with wine, but the suspicious king forced her to drink the cup herself, and she died in 125 BC. By 143 BC, the Jews in the form of the Maccabees had fully established their independence. Parthian expansion continued as well, and in 139 BC, the entire Iranian plateau had been lost to Parthian control. In 64 BC, Syria became a Roman province, and that was the end of the Seleucid Empire.

MACCABEAN REVOLT (THE HASMONEAN DYNASTY)

The Jewish nation was quiet, prosperous, and living in peace for the 400 years during the Persian rule and the Greek rule mainly under the Ptolemaic kingdom in Egypt, Greece, Thrace, and Macedonia. The Hellenization came to Judaea in the fourth century BC when they constructed Greek-style cities, accommodated Greek culture, and the Jewish lived by Greek law. This caused outbreak of violence and the persecution of religious figures in Jerusalem and the formation of Jewish opposition groups, including the Pharisees and Zealots, who influenced the future of Judea for the next 400 years. This action stirred the peace of the Seleucid dynasty and caused anxiety to the newly selected ruler, Antiochus IV.

Antiochus IV was defeated in Egypt by Egyptian forces assisted by the Romans. To recover his pride, he turned in wrath upon Judaea and marched on to Jerusalem to put an end to the Judaean strife. He passed an edict that traditional Jewish practices, such as circumcising males, observing the Sabbath, and adhering to dietary laws, were forbidden.

Antiochos IV. Greek Kings of Syria. 175-164 BC.
AE (21 mm, 6.57 gr.) radiate head/Zeus.

In addition, worship of the God of Israel was forbidden, and all the Jewish in the land of Judaea were forced to worship Zeus and other foreign gods. The punishment was very severe to those who resisted Antiochus's orders, such as death or slavery. The Jewish nation was very restless and fell in bondage again.

According to Josephus, a Jewish priest from Modein named Mattathias Hasmoneas led a rebellion against the Seleucids, which ultimately established the Hasmonean dynasty. The story stated that

Mattathias killed a fellow Jew attempting a pagan sacrifice at the altar, and he also killed a Seleucid royal officer as well. To save his family, the priest fled with his five sons (John, Simon, Judas, Eleazar, and Jonathan) into the hills near Jerusalem. Mattathias put his son Simon, "wise in council," to head the rebellion, and he chose Judas (called Maccabeus, meaning "the hammer") to be the commander of the military. When Mattathias died in 166 BC, the revolt was fresh and had not yet created any major fighting. In only two years, the whole of Judaea, except the large towns, was controlled by the rebel. In 164 BC, Judas took Jerusalem, cleansed the temple from all the foreign deities, rededicated it to Jewish worship, and lit the lamps of the eternal light to the glory of the God of Israel. At this moment, Judas made a history for the Jewish nation and has ever since been celebrated by Jews as the festival of Hanukkah. Judas gained a great victory over the forces of the Seleucid armies. Judas was killed in 160 BC during the battle of Elasa.

Judas's brother Jonathan (160–142 BC) took over the leadership of the revolt. In 152 BC, he marched south with his veteran army and captured many of the coastal cities: Ashdod, Joppa, and Gaza as well as parts of Samaria and Galilee. Jonathan was assassinated in 142 BC. Jonathan's brother Simon (142–132 BC) took over the war against the Seleucid army, and he brought many conquered lands back to the Jewish nation. In 134 BC, Simon and two of his sons were murdered by Simon's son-in-law at the fortress of Dok near Jericho.

The revolt was headed then after Simon's death by his son John Hyrcanus I (134–104 BC). He fought the Seleucids harshly and tried to expand Judaea's borders. During his thirty-year reign, the Jewish nation was divided between the Sadducees, the aristocratic priestly faction, and the Pharisees, a religious group devoted to strict observance of the jewish law. John Hyrcanus I died in 104 BC before the full explosion of this struggle broke over Judaea. His oldest son, Judah Aristobulus, took over the dynasty only less than a year before he died in 103 BC.

Judah Aristobulus. Judaea, Hasmonean Dynasty.
104-103 BC. AE Prutah (15 mm, 2.38 gr.)
double cornucopia/yehudah the high priest.

Alexander Jannaeus (103–76 BC) succeeded his brother in 103 BC. Alexander Jannaeus launched a series of military attacks that added sizable territories to his dynasty. In his twenty-seven-year reign, many civil wars broke out between the Jewish nations. Jewish historian Josephus estimated the cost of these civil wars was at least 50,000 Jews. Alexander Jannaeus claimed himeslf as a king and inscribed his coins "Alexander the King" in Greek, as well as in Hebrew.

Alexander Jannaeus. Judaea, Hasmonean Dynasty.
103-76 BC. AE Prutah (12 mm, 1.4 gr.)
upside down anchor/star of eight rays.

Alexander Jannaeus. Judaea, Hasmonean Dynasty.
103-76 BC. AE Prutah(13 mm, 1.4 gr.)
double cornucopia/Yehonatan the high priest.

Alexander Jannaeus. Judaea, Hasmonean Dynasty.
103-76 BC. AE Prutah (14 mm, 2.4 gr.)
double cornucopia/Yehonatan the high priest.

Alexander Jannaeus. Judaea, Hasmonean Dynasty.
103-76 BC. AE Prutah (14 mm, 2.4 gr.)
double cornucopia/Yehonatan the high priest.

Alexander Jannaeus. Judaea, Hasmonean Dynasty.
103-76 BC. AE Prutah (14 mm, 1.9 gr.)
double cornucopia/Yehonatan the high priest.

Alexander Jannaeus. Judaea, Hasmonean Dynasty.
103-76 BC. AE Prutah (14 mm, 1.5 gr.)
upside down anchor/star of eight rays.

Alexander Jannaeus. Judaea, Hasmonean Dynasty.
103-76 BC. AE Prutah (14 mm, 1.6 gr.)
double cornucopia/Yehonatan the high priest.

Alexander Jannaeus. Judaea, Hasmonean Dynasty.
103-76 BC. AE Prutah (14 mm, 2.26 gr.)
double cornucopia/Yehonatan the high priest.

Alexander Jannaeus was the first king of the Hasmonean dynasty to produce a coinage. Alexander Jannaeus died in 76 BC.

Upon the death of King Alexander Jannaeus, his widow, Salome Alexandra (76–67 BC), took over Judaea instead of her oldest son, John Hyrcanus II. In 67 BC, Salome Alexandra died, and her death sparked a power struggle between John Hyrcanus II and his younger brother, Aristobulus II.

John Hyrcanus II. Judaea, Hasmonean Dynasty.
67-40 BC. AE Prutah (13 mm, 1.5 gr.)
double cornucopia/Yehohanan the high priest.

John Hyrcanus II. Judaea, Hasmonean Dynasty.
67-40 BC. AE Prutah (14 mm, 2.0 gr.)
double cornucopia/Yehohanan the high priest.

John Hyrcanus II. Judaea, Hasmonean Dynasty.
67-40 BC. AE Prutah (14 mm, 1.9 gr.)
double cornucopia/Yehohanan the high priest.

John Hyrcanus II. Judaea, Hasmonean Dynasty.
67-40 BC. AE Prutah (14 mm, 1.5 gr.)
double cornucopia/Yehohanan the high priest.

John Hyrcanus II (67–40 BC) sided with Nabatean King Aretas and promised him to give him a dozen cities in the Transjordan in exchange for an army to defeat his brother. The Nabatean forces under King Areatas defeated Aristobulus II and drove him back into Jerusalem. However, one of Pompey's generals, Marcus Scaurus, defeated King Areatas II, supporter of John Hyrcanus II, in the battle against his brother, Judah Aristobulus II. Two types of coins were minted to commemorate this victory.

A.Plavtius. Roman republic. 55 BC. AR denarius
(18 mm, 3.6 gr.) Turreted head of Cybele/
Bacchius kneeling with camel at his side.

A.Plavtius. Roman republic. 55 BC. AR denarius
(17 mm, 3.7 gr.) Turreted head of Cybele/
Bacchius kneeling with camel at his side.

Marcus Scaurus and Plavtius. Roman republic.58 BC.
AR denarius (16 mm, 3.89 gr.) Nabatean king
Aretas kneeling/Jupiter driving quadriga.

Finally, Rome sent their ablest commander, General Gnaeus Pompeius, (Pompey the Great) who entered the Judaean stage in 65 BC, and dismantled the kingdom of Judaea. The Hasmonean dynasty ended in 63 BC. John Hyrcanus II died in 30 BC after King Herod ordered his execution, even though, according to Josephus, the old man was eighty years old.

The coins for Alexander Jannaeus and Hyranus II have been identified with the "widow's mite," as mentioned in the book of Mark: "But a poor widow came and put in two very small copper coins, worth only a fraction of a penny" (Mark 12:42, NIV). Based on archaeological evidence, these tiny bronze coins were in circulation well after Jesus Christ died.

John Hyrcanus's nephew, Mattathias Antigonus, wanted to be the high priest of Jerusalem, and he sided with the Parthians and attacked King Herod's forces.

Matiathias Antigonus. Judaea, Hasmonean
Dynasty. 40-37 BC. AE 8 Prutah (23 mm, 13.4 gr.)
double cornucopia/mattatayah the high priest.

King Herod escaped to Rome, where he was officially became king of Judaea in 40 BC. King Herod came back and sieged Jerusalem and captured and killed Antigonus.

The Roman Empire

Daniel interpreted the dream of Nebuchadnezzar and explained his own vision of the four beasts: lion, bear, leopard and unnamed terrifying and frightening beast. Daniel explained the meaning of his vision after God instructed the angel Gabriel to tell Daniel the meaning of it. "While I, Daniel, was watching the vision and trying to understand it, there before me stood one who looked like a man, and I heard a man's voice from the Ulai calling 'Gabriel' tell this man the meaning of the vision" (Daniel 8:15–16, NIV). This prophecy had been fulfilled: the lion was the Babylonian Empire, the bear was the Persian Empire, the leopard was the Greek Empire, and the terrifying and frightening beast is the Roman Empire. The first three beasts had been discussed earlier in this book and were wiped out from the face of the earth. The last beast, the Roman Empire, will be the dominant figure in the ancient world for the next 600 years.

THE ROMAN REPUBLIC

Many legends and stories are about the origin of Rome, but the most popular of all legends is the one of a she-wolf and the twins. According to legend, Rome was founded on April 21, 753 BC, by twin brothers who descended from the Trojan prince Aeneas. Romulus and Remus are the grandsons of the Latin king, Numitor of Alba Longa. The king was forced to give up his throne by his cruel brother, Amulius, while Numitor's daughter, Rheasilvia, gave birth. Rheasilvia was a virgin who was raped by Mars, making the twins half-divine. The new king was afraid that when the twins grew up, they would take back the throne, so they threw the twins away. A she-wolf saved and raised the twins, and when they were old enough, they returned the throne of Alba Longa to Numitor.

Antioch, Pisidia. Roman Pisidia. Severus Alexander,
222-235 AD. AE (29 mm, 18.2 gr.) Laureate head/
She-wolf suckling twins Remus and Romulus. Scarce.

The twins then built their own city, but Romulus killed Remus in a fight over which one of them was to reign as the king of Rome. Then the city was named after Romulus. The same legend says that the Latins invited the Sabines to a festival and stole all the unmarried maidens, leading to the integration of the Latins and the Sabines. By the late sixth century BC, The original Latin and Sabine tribes invented their own government by creating a republic.

The Roman Republic was established around 509 BC, and a system based on annually elected magistrates and representatives was established. They did not have emperors or kings, but consuls. The magistracies were originally restricted to aristocrats but were later opened to common people. The Romans secured their conquests by founding colonies in strategic areas, establishing stable control over the region. In the second half of the third century BC, Rome had a war with Carthage in the first of three Punic Wars. These wars resulted in Rome's first overseas conquests of Sicily and Hispania and the rise of Rome as a super imperial power. After defeating the Macedonian and Seleucid empires in the second century BC, the Romans became the dominant power of the Mediterranean Sea.

The Roman Republic struck silver coins called *Denarius*. An example of their coins are presented in this section of this book. The responsibility of minting coins in the republic was primarily that of the *tresviri auro argento aere flando feriundo* (the three men of casting and striking of gold, silver, and bronze). After Julius Caesar, moneyers were increased to four, and the moneyers often placed their names on their coins, although anonymous issues did occur.

Roman Republic. Anonymous. 225-212 BC.
AR didrachm (20 mm, 6.64 gr.)
janiform head of Janus/Jupiter in quadriga. Scarce.

Roman Republic. C. Minucius. 135 BC.
AR denarius (19 mm, 3.91 gr.)
helmeted head of Roma/two togate figures standing.

Roman Republic. L. Minucius. 133
BC. AR denarius (20 mm, 3.90 gr.)
helmeted head of Roma/Jupiter in Quadriga.

Roman Republic. M.Furius. Philus 119
BC. AR denarius (19 mm, 3.8 gr.)
janiform head of Janus/Roma standing. Scarce.

Roman Republic. M. lucilius Rufus. 101
BC. AR denarius (20 mm, 3.90 gr.)
helmeted head of Roma/Victory in a biga.

Roman Republic. Q. Titius 90 BC.
AR denarius (17 mm, 3.69 gr.)
head of Titinus/Pegasus.

Roman Republic. Q. Titius 90 BC.
AR denarius (18 mm, 3.75 gr.)
head of Bacchus/Pegasus.

Roman Republic. C. Norbanus 83 BC.
AR denarius (18 mm, 3.95 gr.)
head of Venus/grain ear and caduceus.

Roman Republic. A.Postumius Albinus. 81 BC.
AR denarius (19 mm, 3.42 gr.)
head of Hispania/togate figure.

Roman Republic. A.Postumius Albinus. 81 BC.
AR denarius (19 mm, 3.75 gr.)
bust of Diana/togate figure.

Roman Republic. L. Procilius. 80 BC.
AR denarius (19 mm, 3.42 gr.)
head of Juno/Juno in Biga.

Roman Republic. CN. Lentulus 76-75 BC.
AR denarius (19 mm, 3.76 gr.) bust of Genius/
EX SC divided by scepter, globe and rudder.

In the early republican period, signs and letters were used to identify the moneyer. From 80 BC onward, men from more prominent families began to hold the office of moneyer. Many of them took the opportunity to show on their coins designs that represented the achievements of their family and ancestors, thereby increasing their own prestige and hope of election to higher offices. All the coins displayed on these pages are Denari (except one, as noted), which were the standard coins of the Roman Republic.

THE ROMAN IMPERATORIAL

This period is referred to by many historians as being from Pompey the Great to Augustus (71–28 BC). Pompey the Great (106–48 BC) was a distinguished military and political leader of the Roman

Imperatorial Period. After military triumphs, he established a place for himself in the ranks of Roman nobility and was granted the title "the Great" for his accomplishments. Pompey was a rival of Marcus Crassus and, at first, an ally to Julius Caesar. The three politicians dominated the late Roman Republic and almost all the Imperatorial Period in 67 BC. Pompey was nominated commander of a special naval task force to campaign against the pirates that dominated the Mediterranean waters.

Roman Imperatorial. Pompey the Great,
42-40 BC. AR Denarius (18 mm, 3.73 gr.)
Bare head of Pompey the Great/Neptune standing
between the Catanaean brothers. Very Rare.

Ultimately, it took Pompey almost a year to clear the Mediterranean of the danger of pirates in 67–66 BC. Pompey, in 66 BC, was nominated to the command that takes charge of the Third Mithridatic War and to fight Mithridates VI of Pontus. In 65 BC, Pompey made Pontus a Roman province. In 64 BC, he marched into Syria, disposed of king Antiochus XIII, and also made that country a Roman province. In 63 BC, he advanced farther south in order to establish the Roman supremacy in Phoenicia, Coele-Syria, and Judea, but he was murdered on landing in Egypt in 48 BC.

The largest conflicts in this era were the wars with Mithridates VI the Great, king of Pontus. He is remembered as one of Rome's most formidable and successful enemies who engaged three of the most prominent generals of the late Roman Republic: Sulla, Lucius Murena, and Pompey the Great. They had three wars with him. The First Mithridatic War under General Sulla (89–85 BC) lasted five years and ended in a Roman victory, which forced Mithridates to abandon all his occupied territories and return to Pontus.

Mithradates VI. Greek Kings of Pontos.
120-63 BC. AV Stater (20 mm, 8.34 gr.)
Kallatis mint. diademed head of deified
Alexander/Athena seated. Very Rare.

Mithradates VI. Greek Kings of Pontos.
120-63 BC. AV Stater (20 mm, 8.38 gr.)
Tomis mint. diademed head of deified
Alexander/Athena seated. Very Rare.

Mithradates VI. Greek Kings of Pontos.
120-63 BC. AV Stater (20 mm, 8.30 gr.)
Istros mint. Diademed head of deified
Alexander/Athena seated. Very Rare.

The Second Mithridatic War (83–81 BC) was fought between Mithridates VI and General Lucius Murena and ended in a victory for Mithridates. The Third Mithridatic War (73–63 BC) was the last and longest of three wars fought between Mithridates VI and the Roman Republic. The Romans won the war under Pompey the Great, and Mithridates committed suicide, ending the Pontic kingdom.

The elder son of Pompey the Great, Cnaeu Pompey, was born in 79 BC. In the course of the African war, he moved to Spain via the Balearic Islands to join his younger brother, Sextus Pompey, following the Pompeian defeat at Thaspus in 46 BC. Their military activities in the Iberian Peninsula brought Julius Caesar's intervention, and in 45 BC, Caesar defeated the Pompeians at Munda.

Roman Imperatorial. Cn. Pompey Jr. 46-45 BC.
AR Denarius (19 mm, 3.81 gr.)
head of Roma/Hispania standing. Rare.

Sextus Pompey, the younger son of Pompey the Great, escaped, but Cnaeu Pompey Jr. was captured and put to death in 45 BC.

Roman Imperatorial. Sextus Pompey, 43-36 BC.
AE As (29 mm, 13.82 gr.) janiform head with
feature of Pompey/prow of galley. Scarce.

After Julius Caesar's death, he formed a fleet, became master of the Mediterranean Sea, and seized the island of Sicily. He was eventually defeated by the fleet of Octavian, and he was taken prisoner and put to death in 35 BC

Julius Caesar, born in 100 BC, was a Roman military and political leader. He played a critical role in the transformation of the Roman Republic into the Roman Empire. Julius Caesar marched into Gaul in 58 BC. The term *Gaul* refers to the Celts, the original people of Europe.

Roman Imperatorial. Julius Caesar, 49-48 BC.
AR Denarius (18 mm, 3.69 gr.) elephant/apex,
Securis and aspergillum. Rare.

With the help of various Gallic tribes, he managed to conquer nearly all of Gaul—this means all of Europe and the southern coast of England. He defeated Pompey in 48 BC and spent the next two years defeating the remnants of the Pompeian family. He then returned to Rome the undisputed master of the Roman world, but after a short time, he was assassinated by a group of senators on the Ides of Mars (15th of March) in 44 BC.

Mark Antony was born in 83 BC and was a Roman politician and general. He was an important supporter and the best friend of Julius Caesar as a military commander and administrator.

Mark Antony. Roman Macedon, Thessalonica.
37 BC. AE (21 mm, 12.36 gr.)
head of Agonothesia/Ant, Kai in two lines. Scarce.

Disagreement between Octavian and Antony erupted into a civil war—the final war of the Roman Republic. In 31 BC, Antony was defeated by Octavian at the naval battle of Actium and a brief land battle at Alexandria. He and his lover, Queen Cleopatra VII of Egypt, committed suicide at Alexandria in 30 BC.

Octavian was born in 63 BC and was adopted by his great-uncle Julius Caesar as his heir shortly before his assassination in 44 BC.

Octavian. Roman Imperatorial.
Autumn 30-Summer 29 BC.
AR Denarius (18 mm 3.70 gr.)
head of Octavian/statue of Octavian. Rare.

The death of Julius Caesar, Mark Antony, Brutus, and Cassius left Octavian the undisputed master of the Roman Empire at the age of thirty-three. In 27 BC, he was granted the title "Augustus," the name by which he is best known to history, and this event is generally accepted as marking the commencement of the Roman Imperial period.

The Roman Imperial section will be discussed in the third part of this book called "The New Testament."

The Parthian
(The Second Persian Empire)

The Parthian Empire, often called the second Persian Empire, was a very important ancient civilization that began at the end of the Greek Empire through the Roman Republic and a good 200 years into the Roman Imperial period, which lasted for over 400 years. The Parthian Empire was the enemy of Rome.

Parthia was originally designated as a territory southeast of the Caspian Sea. It was a satrapy of the Persian Empire from 550 BC when it was subdued by Cyrus the Great until the conquest of the Persian Empire by Alexander the Great in 330 BC. From 311 BC, Parthia became a part of the Seleucid Empire, being ruled by various satraps under the Seleucid kingdom. The Seleucid monarchs tried to stop Parthia from expanding, and Antiochus IV spent the end of his reign fighting the newly emerging Parthian Empire. The Parthian made an even greater gain when Antiochus IV died in 164 BC.

During the reign of Mithridates II and Arodes II, the Parthians conquered all of Iraq, Armenia, eastern Turkey, and eastern Syria. Their army went south and occupied Judaea, Phoenicia, and Arabia.

Mithradates II. Parthia. 123-88 BC.
AR Drachm (22 mm, 3.7 gr.)
diademed bust/archer with bow.

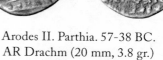

Arodes II. Parthia. 57-38 BC.
AR Drachm (20 mm, 3.8 gr.)
diademed bust/archer with bow.

Arodes II. Parthia. 57-38 BC.
AR Drachm (21 mm, 4.0 gr.)
diademed bust/archer with bow.

The Parthian had many wars with Rome, and they were difficult to defeat. According to sources, they used strategies during warfare unfamiliar to the Romans, such as the famous "Parthian shot," firing arrows backward at the gallop. The Parthian, by their archery, won many battles with the Romans, and the wars between them lasted almost 300 years.

Phraates IV killed his father, King Orodes II, and all his brothers and their families, and he started to advance into Roman territories.

Phraates IV. Parthia. 38-2 BC.
AR Drachm (19 mm, 3.8 gr.)
diademed bust/archer with bow.

Phraates IV. Parthia. 38-2 BC.
AR Drachm (22 mm, 3.9 gr.)
diademed bust/archer with bow.

Mark Antony set out to fight Phraates in 36 BC with an army well over 100,000 men. Antony lost the war, and over 10,000 Romans were killed, and Antony's support and supplies were lost.

Artabanos II (AD 10–38) was one of the most vigorous of the Parthian kings. He was able to expand his monarchy.

Artabanos II. Parthia. 10-38 AD.
AR Drachm (21 mm, 3.5 gr.)
diademed bust/archer with bow.

Artabanos II. Parthia. 10-38 AD.
AR Drachm (21 mm, 3.8 gr.)
diademed bust/archer with bow.

Artabanos II. Parthia. 10-38 AD.
AR Drachm (20 mm, 3.9 gr.)
diademed bust/archer with bow.

Artabanos II. Parthia. 10-38 AD.
AR Drachm (21 mm, 3.9 gr.)
diademed bust/archer with bow.

Vardanes I. Parthia. 40-45 AD.
AR Drachm (20 mm, 3.8 gr.)
diademed bust/archer with bow.

He threatened the Romans to expand the borders of Parthia to include all the territories of the Old Persian Empire under Cyrus the Great. With the help of the Romans, Artabanos II was disposed of and died in AD 38. His son, Vardanes I, took over the throne. Vardanes I successfully controlled the entire empire as far as Aria. Vardanes I was murdered in AD 45 during a hunt.

In AD 51, Parthian King Vologases I (AD 51–78) took over the throne. During his reign, the Parthian Empire began to decay, and finally, he gave Media and Armenia to two of his brothers. Parthia was ruled by many kings after the fall of Vologases I. Vologases III ruled part of the empire from about AD 105. After AD 110, Parthian King Vologases III dethroned the Armenian ruler, and because of that, Roman Emperor Trajan decided to invade Parthia in retaliation. In 116 AD. Trajan took the Parthian capital, Susa and disposed the Parthian king Osroes I. In AD 161, King Vologases IV declared war against the Romans and conquered Armenia. The Roman, with a massive army, marched to fight the Parthians in AD 165. The Parthians were only saved by the outburst of a catastrophic epidemic (smallpox), which temporarily crippled the two empires.

Vologases I.Parthia.51-78 AD. BI Tatradrachm.
(28 mm, 14.12 gr.) diademed bust/
archer with bow. scarce.

Vologases III. Parthia.105-147 AD.
AR Drachm (20 mm, 3.5 gr.)
diademed bust/archer with bow.

Vologases III. Parthia.105-147 AD.
AR Drachm (20 mm, 3.3 gr.)
diademed bust/archer with bow.

Vologases IV. Parthia.147-191 AD.
AR Drachm (21 mm, 3.6 gr.)
diademed bust/archer with bow.

Osroes II. Parthia.190 AD.
AR Drachm (19 mm, 3.5 gr.)
diademed bust/archer with bow.

Osroes II. Parthia.190 AD.
AR Drachm (19 mm, 3.7 gr.)
diademed bust/archer with bow.

Osroes II. Parthia.190 AD.
AR Drachm (19 mm, 3.7 gr.)
diademed bust/archer with bow.

The deciding blow came thirty years later, a few years after King Osroes II (reigned only one year, AD 190), when General Septimius Severus attacked and defeated the Parthians in AD 198. In AD 224, Sasanid King Ardashir revolted, and two years later, he took the capital of Parthia, and this time, it was the end of the Parthian Empire.

The Sasanian Empire will be discussed in part three.

PART III
THE NEW TESTAMENT

The Roman Imperial

After conquering Macedonia, Thrace, Cleopatra VII in Egypt, the Parthians, and the Seleucid Empire, the Romans became the masters of the world. Conquering the armies for Mark Antony and Pompey the Great left Octavian the dominant power of Rome. Octavian became the first Emperor of Rome in 27 BC, and his name changed to Augustus as the Roman honorary title. He was called by that name during his reign form 27 BC to AD 14. The Roman Imperial period lasted almost 500 years before it collapsed and the Byzantine Empire took the lead and lasted approximately 850 years. During the Roman Imperial period, Judea and the Jewish nation suffered more losses and brutal treatment than any other period in Hebrew history. The Christians as well were prosecuted and tortured more than any period in the history of Christianity. The massacres and brutality of both the Jewish nation and the Christians will be discussed briefly later.

Augustus played a very important role in creating the Roman Imperial. Many setbacks affected Augustus during his reign, but over all, he was a very successful leader.

Augustus. Roman Syria, Antioch. 27 BC-14 AD.
AE AS (26 mm, 15.36 gr.)
laureate head/large SC.

He held very great power for a little of over forty years, as the Bible tells us: "In those days Caesar Augustus issued a decree that a census should be taken of the entire Roman world." (Luke 2:1, NIV). Augustus died in AD 14, and he was succeeded by Tiberius (AD 14–37) the oldest son of his wife, Livia, by her first husband.

Tiberius. Roman. Galatia. 14-37 AD.
AE 22 mm 4.22 gr.bare
head left/vailed head of Cybele.

Tiberius proved himself a capable and responsible emperor, and the empire in general prospered during his reign. The biggest problems he faced were the struggle involving the succession of power within the emperor's family. The ministry and crucifixion of Jesus Christ occurred during his reign. Tiberius eventually retired to the island of Capri and never returned to Rome. He died in AD 37.

The story of the "penny" of Tiberius is very well known biblical reference to a coin called "the tribute penny." The Bible says, "Is it right to pay tribute to Caesar? Should we pay or should not, but Jesus knew their hypocrisy. Why are you trying to trap me? He asked. Bring me a denarius and let me look at it" (Mark 12:15, NIV).

The Tribute Penny. Roman. Tiberius. 14-37 AD.
AR Denarius, 18 mm, 3.53 gr.
laureate head/Livia seated. Rare

Emperor Tiberius was also mentioned in the Bible: "In the fifteenth year of the reign of Tiberius Caesar..." (Luke 3:1, NIV).

Emperor Gaius, better known to history as Caligula (little boot), succeeded his great-uncle Tiberius in AD 37. This nickname was given to him by the soldiers when he used to wear a miniature uniform of a private soldier, including the half boot (Caliga), when he was only a few years old.

Caligula. Roman. 37-41 AD.
AE AS 28 mm, 10.98 gr.
bare head left/Vista seated. Scarce

He showed promise to the empire by being a good emperor during his first year when he was under the supervision of his grandmother, Antonia, but later he became ill and possibly insane and became very irresponsible. For the rest of his reign, he was noted for his public oppression and terrifying the imperial palace. He was eventually murdered along with his wife and infant daughter in a group in AD 41.

Claudius took over and was proclaimed emperor by the Praetorian guard in AD 41. A childhood attack of infantile paralysis had left him with a stutter and limp; also, it was generally assumed that he was weak-minded. Claudius is mentioned in the Bible: "There he (Paul) met a Jew named Aquila, a native of Pontus, who had recently come from Italy with his wife Priscilla, because Claudius had ordered all the Jews to leave Rome" (Acts 18:2, NIV).

Claudius. Roman Galatia. 41-54 AD.
AE (18 mm, 5.79 gr.) laureate head/name
of Magistrate in three lines. Scarce.

Claudius was a survivor and tireless worker. It soon became very clear that he was not as weak-minded as people had thought, and in fact, he proved himself a very strong, organized administrator. In AD 43, Claudius invaded Britain, and this was the beginning of the Roman control of Britain, which lasted over 400 years. Claudius married his niece, Agrippina Junior, in AD 49, and in AD 50, he adopted her son, Nero, who then became the heir to the throne. Claudius died in AD 54 after he was poisoned, possibly by the orders of his wife, Agrippina.

Nero became an emperor after Claudius died in AD 54. Apostle Paul stood before Nero when he was taken as a prisoner to Rome for trial. The Roman government was in good shape under capable minds of Seneca and Burrus. The young Emperor Nero could not wait until he could free himself from all restraints, including his controlling mother.

Nero. Roman Imperial. 54-68 AD.
AE AS (28 mm, 10.24 gr.)
bare head of Nero/Victory alighting.

After he ordered her death and the death of Seneca and Burrus, Nero's behavior and conduct was not acceptable and became uncontrolled. His obsession with arts and sport caused him to ignore the basic duties of his government. His cruelty, extravagances, and pride made him very unpopular. According to some legends, he started the great fire of Rome, which destroyed half of the city in AD 64. Many revolts erupted in North Africa, Gaul land, and Spain, and he fled and committed suicide in AD 68.

Four emperors ruled Rome in one year (AD 68–69), including Nero, which was known as the year of four emperors. Emperor Galba reigned for seven months, Emperor Otho ruled for three months, and Vitellius ruled for two months. Galba was governor of Hispania and came to power during the rebellion against Nero.

Galba. Roman Imperial. 68-69 AD.
AR Denarius (20 mm, 3.21 gr.)
laureate head/Diva Livia. Rare.

He had strict discipline and rigid economy, which made him very unpopular with the Roman army. In Rome, Galba was murdered, possibly by Otho, and his severed head was paraded on a pike. Otho proclaimed himself emperor after he put Galba and Calpurnius Piso (Galba adapted heir) to death. He had no qualifications to be an emperor. He was defeated in battle by the army of Vitellius, and he committed suicide.

Vitellius was proclaimed emperor of Rome by his troops after Otho committed suicide. He was appointed governor of lower Germany by Galba to get him as far away from Rome as possible.

Vitellius. Roman Imperial. 69 AD.
AR Denarius (18 mm, 2.73 gr.)
bare head/tripod-lebes, dolphin. Rare.

He was brutal and gave more attention to pleasures and banquets than to the business of government. The army of Vitellius's province revolted and went to Rome, and Vitellius was later captured and murdered by the hands of soldiers loyal to his successor, Vespasian. His body was paraded and dragged through Rome's streets and was finally thrown in the Tiber River.

In AD 69, the legions at Alexandria proclaimed Vespasian (AD 69–79) emperor of Rome. Despite his humble origin, his military skill carried him to a series of important positions, and he was the commander of a portion of the army that invaded Britain under Claudius.

Vespasian. Roman Imperial. 69-79 AD.
AE AS (28 mm, 11.19 gr.)
lauteate head/SC providen, altar.

Vespasian. Roman Imperial. 69-79 AD
AR Denarius (19 mm, 3.45 gr.)
laureate head/shield inscribed SC, two capricorns.

Vespasian. Roman Imperial 69-79 AD.
AR Denarius (19 mm, 3.5 gr.)
laureate head/yoke of oxen.

He was a military man of simple background and tastes. Soon after he became an emperor, he focused on the big task of rebuilding the empire and repairing the damage caused by many civil wars. He proved to be a just and industrious leader with an extraordinary patriotic work ethic. The Roman Empire's condition was soon improved. He died in AD 79 after serving Rome for ten years.

Titus (AD 79–81), Vespasian's eldest son, became an emperor and held the title of Augustus only for two years from AD 79–81.

Titus. Roman Imperial. 79-81 AD.
AR Denarius (18 mm, 3.13 gr.)
Laureate head/rostral column.

He witnessed the opening of the Colosseum in Rome and the volcanic eruption of Mt. Vesuvius, which destroyed the city of Pompeii and ashed the entire bay of Naples. He was always in conflict with his envious younger brother, Domitian, who, according to some legends, murdered Titus in AD 81.

Domitian (AD 81–96) spent most of his life growing up in the shadow of his brother, Titus, who was recognized as a hero during the first Jewish war. He became emperor in AD 81 after the death of his brother, Titus. During the first couple of years, he showed interest and promise to the Roman people and the Senate, but later, he did not maintain his father and brother's reputations.

Domitian. Roman Imperial. 81-96 AD.
AR Denarius (18 mm, 3.47 gr.)
laureat head/clasped hands.

He was very unpopular to those who suffered under his harsh rules. His civil unpopularity resulted in many assassination plots and conspiracies; however, he survived many attempts to kill him until he was murdered in his palace in AD 96.

The period of the twelve Caesars of Rome lasted from about 44 BC to AD 96 being, the first Caesar was Julius Caesar and the last one was Domitian. These twelve Caesars, especially the first two (Julius Caesar and Augustus), initiated the groundwork, forming a government that began as a hereditary monarchy that endured for almost 500 years. After the period of the twelve Caesars passed, more than 125 emperors ruled the Roman Empire, and only the most prominent will be mentioned very briefly on and off in the remainder of this book.

The Herodian Period

The Nabataean kingdom conquered Edom, as mentioned earlier; then, the Hasmonean dynasty re-conquered it under the reign of King John Hyrcanus. Judaea was again annexed to the Judean realm. Antipater, Herod the Great's father, was a very wealthy figure from Idumaea in southern Judaea, where the Edomites were settled. Antipater was married to the daughter of a Nabataean nobleman from Arabia. History is not very clear whether Antipater was an original Jew that descended from the original Israelites that settled in Edom after Moses died or whether he was forced to convert to Judaism when the Hasmoneans invaded Edom. Since Antipater married an Arab woman and Herod I was born in 73 BC, if any—or both—of the two theories above are correct, that would make Herod the Great 100 percent Arab or half Jew. This created many problems later in his reign over the Jewish nation.

HEROD THE GREAT (40–4 BC)

In 40 BC, by declaration of the Roman Senate and the approval of Octavian (later was named Augustus), Herod I was made a king. Of course, this title was honorific, as Judaea was still under the rule of the Parthians; therefore, the Senate also approved to give Herod a Roman army to help him recapture Judaea. In 37 BC, with the help of the Roman army, Herod finally was able to besiege Jerusalem and capture it. Octavian realized the importance of Herod in the east, so he restored to Herod all coastal regions of Judaea. The Roman Senate had already given him Samaria and Idumea, Mark Antony added the Nabataean areas to Herod's territory, and Augustus later awarded Herod large areas in the Transjordan. Herod's territory became as large as it was during the Hasmonean dynasty but stronger because of his Roman allies. Officially, Herod reigned as the "king of Judaea" in 37 BC, and all the Romans and other allies blessed this title. The Jewish nation never blessed his title.

Now Herod had his kingdom, but he still had to be protected and be accepted by the Jewish people, which was more difficult because of Herod's background. Herod's mother was an ethnic Arab, and his father was an Edomite. Even though Herod grew up as a Jew, he lacked the bloodline of the powerful old families in Jerusalem who claimed that they were of pure Jewish blood and were eligible to serve as high priests, as the Hasmonean kings had done. The vast majority of the Jewish, if not all, did not accept Herod to be their king and considered him an outsider.

That caused him to be paranoid and to continue to fight for a Hasmonean theocracy. To strengthen his ties with the royal Hasmonean family, he married Mariamne, a Hasmonean princess, the grand-daughter of Hyrcanus II. Even though Herod was connected to the priestly family bloodline by marriage, the threat remained, and domestic tragedy began to affect Herod's rule. Aristobulus III, Herod's wife's brother, who was the legal heir to the office of high priest, became very popular in the Hasomonaean society. In 30 BC, Herod ordered him to be killed and also ordered the execution of

Hyrcanus II, even though the old man was nearing eighty. In 29 BC, he distrusted his wife, Mariamne, and he had her killed, even though they had five children together. The following year, he executed Mariamne's mother, Alexandra, and his brother-in-law, Kostobar. In the same year, Herod ordered the execution of his two sons by Mariamne, Antipar, and Aristobulus, and later, he executed the remaining three sons by Mariamne. According to legend, when Emperor Augustus heard about all his sons' executions, he said his famous words: "I'd rather be Herod's pig than his son."

Herod the Great. Judaea. 40-4 BC.
AE prutah (15 mm, 1.67 gr.)
anchor/two cornuacopia.

Herod the Great. Judaea. 40-4 BC.
AE prutot (23 mm, 6.94gr.) ceremonial bowl (lebes),
tripod/helmet,star,palms. Scarce.

Herod the Great. Judaea. 40-4 BC.
AE prutot (23 mm, 6.18gr.) ceremonial bowl (lebes),
tripod/helmet,star,palms. Scarce.

Now Herod had eliminated every member of the Hasomanean family who might threaten Herod's throne in the near future. Herod was accused by many scholars through the history as the "killer of the innocents." He ordered the killing of all the male babies in Bethlehem and the surrounding area in order to kill the newborn "King of the Jews," Jesus Christ. As the Bible tells us: "When Herod realized that he had been outwitted by the Magi, he was furious, and he gave orders to kill all the boys in Bethlehem and its vicinity who were two years old and under, in accordance with the time he had learned from the Magi" (Matthew 2:16, NIV).

In spite of all the trouble and turmoil Herod had in his own family, he was one of the most imaginative builders and organizer of the ancient world.

Herod the Great changed the face of the Holy Land. He rebuilt and enlarged Samaria, the former capital of the northern kingdom, and called "Sebaste" in honor of Octavian, who was known then as

Augustus (Sebastos in Greek). He built an enormous, Corinthian-style temple on top of the ruins that was supposedly the site of the palace of former king of Israel Omri and his son Ahab.

Samaria. Greek Samaria. 375-333 BC.
AR Obol (9 mm, 0.80 gr.)
head of Athena/owl. Very Rare.

Sebaste. Roman Judaea. Commodus, 177-192 AD.
AE (25 mm, 9.21 gr.) laureate, draped head/
Demeter standing. Rare.

Sebaste. Roman Judaea. Commodus,177-192 AD.
AE (22 mm, 8.24 gr.) laureate head/
turreted bust of Tyche. Rare.

Sebaste. Roman Judaea. Commodus,177-192 AD.
AE (24 mm, 7.24 gr.) laureate head/
turreted bust of Tyche. Rare.

Caesaraea Maritima. Roman Judaea. 117-138 AD,
Hadrian. AE (24 mm, 11.87gr.) laureate head/
draped bust of Sarapis wearing Kalathos.

Caesaraea Maritima. Roman Judaea. 117-138 AD,
Hadrian. AE (29 mm, 18.17gr.) draped bust/
Hadrian as founder plowing. Scarce.

Around 22 BC, Herod came up with the idea to construct a state-of-the-art port city on the Mediterranean coast, and he called it "Caesarea" (later Caesarea Maritima), in honor of Caesar Augustus. He built many spectacular fortresses and temples during his reign, many of which can still be seen today. Herod was best known and remembered for his rebuilding of the temple in Jerusalem. This massive plan took eighty-four years to be completed, from 18 BC to the first Jewish revolt in AD 66. He turned it into a magnificent Jewish worship place, and it was built to the highest standard of architecture. Herod became very sick, and he died in 4 BC.

During King Herod's reign, coins minted in Judea did not show the king's likeness in respect to the Jewish faith against graven images. Herod was the first Jewish ruler to use Greek inscriptions on his coins. The Herodian kingdom was divided between his three surviving sons: Herod Archelaus, Herod Antipas, and Herod Philip II. Later, the kingdom was ruled by Agrippa I and Agrippa II until AD 95. The Bible described the family of Herod in detail, as shown in chapter 2 of the book of Matthew.

HEROD ARCHELAUS

Herod Archelaus (4 BC–AD 6) was the oldest son of Herod the Great. After Jesus was born, Joseph and Mary took the child to Egypt, because Herod the Great ordered every male child under two years old to be killed. When Joseph heard that Herod the Great died, he decided to go back to Judaea. The Bible tells us a different plan revealed to Joseph: "But when he heard that Archelaus was reigning in Judaea in place of his father Herod, he was afraid to go there. Having been warned in a dream, he withdrew to the district of Galilee" (Matthew 2:22, NIV). Archelaus was appointed king by his father, but the Roman emperor told him that he should be content and happy with the title of ethnarch (national leader) over Judaea, Samaria, and Idumaea.

Herod Archelaus. Judaea. 4 BC-6 AD.
AE prutah (15 mm, 1.4 gr.)
anchor/Greek inscription.

Herod Archelaus. Judaea. 4 BC-6 AD.
AE prutah (12 mm, 0.79 gr.)
two cornucopias/galley.

Augustus promised him that the title "king" would also be granted in the future if Archelaus proved himself a good governor and likeable by his people. Right after his accession, in 4 BC, things began to go wrong, and the Jews hated him and wanted him to reduce the heavy taxes imposed by his father. Two high priests removed the golden eagle from the entrance of the temple, which his father, Herod the Great, put up during his reign. It was a sin to make idols, according to the Ten Commandments. The two priests were burned alive for their doings, and riots broke out all over Judaea, and Archelaus sent his soldiers to face the angry crowd, and some 3,000 Jews were killed, according to Josephus. Archelaus ruled so badly and brutally to his subjects, and the Jews went to Rome and told the emperor about him, "but his subjects hated him and sent a delegation after him to say, we don't want this man to be our king" (Luke 19:14, NIV). Finally, after nine years of bloody reign, he was banished to Vienna in Gaul, and Judaea became a province of the Roman Empire under the direct rule of the Roman procurator Coponius. Most coins of Archelaus carry his title, *ethnarch,* which is Greek for "part of." His coins are usually found in average or below average condition.

HEROD ANTIPAS

Herod Antipas (4 BC–AD 40) was also the son of Herod the Great and full brother to Archelaus. He governed the territories of Galilee and Perea under the title of "tetrach" (ruler of quarter).

Herod Antipas. Judaea. 4 BC-39 AD.
AE (19 mm, 6.74 gr.) branch date across field/
Tibe-Piac in two lines. Very Rare.

He was given his title and his territories by Emperor Augustus and Tiberius after Augustus's death. He was responsible for building projects in Sepphoris, which he initially made his capital. He moved his capital to the city of Tiberias on the western shore of the Sea of Galilee.

Tiberias. Roman Judaea. 98-117 AD, Trajan.
AE (26 mm, 11.3 gr.) laureate
head/Tyche standing. Scarce.

Tiberias. Roman Judaea. 117-138 AD, Hadrian.
AE (23 mm, 12.64 gr.) laureate head/
Zeus seated in tetrastyle temple. Scarce.

Tiberias. Roman Judaea. 117-138 AD, Hadrian.
AE (23 mm, 7.93 gr.) laureate head/
Zeus seated in tetrastyle temple. Scarce.

Herod Antipas built this city and named it in honor of his patron, Roman Emperor Tiberius, who succeeded Augustus in AD 14. The city later became the center of rabbinic teaching. Herod Antipas was married to the daughter of King Aretas IV of the Nabataean kingdom. Herod divorced her and married his brother's wife, Herodias, which created soured relationships between Herod and King Aretas. Antipas was responsible for putting John the Baptist in prison, because, according to Josephus, John's public influences made him fearful of rebellion.

The Bible tells us: "Now Herod had arrested John and bound him and put him in prison because of Herodias, his brother Philip's wife" (Matthew 14:3, NIV). On Herod Antipas's birthday, the daughter of Herodias (unnamed in the Bible but traditionally known as Salome) danced for him and pleased him very much. Salome asked for the head of John the Baptist after Antipas promised her, with an oath, to give her any reward she asked for in reward for her dancing. According to the Gospel of Luke, when Jesus was brought before Pontius Pilate for trial, Pilate handed him to Herod Antipas, and later, Herod Antipas sent him back to Pilate. Agrippa I, grandson of Herod the Great, tried to accuse Antipas of conspiracy against Caligula, the new Roman emperor. Caligula banished Antipas to Gaul, where he died at an unknown date.

HEROD PHILIP II

Herod Philip II (4 BC–AD 34) was the son of Herod the Great and half brother of Herod Antipas. He received the northeastern portion of Herod the Great's kingdom. Philip II was married to his niece, Salome (the daughter of Herodias and Herod Philip I), who had the connection with the execution of John the Baptist. Herod Philip II rebuilt the city of Caesarea Philippi (Paneas), calling it by his own name to distinguish it from the other Caesarea built by his father, Herod the Great, on the Mediterranean coast.

Herod Philip. Judaea. 4 BC-34 AD. AE (22 mm, 8.37 gr.) Dated RY 12 (8/9 AD). laureate head of Augustus/ tetrastyle temple. Very Rare.

Caesaraea Panias. Roman Judaea. 50-100 AD, Agrippa II with Domitian. AE (19 mm, 6.57 gr.) laureate head of Domitian/Nike. Scarce.

The Bible tells us: "In the fifteenth year of the reign of Tiberius Caesar- when Pontius Pilate was governor of Judea, Herod Tetrarch of Galilee, his brother Philip Tetrarch of Iturea and Traconitis..." (Luke 3:1, NIV). According to Josephus, Philip II was a very fair man and a peace-loving person. He proved himself to be a person of moderation and quietness in his personal life and his government affairs. He helped the poor, punished the guilty, and gave mercy to those who had been accused unjustly.

Herod Philip II died in Julias in AD 33, the same year Jesus was crucified, according to the Bible. All his territories were given to Agrippa I in AD 37. Philip II was the first Jewish ruler to strike coins with his own portrait, as was a representation of the Roman temple at Caesarea Philippi. His coins are very rare and seldom found in good conditions, as is the case in most Judaean coins.

HEROD AGRIPPA I

Herod Agrippa I (AD 37–44) was the grandson of Herod the Great and son of Aristobulus. According to the biblical narrative, he is the "Herod" who was mentioned in the book of Acts, verses 1–23: "It was about this time that king Herod (Agrippa) arrested some who belonged to the church, intending to persecute them" (Acts 12:1, NIV). Herod Agrippa's mother, Mariamne, was a Hasmonean and a direct descendent of the Maccabees as well; thus Agrippa was very well respected by the Jews. Even though he was very loyal to Rome, he kept very patriotic feelings toward his country.

After Tiberius died, the new emperor, Caligula, made him tetrarch over the territories of Philip. After the assassination of Caligula in AD 41, the new emperor, Claudius, gave Agrippa dominion over all Judaea, Samaria, and the province of Chalcis ad Labnum at his request. Therefore, Agrippa became one of the most powerful princes of the east, and his territories matched or exceeded that which was held by his grandfather, Herod the Great.

He was a magnificent builder, similar to his grandfather. He built a theater and amphitheater in Berytus (Beriut) and similar magnanimity in Sebaste and Caesarea Maritima. According to legend, after a Passover celebration in AD 44, Agrippa went to Caesarea and performed games in honor of Emperor Claudius. He immediately fell with severe pain in the heart and abdomen, and he died afterward.

Agrippa I. Judaea. 37-44 AD. AE Prutah
(16 mm, 2.0 gr.) canopy/three ears of barley.

Agrippa I. Judaea. 37-44 AD. AE Prutah
(16 mm, 2.0 gr.) canopy/three ears of barley.

Agrippa I. Judaea. 37-44 AD. AE Prutah
(17 mm, 2.8 gr.) canopy/three ears of barley.

Agrippa I. Judaea. 37-44 AD. AE Prutah
(17 mm, 2.9 gr.) canopy/three ears of barley.

Caesaraea Maritima. Roman Judaea. 98-117 AD,
Trajan. AE (25 mm, 9.41 gr.) laureate
head/emperor, veiled standing. Scarce.

Sebaste. Roman Judaea. Geta, 209-212 AD.
AE (21.8 mm, 7.85 gr.) bare head of Geta/
Genius of the colony standing. Rare.

Sebaste. Roman Judaea. Aquila Severa Augusta,
220-222 AD. AE (22 mm, 6.98 gr.)
draped bust/Sphinx seated. Rare.

Berytus. Roman Phoenicia. 218-222 AD,
Elagabalus. AE (31 mm, 22.39 gr.)
laureate bust right/Marsyas within structure. Rare.

HEROD AGRIPPA II

Herod Agrippa II (AD 56–95) was the son of Agrippa I and was only seventeen years old when his father died. For this reason, Roman Emperor Claudius kept him in Rome and sent Cuspius Fadus as procurator of the kingdom and put the kingdom under the Roman rule. Later, Claudius and, after him, Nero had given the right to direct the affairs of the temple in Jerusalem and to appoint the high priest. His sister, Berenice, used to go with him frequently to Rome and Jerusalem. According to Josephus, Berenice had several failed marriages, and she spent the majority of her life with her brother, Agrippa II. The rumors were that she and Agrippa II had an incestuous relationship and that she also began a love affair with Roman Emperor Titus.

Agrippa II. Roman Judaea. 50-100 AD.
AE (24 mm, 12.33 gr.) Dated RY14 (74/75 AD).
laureate head of Titus/Nike. Scarce.

Agrippa II. Roman Judaea. 50-100 AD. AE
(24 mm, 11.59 gr.) Dated RY26 (86/87 AD).
laureate head of Titus/Nike. Scarce.

Caesaraea Maritima. Roman Judaea. 249-251 AD.
Trajan decius. AE (28 mm, 15.08 gr.)
radiate head/Tyche. Scarce.

According to the New Testament, it was before Agrippa II and his sister, Berenice, that the Apostle Paul pleaded his case in Caesarea Maritima in AD 59. As the Bible says, "A few days later king Agrippa [Agrippa II] and Berenice arrived to Caesarea to pay their respects to Festus" (Acts 25:13, NIV). Porcius Festus was the new procurator of Judea under Emperor Nero to whom Paul presented his charges. It was customary back in ancient time for rulers to pay a complimentary visit to a new ruler at the time of his assignment. Agrippa II died childless at the age of seventy in the third year of Trajan, which is AD 100. Josephus cast a serious doubt in the date of Agrippa's II death, and it is believed to be AD 94/95. Agrippa II was the last prince of the Herodian family.

The Roman Procurators
of Judaea (AD 6–66)

Judaea became a Roman province in AD 6. Since this date, five emperors of Rome (Augustus, Tiberius, Caligula, Claudius, and Nero) assigned a position in Judaea called "procurator," or "governor," between AD 6–66. The procurators had the authority to collect taxes and rule the people in Judaea, and they had the power of life and death. There were fourteen procurators appointed to govern Judaea between that time as follows:

Under Augustus:
Coponius, AD 6–9**
Marcus Ambibulus, AD 9–12**
Annius Rufus, AD 12–15
Under Tiberius:
Valerius Gratus, AD 15–26**
Pontius Pilatus, AD 26–36**
Marcellus, AD 36–37
Under Caligula:
Marullus, AD 37–41
Under Claudius:
Cuspius Fadus, AD 44–46*
Tiberius Alexander, AD 46–48
Ventidius Cumanus, AD 48–54
Antonius Felix, AD 52–54
Under Nero:
Antonius Felix, AD 54–59**
Porcius Festus, AD 59–64**
Albinus, AD 62–64
Gessius Florus, AD 64–66
* From AD 41–44, Agrippa I reigned as king of Judaea.
** Only six out of fourteen procurators issued coins during their reign as follows.

Coponius (AD 6–9) was the first procurator of the Judaea province. From the beginning of his rule, he offended the Jews by taking the census of the Jews and imposing very stiff taxes on them.

Coponius. Roman Judaea. 6-9 AD.
AE (16 mm, 2.1 gr.) ear of barley/palm tree.

Coponius. Roman Judaea. 6-9 AD.
AE (17 mm, 1.92 gr.) ear of barley/palm tree.

Coponius was called back to Rome after an incident occurred during the Passover festival. Someone had scattered human bones in the sanctuary. Coponius depicted the palm tree bearing two bunches of dates on his coinage. This was later used to represent Judaea on coins issued by the Jews during the first and second revolts, as well as later Roman-issued Judaean-related coins.

Marcus Ambibulus (AD 9–12) replaced Coponius, and according to Flavius Josephus, very little history is known about him. We know he was procurator from his coins and he must have belonged to the equestrian order, the second class of the Roman elite, after the senator.

Marcus Ambibulus. Roman Judaea. 9-12 AD.
AE (16 mm, 1.96 gr.) ear of barley/palm tree.

No uprising or rebellions occurred during his reign, and that was enough for Josephus to say that he was a good administrator.

Valerius Gratus (AD 15–26) was remembered mainly by the frequent changes he made in the appointment of high priesthood. He deposed Ananus and substituted Ismael, son of Fabi.

Valerius Gratus. Roman Judaea. 15-26 AD.
AE (15.5 mm, 1.90 gr.) TIB, KAI/palm tree.

Valerius Gratus. Roman Judaea. 15-26 AD.
AE (16 mm, 2.0 gr.) TIB,KAI/palm tree.

He put down two powerful bands of robbers that infested Judaea during his reign. Gratus issued several different types of coins representing palm branches, lilies, cornucopia grape leaves, and Amphoras.

Pontius Pilatus (AD 26–36), known as "Pilate," strained relations with the Jewish people. He is best known as the man who presided at the trial of Jesus and, despite stating that he personally found him not guilty of crime meriting death, handed him over to crucifixion.

The Bible tells us that the chief priests and the elders of the Jewish people decided to put Jesus to death: "They bound him, led him away and handed him over to Pilate, the governor" (Matthew 27:2, NIV). Pilate is thus a fundamental character in the New Testament accounts of Jesus. Pilate ordered a sign to be put above Jesus on the cross during crucifixion, stating, "Jesus of Nazareth, the King of the Jews," to give public notice of the legal charge against Jesus for his death. The elders of the people and high priests disagreed that the charge on the sign should read that Jesus claimed to be King of the Jews, and Pilate refused to change the posted charge. This may have been to emphasize the Roman power over Judaea in crucifying a Jewish king or to aggravate the Jewish leaders. According to legend, Pilate was extremely violent, cruel, and brutal to the Jewish. This was the main reason of his being recalled to Rome.

Pontius Pilate. Roman Judaea. 26-36 AD.
AE (15.8 mm, 2.83 gr.)
ears of barley/libation ladle.

Pontius Pilate. Roman Judaea. 26-36 AD.
AE (15.0 mm, 2.2 gr.)
littus/LIH (date year 31 AD).

Anotnius Felix (AD 52–59) rose to the post of procurator from slavery. Legends say that he exercised the duty of a king in the spirit of a slave. Felix's cruelty and disrespectful treatment to the Jewish people led to a severe increase of crime in Judaea province.

Antonius Felix. Roman Judaea. 52-59 AD.
AE (17 mm, 2.82 gr.)
two crossed shields/palm tree.

Antonius Felix. Roman Judaea. 52-59 AD.
AE (17 mm, 1.90 gr.)
Greek inscription/palm branches.

The Apostle Paul stood trial before Felix. Acts 24:24 (NIV) says, "Several days later Felix came with his wife Drusilla, who was a Jewess. He sent for Paul and listened to him as he spoke about faith in Jesus Christ."

Porcius Festus (AD 59–62) inherited all the problems of his predecessor in regard to the Roman practice of creating civic privileges for Jews. This created a severe Jewish hostility to Rome, and the feelings were aroused, which played a big part in the cause of the first Jewish War.

Porcius Festus. Roman Judaea. 59-62 AD.
AE (15 mm, 1.74 gr.)
Greek inscription/palm branch.

Porcius Festus. Roman Judaea. 59-62 AD.
AE (15 mm, 1.40 gr.)
Greek inscription/palm branch.

Porcius Festus. Roman Judaea. 59-62 AD.
AE (16 mm, 1.80 gr.)
Greek inscription/palm branch.

According to the Bible, the Apostle Paul had his final hearing before Festus after his two years of imprisonment: "When two years had passed, Felix was succeeded by Porcius Festus, but because Felix wanted to grant a favor to the Jews, he left Paul in prison" (Acts 24:27, NIV).

Almost all the Roman procurators were not much of a help to the Jewish people. According to Josephus, they robbed the province of Judaea, their cruelty was pitiless, they enforced very heavy taxes, and they used their power to plunder honest citizens. In particular, Gessius Florus robbed whole cities and destroyed whole communities. Most districts were depopulated by his greed. People left their homes and fled into wilderness or into foreign provinces. The Jews destroyed all the leading roads and bridges to the holy sites to prevent Florus from plundering the temple. All these incidents and anger of the Jewish people led to the first Jewish revolt against Rome from AD 66–70 and again in A.D 132–135. The two Jewish revolts will be discussed later in this book.

The Birth of Jesus and His Ministry

Approximately 700 years before the birth of Jesus, the Prophet Isaiah said, "Therefore the Lord himself will give you a sign: the virgin will be with child and will give birth to a son, and will call him Immanuel" (Isaiah 7:14, NIV). The Virgin Mary was pledged to be married to Joseph, but she found herself pregnant with a baby. Joseph found out about her, and he decided to keep quiet about it and not expose her to public disgrace. The Bible tells us an angel appeared to Mary, assuring her that she would conceive in her womb and bear a son, and she will name him Jesus. The angel appeared to Joseph, telling him to take Mary as his wife, because what was conceived in her is from the Holy Spirit. So Joseph took Mary home as his wife, and she gave birth to a son, and she called him Jesus.

The star of Bethlehem was shiny and bright at the birth of Jesus. The magi from the east saw the star, and they came to Jerusalem to worship the newborn king of the Jews. Herod the Great was the king of the Jews and was very disturbed by the idea that another King of the Jews just born was to replace him. Knowing Herod the Great's ruthless behavior—murdering his wife, his five sons, mother-in-law, brother-in-law, uncle, and hundreds of others—he gave orders to kill all the males in Bethlehem and the surrounding area who were two years old and under. The angel of the Lord appeared to Joseph, asking him to take the child to Egypt. After Herod the Great died, the angel of the Lord appeared to Joseph again, asking him to go back to Israel, because those trying to kill the child were dead. When Joseph learned that Herod Archelaus was the king of Judaea, he decided to go to Nazareth, in the district of Galilee.

A revolt of farmers broke out in Galilee as a result of heavy taxes imposed on the Jews by Herod Archelaus. He sent Roman troops and killed about 3,000 Jews, most of them innocent. This event sent a lot of resentment throughout the Jewish world. Another uprising occurred when Herod Archelaus was in Rome to claim the throne and they took the provincial capital of Sepphoris. The Roman army again took the inhabitants and enslaved them and burned the city of Sepphoris to the ground. The revolt was quelled, but the inhabitants were very angry. When Jesus was a teenager (about ten to twelve years old), the city of Sepphoris was in progress of being rebuilt by Herod Antipas. The city was approximately three miles from the city of Nazareth, where Jesus was living.

Sepphoris. Roman Judaea, Diocaesaraea.
98-117 AD, Trajan. AE (23 mm, 11.70 gr.)
laureate head/palm tree. Scarce.

Sepphoris. Roman Judaea, Diocaesaraea.
98-117 AD, Trajan. AE (19 mm, 5.09 gr.)
laureate head/filleted caduceus. Scarce.

Sepphoris was very richly built with many mosaics and buildings. Recent excavations have found what is commonly called the "Mona Lisa of the Galilee" made of mosaics. The city became the capital of the Galilee, and the name changed to Diocaesarea, in honor of "Dio" Zeus, where a temple dedicated to Jupiter, Juno, and Minerva was built by Emperor Hadrian.

History tells us very little about the life of Jesus and his adulthood. Jesus began to be known when he was baptized by John the Baptist, and most literature places it around AD 26. John the Baptist was beheaded by Herod Antipas after Salome, his stepdaughter, danced for him at his banquet. Her mother, Herodias, coaching her, asked for the head of John the Baptist. Earlier, John the Baptist criticized Herod Antipas's marriage to Herodias, because she was married to one of Antipas's brothers. Shortly after Jesus began to teach in many synagogues, he was rejected by his hometown synagogue at Nazareth, which made him move his ministry to the towns around the shores of the Sea of Galilee.

According to the book of Matthew, Jesus was teaching in synagogues throughout Galilee, proclaiming the good news of the kingdom of God and curing every disease and sickness among the people. Jesus focused his teaching on the areas north and west of the Sea of Galilee. He started at the city of Capernaum, which contained a fair balance between Gentile and Jewish. Jesus tried to avoid the cities of just Gentiles and go to Jewish villages, "the lost sheep of Israel." Jesus chose twelve followers called apostles; the number twelve has been interpreted to symbolize the twelve tribes of Israel. The apostles traveled with Jesus to most of the places he went to spread the word, and their loyalty to Jesus was absolute. According to the book of Mark and biblical narratives, Jesus went to most of the towns and villages around the Sea of Galilee (see map number two), such as Abila, Hippos, Tiberias, Gadara, Dium, Pella, Gerasa, Nysa-Scythopolis, and Capitolias. Three of these cities—Hippos, Tiberias, and Nysa-Scythopolis—have already been described, and coins were presented for them earlier in this book; however, only coins (different coins) for them are presented here.

Tiberias. Roman Judaea. 117-138 AD, Hadrian.
AE (12 mm, 3.14 gr.) laureate head/
quinquereme left. Rare.

Tiberias. Roman Judaea. 98-117 AD, Trajan.
AE (25 mm, 14.48 gr.) laureate
head/Tyche standing. Scarce.

Tiberias. Roman Judaea. 98-117 AD, Trajan.
AE (15 mm, 2.45 gr.) Dated CY 90 (109 AD)
laureate head/anchor, date. Rare.

Hippo. Roman Judaea. Antiochia ad Hippum.
161-180 AD, Marcus Aurelius. AE (24 mm, 10.3 gr.)
laureate bust/Tyche holding a horse. Scarce.

Nysa- Scythopolis. Roman Syria, Decapolis.
238-244 AD, Gordian III. AE (23mm,12.01 gr.)
Laureate bust/Tyche-Nysa seated. Very Rare

ABILA

Abila is located about twelve miles southeast of the Sea of Galilee. Based on modern excavations, the city has shown habitation back to the fifth century BC.

Abila. Roman Judaea. 161-180 AD, Marcus Aurelius.
AE (24 mm, 8.51 gr.) laureate bust/
turreted bust of Tyche.Scarce.

Abila. Roman Judaea. 177-192 AD, Commodus.
AE (24 mm, 10.17 gr.) laureate head/
Heracules standing. Scarce.

Abila. Roman Judaea. 198-217 AD, Caracalla.
AE (24 mm, 9.73 gr.) laureate head/
Heracules standing. Scarce.

The city was called Seleukeia after Antiochus III conquered it in 98 BC During the reign of Roman Emperor Nero, Abila was annexed to Herod Agrippa II. Abila is known as Abel in modern-day.

GADARA

In the region of Gadara (Al Hammat), Jesus healed two demon-possessed men: "When he arrived at the other side in the region of the Gadarenes, two demon possessed men coming from the tombs met him, they were so violent that no one could pass that way" (Matthew 8:28, NIV). Gadara is located about four miles from the southwest shore of the Sea of Galilee and was one of the ten cities of the Decapolis. The city was taken by Antiochus III (the Great) in 218 BC when he first invaded Judaea and Palestine. Gadara was given to Herod the Great by Augustus in 30 BC, and the people of Gadara always complained about Herod's harsh and oppressive conduct, but the Roman emperor never listened. During the reign of Vespasian in the second century AD, the Roman aqueduct project started to supply drinking water through the 110-mile-long Qanat. The longest section of the Qanat ran for about sixty miles underground. It was the longest known tunnel from ancient time to date.

Gadara. Roman Syria, Decapolis. 161-169 AD,
Lucius Verus. AE (25 mm, 11.22 gr.)
draped bust/laureate bust of Heracules. Scarce.

Gadara. Roman Syria, Decapolis. 161-169 AD,
Lucius Verus. AE (25 mm, 10.91 gr.)
draped bust/laureate bust of Heracules. Scarce.

Gadara. Roman Syria, Decapolis. 27 BC-14 AD,
Augustus. AE (18 mm, 5.07 gr.) bear head/
veiled bust of Tyche wearing crown. Scarce.

Gadara. Roman Syria, Decapolis. 161-180 AD,
Marcus Aurelius. AE (25 mm, 10.19 gr.)
laureate head/bust of Heracules,lion skin. Scarce.

Gadara continued to be a great and important city during the Byzantine Christian times and was, for a long time, the seat of a bishop. The city fell to Muslim rule following the battle of Yarmouk in AD 638. Gadara was badly destroyed by an earthquake around AD 747 and was abandoned as a city.

DIUM

Dium is located about thirty-five miles southwest of the Sea of Galilee. The city was conquered by Alexander Jannaeus, and later, Pompey the Great captured it in the first century BC

Dium. Roman Syria, Decapolis. 198-209 AD,
Geta. AE (23 mm, 14.27 gr.) draped bust./
War God standing, facing. Scarce.

Dium. Roman Syria, Decapolis. 218-222 AD,
Elagabalus. AE (20 mm, 7.92 gr.) laureate bust/
flaming altar within hexastyle temple. Scarce.

Dium. Roman Syria, Decapolis. 218-222 AD,
Elagabalus. AE (21 mm, 7.78 gr.) laureate bust/
flaming altar within hexastyle temple. Scarce.

Dium. Roman Syria, Decapolis. 198-209 AD, Geta.
AE (24 mm, 14.26 gr.) draped bust./
War God holding scepter and
Nike, recumbent bull to either side. Rare.

This city was one of the Roman Decapolis cities that Jesus did most of his teachings, as the Bible tells us: "Large crowds from Galilee, the Decapolis, Jerusalem, Judea and the region across the Jordan followed him" (Matthew 4:25, NIV). Very little is known about Dium to archeologists and scholars, although some coins were minted in the beginning of AD 205 under Roman Emperor Septimius Severus. Coins for this city are fairly scarce.

PELLA

Pella is another city in the Decapolis located about sixteen miles due south of the Sea of Galilee and in the northern foothills of the Jordan Valley. This city was first mentioned in Egyptian inscriptions in 1800 BC under the name of Pehal.

Pella. Roman Syria, Decapolis. 164-182 AD,
Lucilla. AE (24 mm, 9.68 gr.) draped bust/
Tyche seated, river-God swimming. Rare.

Its name was changed to Pella during the Hellenistic period, perhaps to honor the Macedonian capital and the birthplace of Alexander the Great. The city of Pella was captured by Alexander Jannaeus and was destroyed by him. During the First Jewish Revolt in AD 66–70, it was a refuge for Jerusalem Christians. Pella is known for its spectacular ruins from the Hellenistic and Roman times. The city was badly destroyed by an earthquake in AD 749, and a small village remains in the area called Tabaqat Fahl.

GERASA

Gerasa (Jerash) is another city of the Decapolis and a popular place for Jesus's ministry. Luke 8:26 (NIV) says, "They sailed to the region of the Gerasenes, which is across the lake from Galilee." Gerasa was rediscovered during the Hellenistic period, even though it was already inhabited during the Bronze Age (3200–1200 BC). The Romans renamed the city Antiochia on the Banias River after Seleucid King Antiochus IV. Gerasa was the home of Nicomachus, one of the greatest mathematicians in ancient history, who was known for his work *Introduction to Arithmetic*.

Gerasa. Roman Syria, Decapolis. 161-180 AD,
Marcus Aurelius. AE (15 mm, 3.20 gr.)
laureate head/bust of Artemis. very Rare.

After the Roman conquest of Judaea in 63 BC, Gerasa and the surrounding areas were annexed to the province of Syria and later, in AD 90, were absorbed into the Roman province of Arabia. The city is known by the triumphal arch, which was built by Emperor Hadrian to celebrate his visit to the city in AD 129/130. Also, the remains of the great temple of Artemis, who was the city's main goddess, can be seen standing today. After Constantine I (the Great), around AD 350, large Christian communities have always lived in Gerasa, and at the beginning of the Byzantine Empire (AD 400–600), more than thirteen churches were built, many with magnificent mosaic floors. Today, many ruins have been successfully excavated and preserved, and that is how the city has received the nickname "the Asian Pompeii." Ancient coins from Gerasa are extremely rare.

CAPITOLIAS

Capitolias (Al Hisn) is located roughly about fourteen miles north of Dium.

Capitolias. Roman Syria, Decapolis. 177-192 AD,
Commodus. AE (24 mm, 10.15 gr.)
laureate head/draped bust of Alexander
the great, date flanking. Very rare.

The city is believed to be founded by the Romans under the Greek name of Capitolias, which was derived from the Hebrew *Beth Reisha,* meaning "head." The Arabic name Beit Ras or Al Hisn means about the same. The city began making coins at the time of Emperor Trajan in AD 98 until the rule of Elagabalus in AD 219. Very little is known about this city, and the exact location of the city is still disputed. Coins from this city are very rare.

Jesus was restricted just to the Galilee and the surrounding areas. He withdrew north with his disciples, as the Bible tells us: "When Jesus came to the region of Caesarea Philippi (Panias), he asked his disciples, who do people say the son of man is?" (Matthew 16:13, NIV). At Caesarea Philippi (Panias), Simon Peter gave his great confession, as the Bible tells us: "Simon Peter answered, you are the Christ, the son of the living God" (Matthew 16:16, NIV). Caesaria Panias was first settled in the Hellenistic period after Alexander the Great's conquests in Egypt and Syria around 330 BC Panias is the famous spring named after Pan, the Greek god of desolate places. Herod Philip II (also known as Philip the Tetrach) rebuilt the city and called it by his own name, Philippi, in 3 BC.

Caesarea Philippi. Roman Syria, Paneas.
65 & 63 AD, Diva Poppaea and Diva Claudia.
AE (19 mm. 6.85 gr.) Diva Poppaea seated/
Diva Claudia standing in hexastyle temple. Scarce.

During the first Jewish revolt in AD 66–70, Emperor Vespasian rested his troops in this city in AD 67, holding games over a period of twenty days before advancing on Tiberias to crush the Jewish resistance in Galilee. A woman from Panias, who had been bleeding for twelve years, is said to have been miraculously cured by Jesus in this area.

Jesus did more traveling west on the coast of Phoenicia of the Mediterranean to Tyre and Sidon. During this trip, Jesus got in contact with a daughter of a Gentile woman and healed her there. The Bible tells us: "The woman was a Greek, born in Syrian Phoenicia. She begged Jesus to drive the demon out of her daughter" (Mark 7:26, NIV). The two cities, Tyre and Sidon, were described earlier in this book. Only new coins are presented here.

Tyre. Roman Phoenicia. 218-222 AD,
Elagabalus. AE (30 mm, 10.59 gr.) laureate bust/
Astarte standing, crowned by Nike. Scarce.

Tyre. Roman Phoenicia. 218-222 AD,
Elagabalus. AE (30 mm, 16.21 gr.) laureate bust/
Astarte standing, crowned by Nike. Scarce.

Sidon. Greek Phoenicia. 56-55 BC. AE (23 mm, 8.27 gr.)
Dated year 56 BC. veiled head of Tyche/
Phoenician pentekonter left. Scarce.

Jesus also went to the region of Samaria, where he performed the miraculous healing of the ten lepers, which took place on the border of Samaria and Galilee. One of the lepers threw himself at Jesus's feet and thanked him. He was a Samaritan. Also, as mentioned in the Bible, in the book of John, chapter 4, Jesus encountered a Samartian woman at Jacob's well. He spoke with her about his living water, which would be a spring of water gushing up to eternal life for anyone who would drink it.

Samaria. Roman Caesarea. 117-138 AD, Hadrian.
AE (18 mm, 5.0 gr.) laureate bust/Apollo.

According to legend, Samaria has been associated with John the Baptist, whose body is believed to be buried there. A small basilica, first founded in the fifth century AD, was excavated there and was believed to be the burial place of the head of John the Baptist. In the twelfth century AD, a Latin cathedral, also dedicated to John the Baptist, was built east of the Roman Forum in this city.

It is almost impossible for us to know with certainty all the places that Jesus went to, retreated to, or did all the teaching. He might have gone to Magdala, located on the west shore of Galilee, and met his most important female follower identified by the name of Mary Magdalene. She was one of several women who had been healed or cleansed and who provided support for Jesus and his disciples. As the Bible indicated, Jesus might have gone to the cities east of the Jordan adjacent to the core area where he was teaching, such as Adraa, Bostra, and Phlilippopolis.

ADRAA

Adraa (Edrei) is located about twenty-five miles southeast of the shore of the Sea of Galilee. This city proved to have inhabitants around 1600 BC After the exodus, when Moses wandered around the Sinai for forty years, he finally came to the land of the Amorites and conquered it, and the Israelites settled there. The Israelites captured the surrounding settlements and drove out the Amorites who were there. They then went to the land of Ward Bashen and conquered it and killed the king and all his army in the battle of Adraa. The Bible tells us: "Then they turned and went up along the road to Ward Bashan, and as King of Bashan and his whole army marched out to meet them in the battle of Ederi" (Numbers 21:33, NIV).

Adraa. Roman Arabia. 164-182 AD, Lucilla.
AE (23 mm, 7.13 gr.) draped bust/
turreted bust of Tyche. Rare.

Adraa was built on the banks of the Yarmuk River, and it became a part of the province of Arabia in AD 106. The city is known as Daraa in modern-day.

BOSTRA

Bostra (Basra Ash Sham) is located about twenty miles northeast of Adraa. The settlement in Bostra was first mentioned in the documents of Tutmose III in the fourteenth century BC. At one time, the city was the capital of the Nabataean kingdom and was conquered by Emperor Trajan and put under the province of Arabia in AD 106. The two councils of Arabia were held at Bostra in AD 246 and 247. The city continued to exist under the Byzantine Empire and then, in the seventh century AD, was conquered by the Sasanid dynasty and finally was conquered by Rashidun Caliphate in AD 634. The city of Bostra today stands as a village with many beautiful ruins, such as the second-century Roman theater with covered portico, Roman bridges, Roman citadel, and Nabataean arches.

Bostra. Roman Arabia. 117-138 AD, Hadrian. AE (22 mm, 8.03 gr.) laureate bust/ turreted bust of Arabia holding two infants. Scarce.

Bostra. Roman Arabia. 222-235 AD, Julia Mamaea. AE (18 mm, 3.59 gr.) draped bust/ Marsyas standing, wine skin on shoulder. Scarce.

Bostra. Roman Arabia. 222-235 AD, Julia Mamaea. AE (21 mm, 6.84 gr.) diademed bust/ turreted bust of Tyche left. Scarce.

Bostra. Roman Arabia. 244-247 AD, Philip II. AE (26 mm, 12.10 gr.) radiate, cuirassed bust/ legend in three lines. Scarce.

The city was a very important location during the Romans, Byzantines, and the Arabs, as it was on the trade route of the Roman road to the Red Sea. Roman Emperor Alexander Severus promoted the city to the rank of Roman colony.

PHILIPPOPOLIS

Philippopolis (Shahba) is located about twenty miles southeast of Bostra. This city is known to be the birthplace of Philip I (Philip the Arab). It was founded by him and named after him. After he dedicated himself to building this city and making it a metropolis, he even wanted to turn the city into a replica of Rome. After his death, the building of the city stopped, and today, the city contains well-preserved ruins of triumphal arches, baths, theaters, and a museum, which exhibits beautiful examples of Roman mosaic art.

Philippopolis. Roman Arabia. 247-249 AD,
Philip II. AE (30 mm, 16.21 gr.) laureate bust
Roma seated holding eagle. Scarce.

Jesus, during his ministry, had mentioned many parables and performed many miracles, from healing the blind, raising the dead, walking on water, curing the paralyzed, making the deaf hear, making the crippled walk, feeding the 5,000, healing the demon-possessed, calming the storms, and many, many more. The details of these miracles are well beyond the scope and the purpose of this book. However, one of the parables mentioned in his teaching is worth mentioning, because it relates to a coin. Some of the Pharisees and Herodians tried to ask Jesus about paying taxes to Caesar.

> "Should we pay or shouldn't we?" But Jesus knew their hypocrisy. "Why are you trying to trap me?" he asked. "Bring me a denarius and let me look at it." They brought the coin, and he asked them, "Whose portrait is this? And whose inscription?" "Caesar's," they replied. Then Jesus said to them, "Give to Caesar what is Caesar's and give to God what is God's."
>
> Mark 12:15–17 (NIV)

Since Emperor Tiberius reigned during the ministry of Jesus, it is logical and widely known between scholars and numismatists that the denarius of Tiberius is the best-known biblical reference of the "tribute penny." This Denarius shows the portrait of the emperor on the obverse and a seated female figure on the reverse. The obverse inscription reads, "TI CAESAR DIVI AVG F AVGVSTVS," which means "Tiberius Caesar Augustus, son of the Divine Augustus." The reverse legend reads, "PONTIF MAXIM," which means "high priest," which is the second title for emperor.

The Ttribute Penny. Roman Imperial. 14-37 AD,
Tiberius. AR Denarius (19 mm, 3.71 gr.)
laureate head/Livia, as Pax seated. Rare.

This coin is commonly referred to as the "tribute penny." The reason it is called a penny instead of a denarius is because it was mistakenly translated in the King James Bible in AD 1611. In England, the Latin word *denarius* was transformed into the word *penny*. For hundreds of years, England used the letter "D," meaning denarius, as an abbreviation for penny or pence.

The Crucifixion of Jesus

Jesus Christ had no problems with the Romans, and he did not violate any Roman laws and orders. He was punished by the Romans in accordance with Roman law and executed in such a manner that was reserved mainly for criminals and those guilty of crimes against the Roman Empire. It was very cruel punishment meant to derive the maximum amount of pain. He was crucified between two robbers and died.

The Law of Moses prescribes the three great Jewish festivals: Passover, Pentecost, and Tabernacles. In order to observe these feasts properly, according to the law, male Jews were to be present in the temple at Jerusalem three times a year. According to the Gospel of John, Jesus went to Jerusalem on at least five different occasions during his ministry period. On the last visit to Jerusalem in December, Jesus started preaching in Jerusalem and proclaiming the good word. After the raising of Lazarus at Bethany, opposition from the religious leaders in Jerusalem, especially from Joseph Caiaphas, the high priest, forced Jesus to withdraw to the wilderness. Five days before the Passover, Jesus, seated on a donkey, came down from the Mount of Olives and went toward Jerusalem.

Jerusalem. Roman Judaea, Aelia Capitolina.
Antoninus Pius, 138-161 AD. AE (24 mm, 8.09 gr.)
draped head/Turreted bust of Tyche.

On both sides of the road, people opened their garments, waved palm branches, and shouted "Hosanna!" The Bible tells us the next day Jesus went to the court of the Gentiles and overturned the tables of the moneychangers and the benches of those who sold pigeons. The moneychangers were exchanging money from pilgrims coming from all over to visit the temple. The only money acceptable at the Jerusalem temple was the silver shekel minted in the Phoenician coastal city of Tyre, which was called "the shekel of Tyre." The shekel of Tyre was precise in weight and made of the highest quality of silver and attained a semiofficial status. The shekel of Tyre coins are very rare, especially well-centered specimen.

Judas Iscariot betrayed Jesus for thirty silver coins and had him arrested. Matthew 26:14–16 (NIV) says, "Then one of the twelve, the one called Judas Iscariot, went to the chief priests and asked, what are you willing to give me if I hand him over to you? So they counted out for him thirty silver coins.

From then on Judas watched for an opportunity to hand him over." It is widely believed by scholars, as well as numismatists, that Judas Iscariot received thirty shekels of Tyre for betraying Jesus Christ. Some legends blame the Jews for the death of Jesus, and some legends blame the Roman authorities and the Roman soldiers who put Jesus on the cross. In any case, most Christians believe that it was actually preordained beforehand as part of a divine plan in which Jesus had to suffer and die as a sacrifice to pay for everyone's sins.

Shekel of Tyre. Greek Phoenicia, Tyre. 101-102 BC.
AR Tetradrachm (30 mm, 14.09 gr.)
Laureate bust of Melkart/eagle, EK (date), club,
Phoenician letter between legs. Very Rare.

1/2 Shekel of Tyre. Greek Phoenicia, Tyre. 76-75 BC.
AR Drachm (25 mm, 6.99 gr.)
Lauteate bust of Melkart/eagle standing, EN
(date), club, letter between legs. Very Rare.

Peter and Philip's Journeys

According to Acts 2, after the crucifixion and Jesus's resurrection, his followers were in one place together in Jerusalem for the feast of Pentecost. A sudden voice came from heaven, like the blowing of a violent wind, and filled the house where they were sitting. All of them were filled with the Holy Spirit. Peter stood up, addressed the crowd, and proclaimed the good news. In response to his sermon, some 3,000 people were baptized. This was the first step for the apostles to spread Christianity.

MAP 6: Apostles' Early Travels

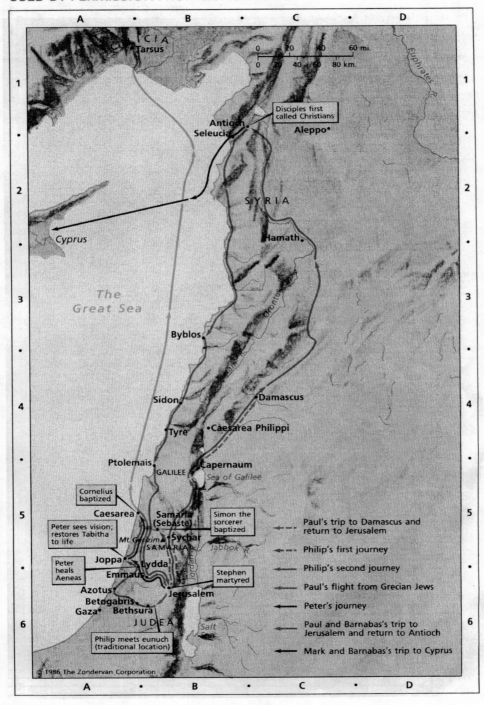

© 1986 The Zondervan Corporation

MAP 7: The Levant 2

COURTESY OF CNG (WWW.CNGCOINS.COM)

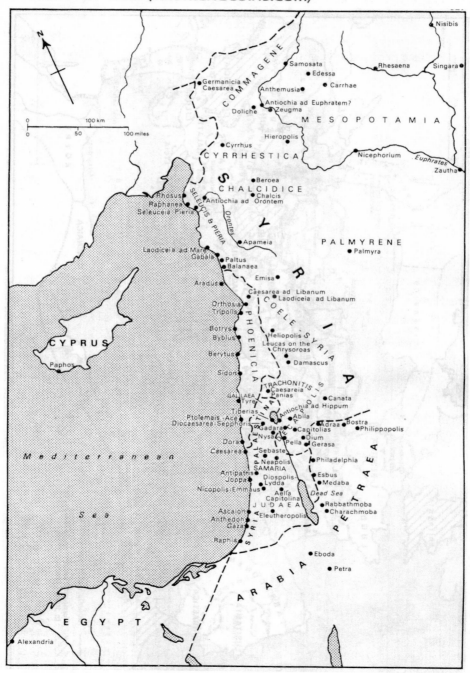

N

0   100 km
0   50   100 miles

Nisibis

COMMAGENE

Samosata
Edessa
Rhesaena
Singara

Germanicia
Caesarea
Anthemusia
Carrhae

Antiochia ad Euphratem?
Doliche
Zeugma

MESOPOTAMIA

Hieropolis

Cyrrhus

CYRRHESTICA

Nicephorium
Euphrates
Zautha

Beroea

CHALCIDICE

Chalcis
Rhosus
Raphanea
Antiochia ad Orontem
Seleuceia Pieria

SELEUCIS & PIERIA

Orontes

PALMYRENE

Apameia

Palmyra

S
Y
R
I
A

Laodiceia ad Mare
Gabala
Paltus
Balanaea

Emisa

Aradus

Caesarea ad Libanum
Laodiceia ad Libanum

Orthosia
Tripolis

COELE SYRIA

Botrys
Byblus

Heliopolis
Leucas on the
Chrysoroas

Berytus

PHOENICIA

Sidon

Damascus

Caesareia
TRACHONITIS
Panias

GALILAEA
Tyre

Canata
Antiochia ad Hippum

Tiberias
Abila

Ptolemais-Ace
Diocaesarea-Sepphoris
Gadara
Adraa
Bostra
Capitolias
Philippopolis
Nysa
Dium
Dora
Pella
Gerasa
Caesarea
Sebaste

SAMARIA

Neapolis
Philadelphia

Antipatris
Joppa
Diospolis
Esbus
Lydda
Medaba

PETRAEA

Nicopolis-Emmaus
Aelia
Capitolina
Dead Sea

Rabbathmoba

JUDAEA
Eleutheropolis
Charachmoba

Ascalon
Anthedon
Gaza

Raphia

ARABIA

CYPRUS

Paphos

Mediterranean

Sea

Eboda

Petra

EGYPT

Alexandria

Ancient Coins Through the Bible   171

The gospel kept on spreading, and more people were baptized. Peter and John healed a cripple who was begging at the gate of Jerusalem. The apostles found the original church in Jerusalem, where they elected seven deacons to run it. They were healing the sick all around the area, but the opposition to the new religion grew to a level that Peter and John and a number of apostles were arrested on orders of the Saducees and brought before the Sanhedrin (the council of priests). Only one member of the Sanhedrin, by the name of Gamaliel, who was honored by all people, spoke on Peter's behalf and asked the council to let these people go because they will only be fighting against God.

Jerusalem. Roman Judaea, Aelia Capitolina.
Geta,198-209 AD. AE (25 mm, 14.35 gr.)
bare head/Dionysos, panther to left. Scarce.

The council let the apostles go after only a flogging and asked them not to preach in the name of Jesus anymore. Peter and John kept spreading the word and teaching in the name of Jesus day after day and from house to house and never stopped proclaiming the good news. Peter was arrested again and again, and the feeling against the followers of Jesus ran high. One of the seven deacons in the church of Jerusalem, named Stephen, was proclaiming his new faith in a Jewish synagogue. Obviously, his words offended the people who dragged him out of the city, and he was stoned to death. History says that he was the first martyr of Christianity. Stephen's death started a general persecution of the followers of Jesus in Jerusalem, which caused many to flee Jerusalem and go to Antioch, Cyprus, Damascus, and other places beyond Judaea, taking with them the message of the good news.

Another of the seven deacons, called Philip, went to a city in Samaria, believed to be Sebaste, where he preached the good news and gained great success. Philip and Peter, according to the Bible, traveled all over Judaea and Samaria, claiming the good news to Shechem (Neapolis), Caesarea, Antipatris, Joppa, Lydda, and Ascalon.

Sebaste. Roman Judaea. 218-222 AD,
Elagabalus. AE (20 mm, 7.35 gr.)
Laureate head/Demeter standing. Rare.

Shechem. Roman Judaea, Neapolis. 159-160 AD,
Faustina Junior. AE (26 mm, 11.94gr.)
draped bust/Artemis standing. Scarce.

Caesarea Maritima. Roman Judaea. 117-138 AD,
Hadrian. AE (28.4 mm, 19.16 gr.)
Laureate bust/Founder plows right. Scarce.

Antipatras, Roman Judaea. Julia Maesa,
218-224 AD. AE (21 mm, 10.25 gr.)
draped bust/Figure reclining. Extremely Rare.

Ascalon. Roman Judaea. Trajan, 98-117 AD.
AE (23 mm, 11.9 gr.) Laureate head/
City Goddess, altar, dove in field. Scarce

Most of these cities have been mentioned earlier in this book and brief descriptions were given then, although different coins are presented here for them. Lydda and Joppa are mentioned here for the first time in this book; therefore, coins and descriptions for them will be presented here.

Lydda

Lydda (Lod) is located about nine miles from Joppa (Jaffa). Based on the Bible, Lod was founded by Shemed of the tribe of Benjamin. The city was abandoned during the deportation of Jews by the Babylonian captivity and was resettled and prospered after the return of the Jews from exile. Under the Maccabean dynasty, Lod was purely a Jewish town. The Roman governor of Syria, Cassius, sold Lydda's inhabitants into slavery in AD 43, while the Roman proconsul of Syria, Cestius Gallus, burned the city on his way to Jerusalem in AD 66. Under the Roman rule, the city grew bigger, and Emperor Septimius Severus made it a colony, renaming it Diospolis, meaning "the city of Zeus." The inhabitants of Lydda were almost all Christians during the Byzantine period.

Lydda. Roman Judaea. Julia Domna, 193-217 AD.
AE (22 mm, 8.69 gr.) draped bust/
veiled bust of Demeter, date behind. Very Rare.

Lydda is the site of Peter's healing of a paralytic man.

> As Peter traveled about the country, he went to visit the saints in Lydda. Where he found a man named Aeneas, a paralytic who had been bedridden for eight years. Aeneas, Peter said to him, Jesus Christ heals you, get up and take care of your mat. Immediately Aeneas got up.
>
> Acts 9:32–34 (NIV)

During the crusader time, for the English crusaders, such as King Richard the Lionheart, Lydda was a place of great significance in the crusader kingdom of Jerusalem. At the present time, Lydda is the home of Israel's main international airport, Ben Gurion International Airport, which was known as Lod Airport in the past. Ancient coins from Lydda are very rare.

Joppa

Joppa (Jaffa) is located on the Mediterranean Sea, about ten miles northwest of Lydda. The biblical town of Joppa is today known as Jaffa—located south of Tel Aviv and is part of the Tel Aviv-Yafo municipality. There is archaeological evidence showing that Joppa was inhabited around 7500 BC. The city's natural harbor has been used since the Bronze Age. The city of Joppa is mentioned four times in the Bible in the books of Joshua, 2 Chronicles, Jonah, and Ezra. It was one of the cities given to the tribes of Dan and a port of entry for the cedars of Lebanon for King Solomon's temple and the place where the Prophet Jonah supposedly was swallowed by the whale. The Bible tells us that Jonah was running away from the Lord, and he was traveling from Joppa to Tarshish, Spain. After leaving Joppa, the sailors threw Jonah overboard and a whale (big fish) swallowed him. Jonah 1:17 (NIV) says, "but the Lord provided a big fish to swallow Jonah, and Jonah was inside the fish three days and three nights." It was also where the Apostle Peter raised the widow Tabitha (Dorcas) from the dead.

> In Joppa there was a disciple named Tabitha (which, when translated, is Dorcas), who was always doing good and helping the poor. About that time she became sick and died and her body was washed and placed in an upstairs room. Peter sent them all out of the room, then he got down on

his knees and prayed, turning toward the dead woman, he said, Tabitha get up. She opened her eyes, and seeing Peter she sat up.

Acts 9:36, 37, 40 (NIV)

In Joppa, later Peter had a vision in which God told him not to distinguish between Jews and Gentiles and to abolish the food restrictions, followed then by the Jews, as mentioned in Acts 10.

Joppa. Roman Judaea. Elababalus, 218-222 AD.
AE (24 mm, 11.7 gr.) draped bust/
Tyche standing within tetrastyle temple. Very Rare.

Since Joppa was a very important port in ancient times, it was frequently conquered. It was conquered by the Assyrians in 701 BC, Alexander the Great in 332 BC, and fell into the Ptolemies' hands in 301 BC. Pompey the Great conquered the city in 66 BC. Herod the Great captured the city, but it was taken from him and given to Cleopatra VII during Mark Antony's reign, but Herod regained it back during Emperor Augustus's reign. Today, the Tel Aviv area is the largest metropolitan area in Israel.

Peter was the only apostle who took the lead in forming and building the early church of Jerusalem. However, according to several sources, including the late first century AD letter of Clement I, the bishop of Rome, and an apocryphal second century AD document, entitled "Acts of Peter," the apostle left Jerusalem to focus on pastoral work. In time, he came to Rome, where the persecutions of Christians under Emperor Nero took place and led to his arrest. According to tradition, Peter was crucified in AD 64 and buried in a rural spot of the Tiber River called "Vatican." At Peter's request, he was crucified with his cross turned upside down, deeming himself unworthy to die in the same manner as Jesus Christ.

A basilica was built on the site of Peter's death in AD 1626. Today, St. Peter's Basilica is located within the Vatican City. Based on some scholars, the Basilica has the largest interior of any Christian church in the world and is regarded as one of the holiest shrines for Christianity.

Paul's First Missionary Journey (AD 47–49)

Paul (Saul) was born into a strict Jewish family in Tarsus, the capital of Cilicia, a Roman province in the southeast corner of Asia Minor (modern-day Turkey). His father was a Pharisee of the tribe of Benjamin, as the Bible said, "of pure and unmixed Jewish blood." Paul followed his father's way of life and inherited his character. Paul was a Roman citizen.

Tarsus. Roman Cilicia. Gordian III, 238-244 AD.
AE (36 mm, 25.46 gr.)
radiate head/Agonistic urn.

The city of Tarsus stood on the banks of the River Cydnus and is a junction point of land and sea routes connecting the Cilician plain, central Anatolia, and the Mediterranean Sea. In ancient times, the city was conquered by the Hittites, followed by Assyria, and then the Persian Empire. Tarsus was the seat of a Persian satrapy from 400 BC onward. Alexander the Great marched through Tarsus and was influenced by the Greek language and culture, and as part of the Seleucid Empire, it became more and more Hellenized. When the province of Cilicia was divided, Tarsus remained the civil and religious metropolis of Cilicia Prima and was a grand city with palaces, marketplaces, roads, bridges, baths, fountains, a gymnasium on the bank of the Cydnus, and a stadium.

From what we learned from literature, Paul (Saul) was raised in a very cultural and influential city. His father sent him to the great Jewish school of sacred learning at Jerusalem, under the celebrated Rabbi Gamaliel. He spent many years studying the Scriptures and all the questions relating to them, which the rabbis themselves practiced. Paul tells us, in Galatians, that he was so advanced in Judaism—more than any person of his age among his own people—and he was so zealous for the ideas of his fathers. His zeal and the fear that the message of Jesus was replacing his ancient Jewish faith led Paul to such strong opposition to the gospel.

Christianity was quietly spreading its influence in the city of Jerusalem after Stephen, one of the seven deacons, gave forth more public and aggressive testimony that Jesus was the Messiah.

Jerusalem. Roman Judaea. Aelia Capitolina.
Marcus Aurelius, 161-180 AD. AE (23 mm, 9.1 gr.)
draped bust/bust of Tyche. Scarce.

This caused much anger among the Jewish society and much disputation in their synagogues. Persecution arose against Stephen and the followers of Christ in general in which Paul took a prominent part. Probably Paul was a member of the great Sanhedrin at the time and an active leader in the Christian persecution by which the rulers then sought to wipe out Christianity. The Christians fled Jerusalem and were scattered abroad preaching the word everywhere in Cyprus, Antioch, and Damascus. The persecutors heard that fugitives had taken refuge in Damascus, and Paul was ordered by the high priest to go to Damascus and root out all the followers of Jesus in the area.

Paul traveled north to Damascus, as he was ordered to do. The trip is about 120 miles, and it perhaps took them at least five to six days to get there.

Damascus. Roman Coele-Syria. Nero, 54-68 AD.
AE (23 mm, 10.98 gr.)
Laureate head/Tyche seated. Scarce

Before he and his companions entered the ancient city of Damascus, suddenly, at midday, a brilliant light was over them, and Paul lay prostrate in fear on the ground. A voice from heaven sounded in his ears, as the Bible tells us: "He fell to the ground and heard a voice say to him, Saul, Saul, why do you persecute me? Who are you, Lord? Saul asked. I am Jesus, whom you are prosecuting, he replied. Now get up and go into the city, and you will be told what you must do" (Acts 9:4–6, NIV). This was the moment of his conversion, the most solemn in all his life, blinded by the dazzling light. His companions led the blinded Paul into Damascus, where he remained for three days without sight and neither ate nor drank, as we learned from the Bible. There was a disciple living in Damascus named Ananias. In a vision, the Lord commanded him to restore Paul's sight and admit him by baptism into the Christian Church. The whole purpose and aim of Paul's life was changed forever. Paul began his work in the synagogues of Damascus, proclaiming Jesus as the Son of God. The Jewish people were very confused and rather angry, and they plotted to kill him. He fled south into Arabia, according to the book of Galatians, and came back to Jerusalem after three years. He began to preach the gospel boldly in the name of Jesus in Jerusalem, but he was again forced to flee from persecution. He went to Caesarea and boarded a ship for his hometown of Tarsus, and he stayed there until Barnabas called on him to come to Antioch.

Peter was the founder of the original Jerusalem church, but Paul was the individual most responsible to helping to create the worldwide churches.

Antioch. Roman Syria, Seleucis and Pieria. Vespasian, 69-79 AD. AE (20 mm, 6.7 gr.) head of Tyche/garlanded altar.

Antioch. Roman Syria, Seleucis and Pieria. Caracalla, 198-217 AD. AR Tetradrachm (26 mm, 14.36 gr.) Laureate head/eagle.

Antioch. Roman Syria, Seleucis and Pieria. Philip I, 244-249 AD. AE (28 mm, 15.09 gr.) Laureate head/turreted bust of Tyche.

The church in the city of Antioch, the capital of Syria, was gaining firm ground on the gospel, and the word of Jesus Christ prospered. This was the first time, and in this town, the disciples were called "Christians." The church in Jerusalem sent a man by the name of Barnabas to Antioch to oversee the activities in the church there. He found out that the activities were, by far, more than he could handle. He set out to Tarsus to seek Paul, and he responded with agreement to go down with him to Antioch. For over a year or so, the two worked hard together, and the church grew and multiplied. Later, a famine broke out in Judaea. The church of Antioch sent Paul and Barnabas to Jerusalem with relief for all the brethren. The two set out by land from Antioch, taking the coastal road of Syria through Sidon, Tyre, Caesarea, and on to Jerusalem.

Sidon. Phoenicia. 43-44 AD. Dated Cy 155
(AE 15 mm, 3.5 gr.) veiled head of Tyche/
Phoenician Pentekonter. Scarce.

Tyre. Roman Phoenicia. 2nd century AD
under Trajan. AE (27 mm, 10.27 gr.)
Laureate head of Melqart/8 columed temple. Rare.

Caesaraea Maritima. Roman Judaea. Hadrian,
117-138 AD. AE (24 mm, 10.53 gr.) draped bust/
bust of Serapis wearing Modius. Scarce.

During the relief mission, persecution of Christians was still going on in Jerusalem. Paul and Barnabas went back to Antioch, taking the same land route on the coast of the Mediterranean, passing through Caeserea, Sidon, Tyre, and most of the northern towns on the coast of Syria leading to Antioch. The church of Antioch was ready to send out missionaries to the Gentiles beyond Jerusalem and Antioch. Sending missionaries all over the known world back then was a great task in the history of the church, and the disciples were now performing what the Lord commanded them to do by preaching and spreading the gospel. The church of Antioch proposed to send Paul and Barnabas, with John Mark as their attendant, for the missionary work.

The three men went forth on the missionary trip. They sailed from the city of Seleucia Pieria (the seaport of Antioch) across to the eastern shore of Cyprus to the city of Salamis.

Antioch. Roman Syria, Seleucis and Pieria.
Gordian III, 238-244 AD. AR Tetradrachm
(27 mm, 12.02 gr.) Laureate head/eagle.

Seleucia Pieria. Roman Syria, Seleucis and Pieria.
Caracalla, 198-217 AD. AR Tetradrachm
(25 mm, 13.86 gr.) Laureate head/eagle. Rare.

Then they went to the southwest shore of Cyprus to the city of Paphos. Paphos was the Roman administrative center for the eastern Roman Empire. At Paphos, the Roman governor, Sergius Paulus, wanted to hear what Paul was preaching. There with the governor was a Jewish false prophet called Bar-Jesus, who Paul prophesied would be struck blind. A sudden darkness fell upon the false prophet, and he became blind. By seeing this, the governor was converted. The missionaries went across to the mainland of Asia Minor.

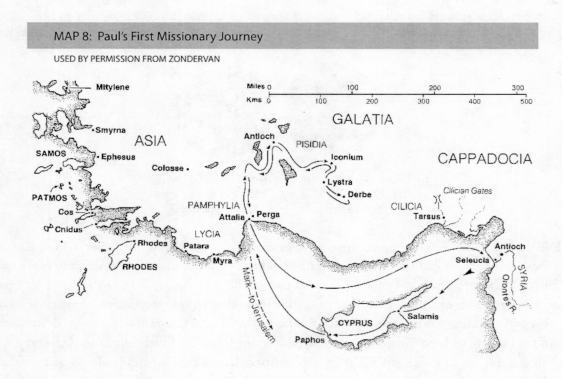

MAP 8: Paul's First Missionary Journey

USED BY PERMISSION FROM ZONDERVAN

They reached Perga, in the province of Pamphylia, where John Mark decided to leave the missionary work and go back to Jerusalem. Paul and Barnabas proceeded north to Antioch in the province of Pisidia. In Antioch, Pisidia, Paul delivered his first address of which we have any record. The inhabitants of Antioch, Pisidia, were infamous, as it was the haven for thieves and illegal slave traders. At Antioch in Pisidia, Paul went to the synagogue and preached to them, but they stirred up persecution against Paul and Barnabas and drove them out of Pisidia.

From Pisidia, the two set out to the province of Lycaonia to the city of Iconium. The same thing happened to them again that the Jews in the synagogues and the Gentiles were on both sides of the issue. Some supported them, and the others opposed their teachings. They stayed a while in Iconium until they learned of a plot to stone them. They traveled south to Lystra, and they did very well by healing a cripple there. This action created a problem throughout the town, and word spread all over the area. Their teaching came to an end in this town. Zealous Jews from Iconium and Antioch, Pisidia, came to Lystra and dragged Paul out of town, leaving him half dead. Paul and Barnabas got some help from friends and Christians there, and shortly after this incident, the two traveled east about fifty miles to the city of Derbe. Later on, they returned by the same route to see and encourage the new converts they had made in those three cities to keep their faith. After their visit to the three cities, they went to Attalia on the coastal portion of Pamphylia province. They found a ship bound for Seleucia Pieria and then back to Antioch, Syria. This missionary journey is mentioned in detail in Acts 13 and 14. The cities that are mentioned in the Bible for Paul's first missionary journey are as follows:

Starting from Antioch, Syria*
Seleucia Pieria, Seleucis and Pieria*
Salamis, Cyprus
Paphos, Cyprus
Perga, Pamphylia
Antioch, Pisidia
Iconium, Lycaonia
Lystra, Lycaonia
Derbe, Lycaonia
Attalia, Pamphylia
Back to Antioch, Syria*
*Only different coins will be presented here, as these cities were previously described.

Salamis, Cyprus

Salamis is located on the northeastern shore of Cyprus Island in the north portion of the Mediterranean Sea. The town, according to archaeological finds, was inhabited in about 800 BC. The Assyrian army broke through the landmass of Mesopotamia and arrived to the coast of the Mediterranean shores in about 875 BC. There, according to some scholars, the king of Cyprus paid homage to Sargon II, the Assyrian king, in about 700 BC.

Salamis. Cyprus. Nikokreon. 331-310 BC.
AE 1/2 Unit (17 mm, 3.79 gr.) Macedonian shield/
Macedonian helmet. Very Rare.

The city was under the Assyrian rule for centuries until it was conquered by Artaxerxes III, the king of Persian Empire, in about 400 BC. After the victory of Alexander the Great and destroying the Persian Empire, one of his generals, Ptolemy I of Egypt, ruled the island of Cyprus. During the Roman times, and after the collapse of the Greek Empire, Salamis was put under the Roman province of Cilicia. The city ceased to be the capital of Cyprus from the Hellenistic period onward when it was replaced by the city of Paphos. The Apostle Paul, with Barnabas, came to Salamis after leaving Seleucia on his first missionary trip. Barnabas was Cypriot born, and he brought Christianity to Cyprus in the early first century AD.

Cyprus. Roman. Koinon of Cyprus. Augustus,
27 BC-14 AD. AE Quadrans (17 mm, 2.14 gr.)
Capricorn, star/scorpion, star. Rare.

Cyprus. Roman. Koinon of Cyprus. Caracalla,
198-217 AD. AE (32 mm, 18.18 gr.)
Laureate head/Conical of Aphrodite. Rare.

According to tradition, Barnabas was stoned to death in the city of Salami about AD 60. Barnabas was considered to be the founder of the Cyprus church, and it is said that his bones are buried in the monastery, which was named St. Barnabas, after his death.

Paphos, Cyprus

Paphos is another city in Cyprus located on the southwest corner of the island. The city was the capital of Cyprus during Alexander the Great and his successors' reign; however, Paphos's history goes back to the seventh century BC.

Paphos. Roman Cyprus. Augustus, 27 BC-14 AD.
AE (21 mm, 7.21 gr.) bare head/Nike. Rare.

Paphos. Greek Cyprus. Ptolemy VI, 163-145 BC.
AR Tetradrachm (26.5 mm, 13.93 gr.)
Dated RY 21 (161/160 BC). diademed head/eagle. Rare.

The city came under Roman rule after the collapse of the Greek Empire. The Roman governor, Sergilus Paulus, was converted to Christianity after the Apostle Paul's visit to Paphos in his first missionary journey around AD 45. The city was, at one time, called "the Land of Aphrodite," as the people believed that the Greek goddess was born there and was worshiped for 700 years. The only remnants of this legend can still be seen today in a number of features, including the Venus rock and the baths of Aphrodite. Paphos lost to Larnaca as a major port in the Middle Ages and experienced a decline during the British colonial period when development of this part of the island come to a standstill.

Perga, Pamphylia

Perga is located in the southern region of the one-time Roman province of Pamphylia and is about seven miles from the coast of the Mediterranean Sea. The city of Perga was founded in about 1400 BC inland as a defensive measure to avoid the pirate gangs that spread terror all over the Mediterranean Sea. The city was conquered by the Persian Empire in 546 BC, and in 333 BC, Alexander the Great arrived at Perga and defeated the Persians.

Perga. Greek Kings of Macedon. 336-323 BC, Alexander the great. AR Tetradrachm (32 mm, 16.96 gr.) Dated yr 26 (196/195 BC) head of herakles wearing lion's skin/Zeus. Scarce.

Perga. Greek Kings of Macedon. 336-323 BC, Alexander the great. AR Tetradrachm (31 mm, 15.68 gr.) Dated yr 18 (204/203 BC) head of herakles wearing lion's skin/Zeus. Scarce.

The citizens of Perga sent out scouts and guides to lead Alexander the Great's army into the city. The Romans occupied the city, and Pamphylia became a Roman province after the defeat of Antiochus III in 190 BC. Perga was the birthplace of great mathematician Apollonius, who composed several books of mathematics describing family curves, circles, and ellipses. Apollonius was a student of the famous physicist Archimedes. According to the Bible, in the book of Acts, the Apostle Paul did not spend much time in Perga on his missionary journey, but he did preach the word going back before he departed from Attalia bound for Seleukia Pieria.

Antioch, Pisidia

Antioch is located on the northern tip of the province of Pisidia, on the border of Pisidia and Phrygia. The city was refounded during the Seleucid dynasty in early third century BC, although there were inhabitants in the city about 1500 BC. It was the land of the Hittites and was named Arzawa back then. The Persians conquered the city in the sixth century BC and attempted to rule the area by dividing Pisidia into satrapies.

Antioch, Pisidia. Roman Pisidia. Valerian, 253-260 AD. AE (23 mm, 5.52 gr.) radiate head/vexillum, between two standards.

Antioch, Pisidia. Roman Pisidia. Philip I, 244-249 AD. AE (25 mm, 7.35 gr.) radiate head/river god.

Antioch, Pisidia. Roman Pisidia. Gordian III, 238-244 AD. AE (26 mm, 12.48 gr.) radiate head/Aquila, signa.

Uprisings between most of the provinces against the Romans increased because of the way the Romans operated, but the Roman rule was restored in Pisidia in 102 BC. Pisidian Antioch was the center of culture of many different groups and was the economic and military capital of Pisidia. That is why the Apostle Paul visited this city on every missionary journey he conducted, hoping he would make the city the center of Christianity in Asia Minor. The city fell to Turkish rule (Anatolia), and all the ancient names were changed by the Turks, who called Antioch Yalvac, which means "prophet"— maybe after the Apostle Paul. Today, Pisidian Antioch is a great tourist spot in Turkey because of all the history and antiquity.

Iconium, Lycaonia

Iconium is located in Asia Minor on the central plateau of Anatolia, which was the Lycaonia province. The city of Iconium had inhabitants, according to excavations, during the copper age (around 3000 BC). The Hittites invaded the city around 1500 BC and the sea people from the north and west took the city from the Hittites around 1200 BC. The city was part of the Persian Empire until Alexander the Great's conquest in 333 BC.

Iconium. Roman Lycaonia. Nero, 54-68 AD.
AE (26.2 mm, 11.72 gr.) Laureate head/
Poppaias as Kore seated. Scarce.

The Apostle Paul visited this town, according to the book of Acts, several times, perhaps on all of his missionary journeys. During the Byzantine Empire, the city was conquered and destroyed several times within 200 years from the seventh century to the ninth century AD. Finally, the city was captured by the Seljuk Turks in AD 1671 when the name of the town changed to Konya. The inhabitants of this city, at the present time, are mainly Muslims, and it has a reputation of being one of the more religiously conservative metropolitan centers in Turkey. It was known, at one time, as the "Citadel of Islam." At the same time, the city was a prominent source for exporting of Turkish carpets to Europe during the Renaissance period.

Lystra, Lycaonia

Lystra is located approximately twenty miles south of Iconium, in the province of Lycaonia in Asia Minor, modern-day Turkey. Lystra was one of the big trade centers between Persia and Asia Minor, being situated on the famous Persian Royal Road. The Roman Empire made Lystra a Roman colony in 6 BC to get a better hold of all the tribes around the area.

llistra. Roman Lycaonia. Marcus Aurelius,
161-180 AD. AE (25 mm, 13.03 gr.)
Laureate head/Zeus enthroned, eagle. Rare.

The Apostle Paul visited Lystra with Barnabas, and he healed a man lame from birth, and the lame began to walk. The locals were very impressed and took Paul for Hermes (the messenger of the gods in Greek mythology) because he was the main speaker. They took Barnabas for Zeus (chief of the gods, the ruler of Mount Olympus and the god of the sky and thunder in Greek mythology). Paul was nearly stoned to death by the Jews in this town, and they had to leave Lystra and go east to Derbe. Paul returned to this town again in his future journeys, where he met Timothy, a young disciple from Lystra, and accompanied Paul and Silas in the second missionary journey. Timothy and his mother and grandmother were Jews from Lystra.

Derbe, Lycaonia

Derde is located about fifty miles due east from Lystra. The Apostle Paul and Barnabas escaped from Lystra to Derbe, where they preached and proclaimed the word in peace and made many converts there.

Lycaonia. Roman Savatra. Antoninus Pius,
138-161 AD. AE (26 mm, 11.2 gr.)
Laureate head/Tyche seated.

It is widely believed that the city of Derbe was used as refuge for escaping Christians from Roman persecution. There are many churches built to commemorate the visits of the Apostle Paul in mid-first century AD. History tells us that many Christian churches were burned and destroyed during the great Christian persecution conducted by Roman Emperor Diocletion between 284 and 305 AD. After the destruction of Derbe, there was a mass exodus of the Christian population scattered eastward to Mesopotamia and westward to Europe. Ancient coins from Derbe are extremely rare, and over the years I never had the chance to purchase any of them. The coin presented here is a substitute.

Attalia, Pamphylia

Attalia is the furthermost southern city in the province of Pamphylia. The city is located on the Mediterranean coast and was built on cliffs overlooking the Mediterranean Sea, which made the city an international tourist spot. According to tradition, King Attalos II of Pergamon gave the order to scouts and his men to go and find "heaven on earth." After they traveled all around the known world, they found this land and said, "This must be heaven." It is believed that Attalos II, king of Pergamon, found this city as a naval base for his famous fleet around 150 BC and called it Attalia.

Attaleia. Greek Pamphylia. 2nd-1st century BC.
AE (15mm, 4.84 gr.) Jugate bust of Athena/
Zeus seated. Very Rare.

King Attalos II willed his kingdom to Rome at his death in 133 BC, and it came under the Roman Republic. The city prospered and became larger during the Roman Empire period. Christianity started in this region when the Apostle Paul and Barnabas preached to the Gentiles and Jewish before departing to Antioch in his first missionary journey. The city and the surrounding areas were conquered by the Seljuk Turks in early thirteenth century AD, and they grew to a population from a few thousand in ancient days to over a million today. The last city in Apostle Paul's first journey was Antioch, Syria.

Antioch. Roman Syria. Elagabalus, 218-222 AD.
AE (19 mm, 5.6 gr.) Laureate head/Large AE.

Now Paul and Barnabas were back in the church of Antioch, Syria, after having been away for as much as two years. They told all about their journey and how Paul planted the seeds of faith in the Jewish people, as well as the Gentiles, during his first journey. A great controversy had broken out in the church of Jerusalem about how the Gentile converts that Paul had accomplished had not been circumcised and were not keeping the mosaic law of Judaism. This controversy escalated to a point that a crisis was threatening the infant church of Jerusalem. So Paul, Barnabas, and others were asked to go to Jerusalem and discuss the matter with the apostles and the elders there.

The Bible tells us, in Acts 15, that Paul and Barnabas went to Jerusalem from Antioch, Syria, by land, taking the coastal route (see maps six and seven), passing through Phoenicia and Samaria, converting the Gentiles on the way to Jerusalem. But the Bible did not give details on this trip nor the cities/towns that Paul and Barnabas went through. To convert Gentiles on the way to Jerusalem, Paul and Barnabas had to go through the coastal towns that had existed thousands of years before Paul's time. There were very limited roads in ancient times. The known ancient trade routes were the Silk Road, connecting the Orient to Mesopotamia and northern Syria; the caravan route, connecting Mesopotamia to Syria, Judaea, Phoenicia, and Egypt; the way of Philistines, connecting Samaria, Judaea, and Egypt; the Kings' Highway, connecting Mesopotamia through the Palmyrene Desert to Arabia and on to Egypt; and finally the coastal trade route (which Paul and Barnabas took), the only road connecting Asia Minor, Syria, Phoenicia, Samaria and Judaea.

Coin of Syria. Roman Koinon of Syria. Tiberius, 14-37 AD. AE (29 mm, 14.75 gr.) Laureate head/crossed cornoacopia. Scarce.

Coin of Syria. Roman Koinon of Syria. Trajan, 98-117 AD. AE (29 mm, 13.94 gr.) Laureate head/legend in two lines. Scarce.

Antioch. Roman Syria. Caracalla,198-217 AD. AR Tetradrachm (26 mm, 13.38 gr.) Laureate head/eagle standing.

One can reasonably assume that Paul and Barnabas, after they left Antioch, Syria, had to go through the cities/towns on the coastal road to Jerusalem. The towns that are located on the coastal road are: Raphanea*, Laodiceia ad Mare, Gabala*, Paltus*, Balanaea*, Aradus (an island two miles offshore), Marathus, Orthosia*, Tripolis, Botrys*, Byblos, Berytus, Sidon, Tyre, Ptolemais-Ake, Dora, and then to Jerusalem.

Raphanea. Roman Syria. Caracalla, 198-217 AD. AE (24 mm, 7.4 gr.) draped bust/Genius. Rare.

Laodicea ad Mare. Roman Syria. 138-161 AD, Antoninus Pius. AE (26 mm, 9.87 gr.) Laureate bust/Bust of Tyche, wearing head dress.

Laodicea ad Mare. Roman Syria. 198-217 AD,
Caracalla. AE (29 mm, 16.16 gr.) Laureate head/
she-wolf, suckling the twins, Romulus and Remus.

*These cities are mentioned for the first time in this book; therefore, coins and city description will be presented here. As far as the rest of the cities, only different coins are presented, as these cities were previously described.

Gabala

Gabala (Jableh) is a coastal city on the Mediterranean Sea and is located about eighteen miles south of Laodiceia ad Mare. The ancient site of Gabala is located about half a mile from the city center of Jableh and was reported to be inhabited back to 2000 BC.

Gabala. Roman Syria. Caracalla, 198-217 AD.
AE (27 mm, 14.64 gr.) Laureate head/
Tyche seated, holding rudder and cornucopia. Scarce.

Gabala. Roman Syria. Caracalla, 198-217 AD.
AE (21 mm, 6.21 gr.) Laureate
head/Tyche standing. Scarce.

Gabala. Roman Syria. Macrinus, 217-218 AD.
AE (27 mm, 12.38 gr.) bare head/
Tyche seated. Scarce.

Gabala. Roman Syria. Elagabalus, 218-222 AD.
AE (22 mm, 5.52 gr.) Laureate
head/Tyche seated. Scarce.

Gabala. Roman Syria. Trajan, 98-117 AD.
AE (22 mm, 9.44 gr.) Laureate head/
Tyche seated. Scarce.

The city of Gabala was under the municipality of Laodiceia ad Mare, and the inhabitants who lived in it were famous boat builders. The city had a natural port that accommodated all the boats used by the people. The Persians, Greeks, and the Romans occupied this coastal town, and one of the main remains of antiquity is the Roman theater, which was capable of seating more than 7,000 people. There are some older remains a little south of the city that belong to the Phoenician era. The crusaders were stationed in Gabala and were captured by Saladin in AD 1189 when he had victory over the crusaders' armies. Anceint coins from Gabala are scarce.

Paltus

The ruins of ancient Paltus are located on the coast of the Mediterranean Sea between Gabala and Balanaea. Paltus, at one time, was part of the Aradus colony in about 400 BC and was later part of the Roman province of Seleucis and Pieria in northern Syria.

Paltus. Roman Syria. Septimius Severus,193-211 AD.
AE (25 mm, 11.7 gr.) Laureate head/
draped bust of Julia Domna. Rare.

During the Byzantine Empire, the city became a province of Theodorias under Byzantine Emperor Justanian. Ancient coins from Paltus are rare.

Balanaea

Balanaea (Baniyas) is another coastal city on the shore of the Mediterranean Sea between Gabala and Orthosia. The city was a very important seaport during the Phoenician era. The Romans called the city Balanaea because of its famous natural baths (Latin: *balneum*).

Balanea. Roman Syria. Augustus, 27 BC-14 AD. AE (23 mm, 8.42 gr.) bare head/uncertain Deity driving Quadriga. Scarce.

Balanea. Roman Syria. Domitian, 81-96 AD. AE (20 mm, 5.44 gr.) Laureate head/ veiled, draped bust of Tyche. Rare.

Balanea. Roman Syria. Domitian, 81-96 AD. AE (21 mm, 7.32 gr.) Laureate head/ uncertain deity wearing Tiara, driving Quadrirga. Scarce.

Balanea. Roman Syria. Trajan, 98-117 AD. AE (21 mm, 8.55 gr.) Laureate head/ Trajan in Quadriga. Scarce.

Balanea. Roman Syria. Caracalla, 198-217 AD. AE (25 mm, 9.79 gr.) Dated CY 251 (213/214 AD). Laureate head/Sol driving facing Quadriga, date in exergue. Scarce.

Arados. Greek phoenicia. 130-129 BC. AE (20 mm, 6.69 gr.) Head of Tyche/Poseidon.

Arados. Greek phoenicia. 132-131 BC. AR Tetradrachm, Dated CY 196 (64/63 BC). (26 mm, 12.7 gr.) Head of Tyche/Nike advancing, Aramaic letters. Scarce.

The city became part of Arvad (Aradus). Balanaea is built on hilly ground overlooking the sea, and on one of the hills is the magnificent Margat citadel, a big fortress of black basalt stone. Ancient coins from Balanaea are scarce.

Orthosia

Orthosia (Tartus) is the second largest city on the Syrian coast. The city was known as Antartus during the Greek and Roman times and Tartosa during the crusaders' era. The city is called Tartus in modern-day.

Orthosia. Roman phoenicia. Elagabalus, 218-222 AD.
AE (23 mm, 7.51 gr.) Laureate head/
statue of Astarte, being crowned by Nike
within tetrastyle temple. Extremely Rare.

The city is located on the coastal plains between the Mediterranean Sea and the Alawite Mountains. The city of Arvad (Aradus), the only inhabited island in Syria, is located about two miles offshore of Orthosia. According to tradition, the history of the city of Orthosia goes back to about 1500 BC. It was found as a Phoenician colony of Arvad (Aradus), along with the city of Marathus (as mentioned earlier in this book), just south of Tartus.

Marathos. Greek phoenicia. 156 BC.
AE (16 mm, 2.92 gr.)
Head of Tyche with palm/Marathos
standing, Phoenician letters, date. Scarce.

Tripolis. Roman phoenicia. Hadrian, 117-138 AD.
AE (25 mm, 11.28 gr.) draped bust/
jugate Laureate busts of the Dioscuri. Scarce.

Tripolis. Roman phoenicia. Hadrian, 117-138 AD.
AE (21 mm, 6.6 gr.) draped bust/
Nike on Roman Galley, date in front. Scarce.

Marathus and Orthosia were the largest settlements in the Aradian colonies. The Muslims conquered the city, and the crusaders recaptured Tartus and built the Church of Our Lady of Tartosa. This church was converted to a mosque after Saladin recaptured the city from the crusaders, and it is now the city museum containing many artifacts and antiquities discovered in Marathus (Amrit) and all the surrounding areas. Ancient coins from Orthosia are very rare.

Botrys

Botrys (Batroun) is located between Tripolis and Berytus, or the modern cities of Tarabulus and Beirut, Lebanon.

Botrys. Roman phoenicia. Elagabalus, 218-222 AD.
AE (27 mm, 18.97 gr.) draped bust/
Astarte standing in Octastyle temple. Very Rare.

Botrys is considered to be one of the oldest cities in the world and dates back to the fourteenth century BC. This city was mentioned by most ancient geographers and was said to be refounded by king of Tyre Ethbaal, whose daughter, Jezabel (897–866 BC), married Ahab there. Botrys came under the Roman rule as a part of the Phoenicia Prima province. The city was a major Christian town, and it is known that three Greek Orthodox bishops came from Botrys between AD 450 and 550. After the Muslim conquest, the city was renamed to Batroun. The modern-day city of Batroun is the home of the Lebanese Red Cross and is a major tourist destination in north Lebanon. The city contains many historic churches, such as the Church of St. Stephen and the Church of our Lady of the Seas. Coins from Botrys are very rare.

Byblos. Greek phoenicia. Addirmilk & Iyyenael,
348-332 BC. AR 1/16 Shekel (10 mm, 0.75 gr.)
galley/lion attacking bull. Very Rare.

Berytus. Roman phoenicia. Septimius Severus,
193 211- AD. AE (22 mm, 9.45 gr.)
confronted busts of Caracalla and Severus/Astarte. Scarce.

Berytus. Roman phoenicia. Elagabalus,218-222 AD.
AE (30 mm, 20.32 gr.) draped bust Marsyas
in distyle temple, lion above. Scarce.

Sidon. Greek Egypt. Ptolemy II, 285-246 BC.
AR Tetradrachm (28 mm, 14.2 gr.) diademed
head/AB (date, RY 32 (254/253, BC). eagle.

Tyre. Roman Phoenicia. Caracalla, 198-217 AD.
AR Tetradrachm (24 mm, 12.2 gr.)
Laureate head/eagle standing.

Acco. Roman Phoenicia. Ace-ptolemais.
Valerian I, 253-260 AD. AE (26 mm, 13.09 gr.) Laureate
head/Tyche crownrd by Nike in hexastyle temple. Scarce.

Dora. Roman Phoenicia. Caracalla, 198-217 AD.
AE (25 mm, 7.38 gr.) Laureate head/
Laureate head of Doros. Rare.

Jerusalem. Roman Judaea, Aelia Capitolina.
Antoninus Pius & Marcus Aurelius,
138-161 AD. AE (22 mm, 6.51 gr.)
Pius bust/Aurelius bust. Rare.

Now Paul and Barnabas arrived to Jerusalem to present their case before the church apostles and the elders. Peter and James and most leaders of the church agreed with Paul and Barnabas and voted against the Judaizing of Gentiles. Paul and Barnabas went back to Antioch, Syria, using the same coastal road or the caravan road through Damascus to Antioch. Along with them were Judas Barsabbas and Silas.

Paul's Second Missionary Journey (AD 49–51)

Paul and Barnabas decided to go again to visit the brethren they had met and converted in their first missionary journey and see how they were doing. Barnabas asked Paul to take John Mark with them, but Paul refused to take him because he left them during their first mission and had not done any work with them. Barnabas decided to take John Mark with him to Cyprus, and Paul took Silas with him as a companion on his second missionary journey. Paul and Barnabas were separated, and according to tradition, they never met again. The Apostle Paul and Silas took off from Antioch, Syria. By land, along the coastal trade route road north of Antioch leading to Cilicia, after passing through the cities of Raphanea, Rhosus, Alexandria ad Issum, and the city of Issus, they arrived to Tarsus, the birthplace of Paul. At Tarsus, Cilicia, they traveled north around the Taurus Mountains. The geography of this region is described as a mountain range in Cilicia from which the famous ancient rivers, the Euphrates and Tigris, descend into Syria and Iraq. The road that Paul and Silas took had to curve north to avoid the high mountain range, which had many peaks rising 3,000–3,500 meters (10,000–12,000 feet). They went along the southern edge of Cappadocia before heading west.

Cilicia. Roman Ninica-Claudopolis.
Maximinus I, 235-238 AD. AE (31 mm, 14.53 gr.)
draped bust/She-wolf standing under fig tree,
suckling Remus and Romulus.

Cilicia. Roman Flaviopolis-Flavias. Gallienus,
253-268 AD. AE (25 mm, 8.45 gr.)
Dated CY181 (253/254 AD. draped bust/Herakles.

Cilicia. Roman Anazarbus. Caracalla,
198-217 AD. AE (37 mm, 25.78 gr.)
Dated (213/214 AD). draped bust/Koinoboulion
seated left, dropping pebble in Urn, holding
cornucopia, tree, date in legend. Rare.

Cappadocia. Greek Kings of Cappadcia.
Ariobarzanes I, 95-63 BC. AR Drachm
(17 mm, 3.5 gr.) Ir (date), year 13 (83/82 BC).

Cappadocia. Greek Kings of Cappadcia.
Ariobarzanes II, 63-52 BC. AR Drachm
(16 mm, 3.9 gr.) Z (date), year 7(57/56 BC).

Cappadocia. Greek Kings of Cappadcia.
Ariobarzanes III, 52-42 BC. AR
Drachm (17 mm, 3.7 gr.).

Cappadocia. Roman Caesaraea-Eusebia.
Trajan, 98-117 AD. AR Didrachm
(21 mm, 6.75 gr.) Laureate bust/Apollo.

Cappadocia. Roman Caesaraea-Eusebia. Gordian III,
238-244 AD. AE (26 mm, 11.23 gr.)
Laureate bust/. Agalma of mount Argaeus on altar.

Cappadocia is extended through the northeast part of Asia Minor bordering the Black Sea in the north. This land is as ancient as any land in this area. It was the home of the Hittites. Persian King Darius established a Persian satrapy in Cappadocia before he was defeated by Alexander the Great in 333 BC. Cappadocia is famous for sedimentary rocks that erupted by ancient volcanoes, forming what is called today "fairy chimneys of Cappadocia." The Bible mentioned Cappadocia in Acts 2. The Cappadocians were a group of "God-fearing Jews." The region contains several underground places largely used by early Christians as hiding places before Christianity became a legitimate religion. Today, Cappadocia compromises more than thirty rock-carved churches and chapels that date back to AD 800.

The pass that Paul and Silas took was known in ancient time as the famous Cilician Gates. They went from the gate toward Derbe, Lystra, and Iconium. Paul informed all the friends and churches already founded in Asia Minor about the decision of the elders and apostles of the Jerusalem church for the people to obey. In Lystra, there was a disciple named Timothy, whose mother was a Jewish Christian and father was a Greek. He joined the missionary journey with Paul. Brothers in Lystra and Iconium spoke very highly of Timothy. They went from Iconium to Antioch, Pisidia, and they met with the apostles and the church elders there.

From there, Paul, Silas, and Timothy went through Galatia, which is an area in the highlands of central Anatolia. Most Galatians were a part of the great Celtic migration, which invaded Macedon coming through Thrace to settle in Galatia, in about 270 BC. Galatia became a Roman province in 64 BC after they defeated the Seleukid kingdom. Paul was detained in Galatia by sickness and thus had a longer opportunity of preaching the gospel to them.

Galatia. Roman Koinon of Galatia.
Vespasian, 69-79 AD.
AE (28 mm, 14.97 gr.) Laureate bust/eagle.

Paphlagonia. Roman Neoclaudiopolis.
Antoninus Pius, 138-161 AD.
AE (31 mm, 20.75 gr.) Laureate bust/Tyche.

From Galatia, they traveled north, heading to Bithynia through Pontos and Paphlagonia, which were regions just south of the Black Sea. Bithynia was an ancient region in the northwest corner of Asia Minor adjoining the Propontis and the Thracian Bosporus. The region was occupied by mountains and forests but had valleys and coastal plains of great fertility. Paul wanted to go through Bithynia and Pontos, but the way was shut spiritually. Here again, the spirit of Jesus did not allow them to enter the region. According to legend, they traveled over a hundred miles north and then southwest along the shore of Marmara Denizi.

Bithynia. Roman Nicaea. Caracalla, 198-217 AD.
AE (23 mm, 7.16 gr.) Laureate bust/Hexastyle temple.

Pontus. Roman Amasia. Commodus, 177-192 AD.
AE (33 mm, 22.74 gr.) Laureate bust/Tyche.

Pontus. Roman Comana. Septimius Severus,
193-211 AD. AE (30 mm, 17.05 gr.)
Laureate bust/Nike standing in tetrastyle temple.

Kings of Bosporos. Roman Bosporos. Mithradates
III, 39-44 AD. AE (21 mm, 8.35 gr.)
diademed head/lion skin on club.

Kings of Bosporos. Roman Bosporos. Sauromates I,
93-123 AD. AE (27 mm, 15.31 gr.)
diademed head/shield, horses head, helmet.

Byzantium. Greek Black Sea area. 380-366 BC.
AR Siglos (17 mm, 5.4 gr.) cow/incuse square.

The Bosporus is located on the Sea of Marmara, which connects it to the Black Sea. The Bosporus is known as the world's narrowest strait that separates Europe from Asia. In ancient time, the Bosporus was a Greek colony, had its own kings, and later became a Roman province.

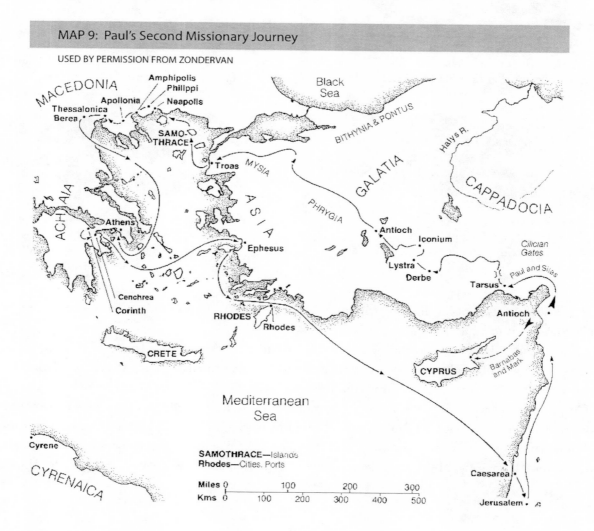

MAP 9: Paul's Second Missionary Journey

USED BY PERMISSION FROM ZONDERVAN

The prosperity of the Bosporus kingdom was based on the export of wheat, fish, and slaves. The city of Constantinople—Byzantium (Istanbul)—is located on the Bosporus. From there, the three went through Mysia province, where, according to some scholars, they went through the coastal towns of Cyzicus and Lampsacus in Mysia. Mysia was a region in northwest Anatolia and is located on the southeast of the Sea of Marmara. The entire seacoast of Mysia was scattered with Greek towns, several of which were places of considerable importance. They continued their journey west until they came down to the shores of the Aegean Sea and arrived to Alexandria in Troas. Alexandria was approximately ten miles from the legend ancient city of Troy (Ilium) and the city of Skepsis.

Kyzikos. Greek Mysia. 2nd-1st Century BC.
AE (29 mm, 10.02 gr.)
wreathed head of Kore Sotiera/Tripo.

Lampsakos. Greek Kings of Macedonia.
336-323 BC. AR Drachm (17 mm, 4.23 gr.)
head of Herakles wearing lion skin/Zeus. Scarce.

Skepsis. Greek Troas. 400-310 BC.
AE (20 mm, 7.12gr.) Rhyton/
palm tree within linear square. Rare.

Ilium (Troy). Roman Troas.
Vespasian, 69-79 AD.
AE (20 mm, 6.96gr.) Laureate head/heads of
Titus and Domition, statue of Athena. Rare.

We have no account for this long trip from Antioch in Pisidia to Alexandria, Troas, except for some references to it in Paul's Epistle to the Galatians.

Now Paul, Silas, and Timothy were in the busy harbor of Alexandria, Troas, waiting for indications of the will of God as to their future mission. According to Acts 16, in Alexandria, Troas, Paul had a vision in the night of a man from the opposite shore standing before him, and he heard him cry, "Come over to Macedonia and help us." In Alexandria, Troas, the Gentile Luke (who would later write one of the four gospels) joined Paul, Silas, and Timothy in their missionary journey. The next morning, all four sailed from Troas west to the island of Samothrace, where their ship anchored for the night. Samothrace is an island in the northeastern Aegean Sea, which became a convenient place for ships to anchor rather than risk sailing at night. Some scholars believe that all four of them went to the region of Mosia and Thrace where both of these regions are located in the northern part of Macedonia.

Samothrace. Greek Island off Thrace. 3rd-2nd centuries BC. AE (18 mm, 6.03 gr.) helmeted bust of Athena/Cybele seated. Rare.

Macedon. Roman Koinon of Macedon, under Severus Alexander, 222-235 AD. AE (27 mm, 12.96 gr.) Head of Alxander the Great/horsman.

Thasos. Greek Island off Thrace. 500-463 BC. AR Drachm (18 mm, 3.88 gr.) Satyr abducting protesting Nymph/incuse square. Rare.

Thasos. Greek Island off Thrace. circa 148 BC. AR Tetradrachm (34 mm, 16.48 gr.) head of young Dionysos/Nude Herakles, club, lion skin.

Thrace. Roman Anchialus. Geta, 198-209 AD. AE (29 mm, 14.61 gr.) Laureate head/Geta on galley. Scarce.

Thrace. Roman Anchialus. Gordian III, 238-244 AD. AE (26 mm, 12.62 gr.) confronted heads of Gordian III and Tranquillina/City gate.

Thrace. Roman Deultum. Gordian III, 238-244 AD. AE (23 mm, 7.98 gr.) Laureate head/Diana

Moesia Inferior. Roman Marcianpolis. Caracalla, 198-217 AD. AE (27 mm, 11.7 gr.) Laureate bust of Caracalla, draped bust of Julia Domna/Hera standing.

Moesia Inferior. Roman Nikopolis ad Istrum.
Elagabalus, 218-222 AD. AE (26 mm, 10.0 gr.)
radiate bust/legend in seven lines.

Moesia Inferior. Roman Marcianpolis. Macrinus and
Diadumenian, 217-218 AD. AE (27 mm, 12.8 gr.)
confronted Laureate bust/Hera.

Moesia Superior. Roman Viminacium. Herennius
Etruscus, 249-251 AD. AE (26 mm, 10.5 gr.)
draped bust/Moesia, bull, lion.

The next day, they reached the city of Neapolis in Macedonia, possibly going by the island of Thasos north of the Aegean Sea. Since the Hellespont is the dividing line between Asia Minor and the west, by crossing the Hellespont, Paul carried the tidings of the gospel from Asia to the western world. From there, Paul went to the city of Philippi and stayed there for a week or so. Paul could not find a synagogue in Philippi, but on the Sabbath, he went out of the city gate to pray by a river. Paul spoke to the women who were gathered there. According to the Bible, one of the women, named Lydia, believed in Paul's message and was converted. Lydia was Paul's first convert in Europe. Lydia insisted that the four apostles stay at her house. On the way to the place of prayer, they met a slave girl that made a great deal of money for her owners by fortune-telling. Paul and Silas commended the spirit to come out of the girl, and it did. Her owners lost hope of profiting from the girl, so they seized Paul and Silas and put them in prison after taking them in to the magistrates. An earthquake damaged the jail and made their escape possible. The jailer and his family were later converted and baptized. Here, Luke decided to remain in Philippi.

The Bible tells us that Paul, Silas, and Timothy set off from Philippi southwestward, passing Amphipolis and Apollonia, and arrived to the great Macedonian city of Thessalonica. In Thessalonica, Paul was preaching in the synagogue and explaining that Jesus had to suffer and rise from the dead. The Jews there were jealous and stirred up a mob and attacked the house of Jason, where Paul and the others were staying, searching for Paul. Paul, Silas, and Timothy took off during the night to Beroea. In Beroea (Berea), Paul went to synagogue, and the Jews there received the message with great eagerness, as they were more noble men than the Thessalonians. When the Jewish men from Thessalonica found out that Paul was preaching in synagogues in Beroea, they chased him, causing him to leave to Athens, leaving behind Silas and Timothy in Beroea. In Athens, Paul was disappointed, as he saw the city was full of idols. Since there was no church in Athens, Paul went to synagogue and started preaching and arguing with the Jews there, and the Athenians received him with cold disdain. Paul made a few converts in Athens and went west to Corinth before Silas and Timothy arrived from Beroea. According to tradition, Paul never went back to Athens.

Corinth was one of the greatest commercial centers of the empire. Paul met a Jew named Aquila with his wife, Priscilla, who recently came from Italy after Roman Emperor Claudius commanded all the Jews to leave Rome. Silas and Timothy arrived to Corinth from Beroea and joined Paul in the teaching. Most of the Jews rejected Paul's teaching in Corinth, but Crispus, the ruler of the synagogue, believed in Paul's teaching. Then Paul turned to the Gentiles of the city, and he had great success. Paul stayed in Corinth about one and a half years, doing the second aspect of his ministry by writing letters to Christian Churches. It is believed that, from Corinth, Paul wrote letters twice to the Thessalonians, and they were the earliest Epistles of Paul. After eighteen months, Paul traveled to Ephesus, accompanied by Aquila and Priscilla, leaving Silas and Timothy in Corinth. Paul left the couple in Ephesus and found a ship bound for Caesarea. After landing in Caesarea, he went to Jerusalem to greet the elders and the apostles of the church. After a short while, Paul returned to Antioch in Syria.

Cities that are mentioned in the Bible for Paul's second missionary journey are shown below:

Starting from Antioch, Syria*
Tarsus, Cilicia
Derbe, Lycaonia*
Lystra, Lycaonia*
Iconium, Lycaonia*
Antioch, Pisidia*
Alexandria, Troas
Neapolis, Macedonia
Philippi, Macedonia
Amphipolis, Macedonia
 Apollonia, Thrace
Thessalonica, Macedonia
Beroea (Berea), Macedonia
Athens, Attica
Corinth, Corinthia (Achaia)
Ephesus, Ionia
Caesarea, Samaria*
Jerusalem, Judaea*
Back to Antioch, Syria*
*Only different coins will be presented here, as these cities were previously described.

Tarsus

Tarsus is a large city located in the east corner of Cilicia province. Tarsus is the birthplace of the Apostle Paul and a very important trading city, as it is located on the ancient trade route. Tarsus's history goes back to about 9000 BC, and some legends say that the settlement came to this city from people from Argos that were exploring the coastal plain of Cilicia. Just like any city in Anatolia, the Hittites ruled the area, then the Assyrians, Babylonians, Persians, and the Greeks. During the Roman Republic, Pompey the Great occupied Cilicia in 66 BC and made Tarsus the capital of the Roman province of Cilicia.

Antioch, Syria. Roman kings of Syria. 244-249 AD, Philip I. AR Tetradrachm (26 mm, 13.3 gr.) draped head/eagle.

Tarsus. Roman Cilicia. Caracalla, 198-217 AD. AE (34 mm, 18.12 gr.) draped bust/athlete crowning self with a gonistic crown. Rare.

Iconium. Roman Lykaonia. Antoninus Pius, 138-161 AD. AE (17 mm, 3.7 gr.) Laureate bust/helmted bust of Athena. Scarce.

It was said that Cleopatra VII and her lover, Mark Antony, met in Tarsus, and they gave a big feast celebrating the construction of their fleet in 41 BC.

Tarsus is the home of the Seven Sleepers Cave, which has many legends presented by historians and scholars. The best legend I found of many is this: During the Christian persecutions by Roman Emperor Decius around AD 250, seven men were accused for their Christian beliefs. They retired to a mountain to pray, and they fell asleep in a cave. The emperor, seeing that their attitude toward paganism had not improved, ordered the opening of the cave to be sealed. During the reign of Emperor Theodosius (AD 379–395), which is 150 years later, the landowner decided to open the sealed opening of the cave. He planned to use it as animal shelter. After he opened the cave, the seven men woke up, imagining that they had slept only one day. One of them went to Ephesus, and he was shocked to see new buildings with crosses on them, and the people were also astonished to see a man trying to spend old coins from Emperor Decius's reign. The bishop interviewed the sleepers, and they told him their miracle story, and he died then, praising God. In modern times, tourists in the city of Tarsus are still taking pictures of the Seven Sleepers Cave.

Alexandria, Troas

Alexandria, Troas, is located on the Aegean Sea in the northwestern part of Anatolia and in the vicinity of the area containing the ruin of the ancient city of Troy. Troas was raided by the Hittites many times during the twelfth century BC. The Persians, Greeks, and Romans occupied this region, and it finally became a Roman colony and later became part of the province of Asia.

Alexandria, Troas. Roman Troas. Caracalla,
198-217 AD. AE (24 mm, 7.6 gr.)
draped bust/Apollo standing.

Antioch, Pisidia. Roman Pisidia. Trajan Decius,
249-251 AD. AE (26 MM, 7.96 gr.)
Bust of Dacius/Two standards.

The city was refounded by Antigonus, king of Greece, in about 310 BC under the name of Antigonia, Troas; and later, Lysimachus, king of Thrace, called it Alexandria, Troas, in memory of Alexander the Great of Macedon. Alexandria is the chief port in northwest Asia Minor and prospered greatly in Roman times due to its location, which links Europe to Asia. Constantine the Great considered making Alexandria the capital of the eastern Roman Empire before he settled on Constantinople. The Apostle Paul had a dream of a man calling him from across the Aegean Sea to come and help them, and that episode marked a very important point in Christian history by spreading Christianity over Western Europe.

Neapolis, Macedonia

Neapolis is the principle seaport in eastern Macedonia and is located off the bay of Kavala, across from Alexandria, Troas. The city was founded by settlers from Thasos in about 5000 BC, and they called it Neapolis (new city). The city was a navy base for Brutus's fleet (he was accused of assassinating Julius Caesar) in about 42 BC before he was defeated in the battle of Philippi.

Neapolis. Greek Macedonia. 424-350
BC. AR Hemidrachm (15 mm, 1.78 gr.)
Gorgoneion/head of Nymph. Scarce.

During the Byzantine Empire in the sixth century AD, Emperor Justinian I fortified the city to prevent the barbaric tribes from invading it. But during the Ottoman Empire, the city was totally destroyed by Sultan Bayezid I in AD 1391 and was not rebuilt until the end of the fifteenth century AD. Neapolis had a Greek navy base and played an important role during the Greco-Turkish War in 1919. Neapolis today is a very prosperous harbor and is famous in their tobacco industries.

Philippi, Macedonia

Philippi is located approximating eight miles from Neapolis in the northeast portion of the mainland of Greece. The city was found by Philip II of Macedon, Alexander the Great's father, in 356 BC. Philippi was famous for its gold mines, and the king improved the techniques of mining the gold, which offered King Philip an immense amount of money—some legends said about 1,000 talents of gold (about 75,000 pounds of gold).

philippi. Roman Macedonia. Augustus,
27 BC-14 AD. AE (18 mm, 4.16 gr.)
Nike/standards.

The city of Philippi is famous for the battle of Philippi, where Mark Antony and Octavian defeated the Republican army in 42 BC under Marcus Brutus and Gaius Longinus, the assassins of Julius Caesar. This battle was very important in the history of the Romans because it ended the Roman Republic and started the Roman Imperial era. In Philippi, the Apostle Paul baptized a woman called Lydia, who was the first Christian convert in Europe. As before, Paul visited many Christian families and synagogues and stayed in Philippi a good while until some of the Jews captured him and he was thrown in prison along with Silas after they cast an evil spirit out of a slave girl. They were miraculously freed from the prison by an earthquake, as mentioned in Acts 16. Philippi survived all the invasions by Slavs, Bulgars, crusaders, and the Turks, but it appears to have been abandoned in the fifteenth century AD.

Amphipolis, Macedonia

Amphipolis is another city in northern Macedonia located about twenty-five miles southwest of Philippi.

Amphipolis. Greek Macedonia. 187-168 BC.
AE (30 mm, 14.39 gr.) bust of Artemis/
Artemis seated on bull. Rare.

The history of Amphipolis goes back to about 3000 BC. It was fortified at an early age due to its strategic location. According to legend, King Xerxes I of Persia, during his invasion to Greece in 480 BC, buried nine men and nine women alive in Amphipolis as a sacrifice to the river god. A year later, near the same site, Alexander I of Macedon defeated the remains of Xerxes's army in 479 BC. Philip II of Macedon conquered the city in 357 BC and immediately incorporated it into his kingdom. The city was a very important naval base to the Macedonian kingdom and was the birthplace of the most famous Macedonian admirals. Later, the Romans conquered the city and made it part of the Roman province of Tracia. Amphipolis prospered during the Christian era when many Christian churches were built, but they were restricted to some areas of the city and sheltered by the walls of the Acropolis. The city lost its amphipolitan lifestyle after the Slavic invasions in late sixth century AD.

Apollonia, Thrace

Apollonia is another city on the Aegean Sea located about twenty miles from Amphipolis. This city's name is one of several cities in the ancient world with the same name.

Apollonia, Thrace is on the landmass of northern Greece and exhibits a beautiful wooded region with a good variety of lakes and riverbeds. Just like some historians said, "An ideal place to restock supplies on a journey." Paul and Silas passed through this city on their way to Thessalonica. No one knows if they stayed in Apollonia. The Bible did not tell us if Paul and Silas did preaching or ministered there. Apollonia is almost halfway between Amphipolis and Thessalonica.

Apollonia. Greek Thrace. 187-168 BC.
AE 20 mm, 7.34 gr.)
Laureate head/Amphora. Very Rare.

Thessalonica, Macedonia

Thessalonica was founded by King Cassander in 315 BC. The city soon became one of the most commercial and cultural centers of Macedonia.

Thessalonica. Roman Macedonia. 14-37 AD,
Tiberius. AE (23 mm, 8.23 gr.) draped bust of Tiberius/
draped bust of Julia Augusta. Rare.

Thessalonica. Roman Macedonia. 14-37 AD,
Tiberius. AE (22 mm, 8.79 gr.) bare head of Tiberius/
draped bust of Livia.

Thessalonica. Roman Macedonia. 41-54 AD,
Claudius. AE (22 mm, 11.68 gr.) head of Claudius/
head of Augustus.

Thessalonica. Roman Macedonia. circa 70 AD.
AE (17 mm, 4.58 gr.) Turreted head
of city Goddess/Kaberiros.

The city fell to the Roman rule and became the capital of the Roman province of Macedonia in 168 BC. The large and unique city harbor played a big role in the prosperity of the city. Thessalonica is one of the few cities in Greece that experienced constant cultural development and has continuously played a significant role in both Greek and world history. King Cassander of Macedonia gave the city its name after his wife, Thessaloniki, whom was the half sister of Alexander the Great. In Thessalonica, the Apostle Paul preached for three weeks in the synagogue as he always did when he arrived to a new city. Some of the Jewish stirred up a mob and attacked the house of Jason, where Paul and the others were staying. But in Thessalonica, Paul later found the second Christian Church on the European continent and wrote his two Epistles to the Thessalonians. During the Byzantine rule, the city largely adopted the Christian faith under the Greek culture. It was called the "eye of Europe." In modern days, Thessalonica became a commercial, industrial, and spiritual center of international importance and can satisfy the demands of any visitor.

Beroea, Macedonia

Beroea (Berea) is located about forty miles west of Thessalonica and was built at the foot of Vermion Mountains in northern Greece. Evidence indicated that the city was populated as early as 1000 BC.

Paroreia. Greek Macedonia. 185-168 BC.
AE (22 mm, 8.15 gr.) Zeus/Eagle.

During the Roman Empire, Beroea became the site of worship for the Roman citizens. The city housed many Jewish settlements and contained many synagogues. The Apostle Paul preached in the synagogues, and most of the Jews received the word with eagerness, but they examined the scriptures to see if the things Paul was saying were so. Paul had to leave the city because the Jews from Thessalonica pursued him to Beroea, threatening to kill him. In the Byzantine time, the city grew and prospered until the Bulgarians invaded it in the ninth century AD. The city was conquered by the Normans in 1185, during the crusaders' rule, and by the Franks in 1204. The city came under the Ottoman Empire in AD 1436 and remained in their control almost until World War I.

Some of the Greek Imperial coins do not bear the name or portrait of the reigning Roman emperor or any other member of the imperial family. Coins for the province of Macedon were mostly struck at Beroea and are very rare. The specimen presented here is one of these coins, and only a few of them add the word O^VM II IA (Olympia) on the reverse above and below the temple.

It is widely believed by many numismatists that this issue commemorates games that were held in Beroea around AD 242, probably in the presence of Roman Emperor Gordian III. This coin is extremely rare.

Beroea. Roman Macedonia. 238-244 AD,
Gordian III. AE (27 mm, 10.97 gr.)
Diademed head of Alexander the Great/two temples
with OLYMPIA above and below. Extremely Rare.

Athens, Attica

Athens (Athina) is considered to be one of the oldest cities in the world. Its recorded history goes back to 4500 BC. Athens; Alexandria, Egypt; and Antioch, Syria, were the largest, most cultural, most powerful centers of the arts and learning literature and philosophy in the ancient world. Athens is the home of Plato's Academy and Aristotle's Lyceum. Also, Athens was the birthplace of Socrates, Pericles, Sophocles, and many other prominent philosophers, writers, and politicians of the ancient world. It is widely believed that the city of Athens was the cradle of Western civilization and the birthplace of democracy.

Athens. Greek Attica. AR Tetradrachm,
393-300 BC. (24 mm, 17.0 gr.)
helmeted head of Athena/owl standing right.

Athens. Greek Attica. AR Tetradrachm, 144-143 BC.
(34 mm, 16.5 gr.) helmeted head of Athena/
owl standing right on amphora.

Athens. Greek Attica. 136-135 BC. new style,
AR Tetradrachm (30 mm, 16.5 gr.)
helmeted head of Athena/owl on amphora. Scarce.

The Apostle Paul came to Athens from Beroea, and he was astonished, rather angry, and—as the Bible said—"provoked," as he saw all the idols and statues of gods and goddesses all over the city of Athens. A metropolitan with multicultural city like Athens is not a paradise for an evangelist like Paul to proclaim the Word of God. He preached in synagogues and marketplaces and spoke to anyone he could. He could not find a church there; therefore, he left for Corinth. The city of Athens prospered during the crusaders' period, but it declined during the rule of the Ottoman Empire. In the nineteenth century, it reemerged as the capital of the independent Greek state and hosted the first modern Olympic Games in 1896.

Corinth, Achaia

Corinth is located approximately forty miles west of Athens. The city was founded in the Neolithic Age, circa 6000 BC, by the goddess Ephyra (according to myth), a daughter of the Titan Oceanus, thus the ancient name of the city was "Ephyra." Around the mid-sixth century BC, Corinth was a major exporter of black-figure pottery to the civilized world. Corinth played a very important role in the Persian wars—they offered 40 warships and 5,000 armed soldiers in the battle of Salamis. Corinth was destroyed by Lucius Mummius, Roman Republic general, in 146 BC. He put all the men to the sword and sold women and children into slavery, and then he burned the city.

Corinth. Roman Corinthia. Domitian, 81-96 AD.
AE (22 mm, 7.24 gr.) Laureate head/Victory.

Julius Caesar re-found the city in 44 BC right before his assassination. The city later grew and multiplied and was noted for the luxurious immoral lifestyle. The city became a large metropolis with mixed population of Romans, Greeks, and Jews. The Apostle Paul visited this city and stayed there eighteen months, enjoying great success. Paul turned to a different aspect of his ministry by writing letters to Christian Churches in other places. Paul visited Corinth one more time in his third missionary journey, where, according to the Bible, Paul wrote two Epistles to the Corinthians, two Epistles to the Thessalonians, and the Epistle to the Romans. During the Byzantine reign, Emperor Justinian I erected a stone wall around the Corinthian gulf to protect the city from the Barbarian invasions of the north.

Ephesus, Ionia

Ephesus is located on the western coast of Anatolia in Asia Minor in the province of Ionia. The history of Ephesus goes back to about 6000 BC, as indicated by excavations.

Ephesus. Roman Ionia. Augustus, 27 BC-14 AD.
AE (18 mm, 7.67gr.) conjoined heads of
Augustus and Livia/stag standing. Scarce.

The city came under the Persian rule, and the Ephesians raged in a revolt against the Persians for the continued rising of taxes in the battle of Ephesus in 498 BC. All the Ionian cities, together with Sparta and Athens, were able to drive the Persians from Anatolia in 479 BC. Alexander the Great defeated the Persians, and he liberated all the Greek cities of Asia Minor. After Alexander's death, the city of Ephesus came under the rule of Lysimachus, one of Alexander's ablest generals, in 290 BC. The city fell under the Romans and the taxes rose sky high. Ephesus invited and welcomed Archelaus, a general of Mithridates the Great, king of Pontus, when he conquered Asia Minor. This welcome led to the Asiatic Vespers (First Mithridatic War), where according to legend, about 80,000 Romans and/or those who spoke with a Latin accent were slaughtered.

Caesaraea Maritima. Roman Judaea. Trajan Decius,
249-251 AD. AE (26 mm, 14.97gr.) Laureate head/
Dacius receiving wreath from Nike. Scarce.

Jerusalem. Roman Judaea, Aelia Capitolina. Antoninus
pius, 138-161 AD. AE (22 mm, 11.06 gr.)
Laureate head/Dioskourois. Scarce.

Antioch, Syria. Roman Syria. Elagabalus, 218-222 AD.
AR Tetradrachm(26 mm, 13.06 gr.)
Laureate head/eagle.

The Apostle Paul visited Ephesus in his third missionary journey and stayed there more than two years, and he used the city as a home base of his missions. Paul later wrote a letter to the Christian Church of Ephesus. Apostle John lived in Asia Minor after Paul's death, and he guided all the churches of the province from Ephesus. The house of the Virgin Mary supposedly is located on the edge of Ephesus and, according to tradition, is believed to have been the last home of Mary, mother of Jesus. Today, the place is a very popular place to visit by pilgrims and was visited by three recent popes.

Paul's Third Missionary Journey (AD 52–57)

After Paul spent some time in Antioch, after his second journey, he went in depth to the provinces in Galatia and Phrygia to strengthen his converts and the disciples.

Galatia. Roman Galatia. Koinon of Galatia.
Nero with Poppaea, 54-68 AD.
AE (26 mm, 12.52 gr.) head of Nero/bust of Poppaea.

The biblical scholars believe that the main reason for Paul's third journey was the pressure caused by conflict created by the legalistic Christians in Jerusalem's church. The justification was through the law, not just the faith as they claimed. Paul argued and confronted these legalistic believers, including Peter, accusing them that they were not straightforward with of the gospel. Paul's theological objectives were living by faith in the son of God.

Paul told the elders in the church of Jerusalem if justification were through the law, then Jesus Christ died for no reason. The church of Jerusalem sent evangelists to challenge the teaching and the authority of Paul all over Asia Minor. So Paul went on this journey to retrieve the freedom of the gospel.

The Bible tells us that Paul retraced his steps of the second journey by leaving Antioch to Tarsus, and from there, he went through the Cilician Gates to Derbe, Lystra, and Iconium.

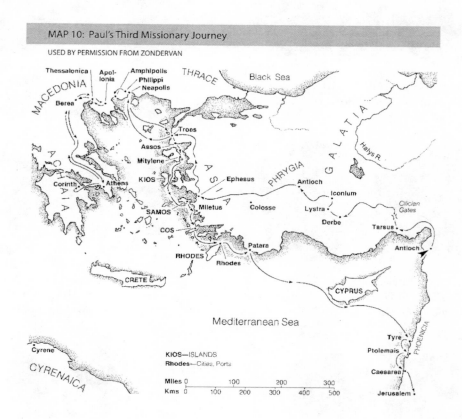

He continued west to Antioch, Pisidia, and from Antioch, he passed through the city of Laodicea, Phrygia, before reaching Ephesus. Ephesus was a splendid city. It was the Liverpool of the Mediterranean Sea. It contained a great harbor, which concentrated the traffic of the sea and the highways of the nations. The city of Ephusus was famous in its theaters, given over to every kind of pleasure, and a city of vast wealth.

Antioch, Syria. Greek Syria. 149-147 BC.
AE (23mm, 12.3 gr.) head of Zeus/Zeus enthroned.

Antioch, Syria. Roman Syria. Elagabalus, 218-222 AD.
AE (32mm, 19.49 gr.) Laureate head/Tyche seated.

Tarsus. Roman Cilicia. Gordian III, 238-244
AD. AE (36mm, 23.76 gr.) radiate head/Tyche.

Tarsus. Roman Cilicia. Trajan Decius,
249-251 AD. AE (35mm, 19.63 gr.)
radiate head/Herakles standing,club,lion skin.

Iconium. Roman Lycaonia. Gallienus, 253-268 AD.
AE 31.8mm, 17.92 gr.) diademed head/She wolf,
suckling twins Romulus and Remus .Scarce.

Antioch, Pisidia. Roman Pisidia. Philip II,
247-249 AD. AE (26mm, 10.97gr.)
radiate head/sacrificial Implements.

Antioch, Pisidia. Roman Pisidia. Gallienus,
253-268 AD. AE (27.5mm, 13.98 gr.)
Laureate head/she-wolf suckling twins
Romulus and Remus.

Ephesus. Roman Ionia. Augustus,
27 BC-14 AD. AE (20mm, 5.35 gr.)
conjoined heads of Augustus and
Livia/stag standing. Scarce.

Ephesus. Greek Ionia. 150-140 BC.
Cistophoric AR Tetradrachm (31 mm, 12.10 gr.)
Cista Mystica within ivy/bow case with serpents.

This kind of metropolis opened a big, wide door for Paul to proclaim the word. Paul sent his assistants up the valleys to evangelize and carry the gospel to Colossae and Laodicea and other places while he worked in Ephesus.

Paul stayed in Ephesus, as the Bible tells us, more than two years, preaching and spreading the word. He taught in synagogues and spoke boldly in the market places about the kingdom of God. Paul performed many miracles, cured many sick, and drove the evil spirit out of many. At the end of two years, many of the Jews, Gentiles, and Greeks that lived in Asia Minor had heard the word of God, and the name of the Lord Jesus was held in high honor. When this became known between the Jews and Greeks living in Ephesus, they were scared. For many centuries, Ephesus was the pilgrim center bringing worshipers to the temple of the fertility goddess, Artemis, which, according to legend, was one of the Seven Wonders of the World. All of the worshipers would buy silver, gold, marble, and little silver-image statues of the multi-breasted goddess. So after the word of the Lord spread widely and grew in power, Paul's converts abandoned their worship, and all the businesses fell off. Demetrius, the silversmith of Ephesus, stirred a riot against Paul, and then Paul had to leave Ephesus.

Paul went through the city of Adramyttium, Mysia, which is a city located between Ephesus and Alexandria, Troas. According to the Bible, this is the ship in which Paul embarked on in Caesarea, going to Rome as prisoner. The ship belonged to this city, and he traveled on it to Myra, Lycia. Acts 27:2 (NIV) says, "We boarded a ship from Adramyttium about to sail for posts along the coast of the province of Asia." After passing Adramttyium, Paul arrived at Alexandria, Troas. Paul was sad of heart and weary of body for what happened to him in Ephesus and the concern with the legalistic faction in the Jerusalem church. From Troas, he went to Neapolis and was discouraged when Titus told him the news that the Corinthians had accepted the legalistic discipline in the church. During the summer and autumn, Paul spent his time with the churches of Philippi, Thessalonica, Beroea, Amphipolis, and Apollonia, and he probably penetrated into the interior of the shores of the Adriatic.

Adramyttium. Greek Mysia.
circa 350 BC. AE(16 mm, 4.38gr.)
bust of Zeus/forepart of winged horse. Rare.

Adramyttium. Greek Mysia.
circa 300 BC. AE (10 mm, 0.90 gr.)
bust of Zeus/forepart of winged horse. Rare.

Adramyttium. Roman Mysia.
Antonine period, 98-192 AD.
AE (22 mm, 4.05 gr.)
Dionysos, wearing ivy wreath/Demeter. Rare.

Alexandria, Troas. Roman Troas.
177-192 AD, Commodus.
AE (24 mm, 4.7 gr.) draped bust/horse gazing.

Alexandria, Troas. Roman Troas.
198-217 AD, Caracalla.
AE (27 mm, 10.28 gr.) draped bust/horse gazing.

Neapolis. Greek Macedonia. 424-350 BC.
AR Hemidrachm (15 mm, 1.80 gr.)
Gorgoneion/head of Nymph. Scarce.

Philippi. Roman Macedonia. 27 BC-14 AD,
Augustus. AE (19 mm, 5.54 gr.) bare head/two
pontiffs behind team of oxen plowing. Scarce.

Philippi. Roman Macedonia. 27 BC-14 AD,
Augustus. AE (18 mm, 4.45 gr.)
Nike advancing/three military standards.

Amphipolis. Kings of Macedon under
Roman rule, 158-149 BC. AR Tetradrachm
(31 mm, 16.7 gr.) diademed head of Artemis/
club of Herakles within a wreath. Scarce.

Amphipolis. Roman Maccedonia. 14-29
AD, Julia Augusta. AE (23 mm, 7.11 gr.)
draped bust of Artemis/Artemis on bull. Scarce.

Beroea. Roman Macedonia. 238-244 AD,
Gordian III. AE (27mm, 10.97 gr.)
Diademed head of Alexander the Great/two temples
with OLYMPIA above and below. Extremely Rare.

Corinth. Greek Corinthia. Alexander the Great,
336-323 BC. AR Tetradrachm (29 mm, 17.12 gr.)
head of Herakles wearing lion skin/Zeus seated. Scarce.

Thessalonica. Roman Macedonia. 27 BC-14 AD,
Augustus with Caius Caesar. AE (23 mm, 9.14 gr.)
Laureate head of Augustus/bare head of Caius.

Thessalonica. Roman Macedonia. 27 BC-14 AD,
Augustus with Caius Caesar. AE (22 mm, 8.29 gr.)
Laureate head of Augustus/bare head of Caius.

Thessalonica. Roman Macedonia. 14-37 AD,
Tiberius with Livia. AE (23 mm, 9.34 gr.)
Laureate head of Tiberius/veiled head of Livia.

Thessalonica. Roman Macedonia. 235-238 AD,
Maximus. AE (25mm, 11.2 gr.) bare head/Kabir.

Apollonia. Greek Thrace. 5th-4th Century BC.
AR Drachm (15 mm, 2.85 gr.) facing head
of Medusa/anchor,A,cray fish. Scarce.

Then he went to Corinth to challenge the people who came from Jerusalem's church to question his teaching authority. After three months in Corinth, Paul decided to go back to Jerusalem, and he found a ship bound for Syria. When he learned that there was a plot against his life, he went through Macedonia by road. He celebrated the Passover at Philippi, and then he sailed to Alexandria, Troas, where he stayed for seven days. The Bible tells us, on the first day of the week, Paul gave a sermon that lasted until midnight in a third-floor room. A young man named Eutychus was seated in a window, and when he was sound asleep, he fell to the ground from the third story and was taken up dead. By a miracle, Paul put his arms around him and informed the people, "Don't be alarmed; he is alive" (Acts 20:10, NIV).

From Alexandria, Troas, Paul sailed to Assos, Troas, and went south to Mytilene and Samos en route to Miletus. Paul had purposely bypassed Ephesus, because he was in a hurry to get to Jerusalem. From Miletus, he sailed for Cos, then Rhodes, and finally to Patara. In Patara, Paul changed ships to a cargo vessel bound for Phoenicia. The Bible tells us that he sailed within sight of Cyprus on their left (did not go to Paphos) and finally arrived to the city of Tyre. Paul talked to the Christians in Tyre. They warned him not to go to the Holy City of Jerusalem. From Tyre, he went to Ptolemais-Ake and then to Caesarea, where Paul and his group stayed in the house of Philip, one of the seven deacons in the Jerusalem church. In Caesarea, Paul was warned again not to go to Jerusalem, but in spite of all the warnings, Paul arrived to Jerusalem.

Cities that are mentioned in the Bible for Paul's third missionary journey are shown below:

Started from Antioch, Syria*
Tarsus, Cilicia*
Derbe, Lycaonia*
Lystra, Lycaonia*
Iconium, Lycaonia*
Antioch, Pisidia*
Ephesus, Ionia*
Alexandria, Troas*
Neapolis, Macedonia*
Philippi, Macedonia*
Amphipolis, Macedonia*
Beroea, Macedonia*
Corinth, Corinthia (Achaia)*
Thessalonica, Macedonia*
 Apollonia, Thrace*
Assos, Troas
Mytiline, Lesbos
Chios, island off Ionia
Samos, island off Ionia
Miletus, Ionia
Cos, island off Caria

Rhodes, island off Caria
Patara, Lycia
Tyre, Phoenicia *
Ptolemis-Ace, Phoenicia *
Caesarea, Samaria *
Arrived to Jerusalem, Judaea *
*Only different coins are presented in this section, as these cities were previously described.

Assos, Troas

Assos is located on the southwest shore of Troas province, approximately twenty-five miles south of Alexandria, Troas. The city is across the gulf where the island of Lesbos is located, about six miles offshore. Assos was founded by the Aeolic immigrants that came from Methymna in Lesbos about 1000 BC. Assos is a harbor city on the gulf of Adramyti.

Assus. Roman Troas. Augustus, 27 BC-14 AD.
AE (19 mm, 3.71 gr.)
bare head/Griffin reclining. Vary Rare.

The city came under the rule of the Persians before it fell to Alexander the Great in 334 BC. After Alexander died, the city was ruled by Lysimachus, one of Alexander's ablest generals. It was said that Aristotle founded a Platonic school in Assos (348–345 BC) and the stoic philosopher Cleanthes was born in Assos. Ancient coins from Assos are rare.

Mytilene, Lesbos

Mytilene is located on the Greek island of Lesbos in the northern region of the Aegean Sea. The city became the largest and most prosperous on the island of Lesbos and became its capital around 640 BC. The mineral electrum was abundant around Mytilene, where a great output of electrum coins were minted during the sixth and fifth century BC.

Mytilene. Greek Lesbos. 521-478 BC. EL Hekte
(10 mm, 2.42 gr.)ram's head/Incuse,
head of Herakles right. Very Rare.

According to legend, Aristotle lived in Mytilene for a couple of years, 337–335 BC, after becoming the tutor to Alexander III (the Great), son of King Philip II of Macedon. The city came under the Roman rule and later under the Byzantine Empire before it was captured by the Seljuk Turks. Recent archaeological excavations revealed five altars in Demeter sanctuary used for sacrifices to Demeter and Kore and later to Cybele, the great mother goddess of Anatolia.

Chios, Island off Ionia

Chios is considered to be the fifth largest island of the Greek Isles. It is located to the west off the province of Ionia. The history of Chios goes back to about 1600 BC from cave dwelling in the north and a settlement later at the far south of the island.

Chios. Greek Ionia. 3rd century BC.
AE (14mm 2.03, gr.)
Sphinx seated/Amphora. Rare.

Chios. Greek Ionia. 2nd-1st century BC.
AE (14mm, 2.1 gr.)
Sphinx seated/Amphora. Rare.

During the Hellenistic period, the island became one of the largest exporters of high-quality Greek wines with a characteristic sphinx emblem and bunches of grapes to symbolize the city. The city fell to Roman rule and became a province of Asia Minor. Chios was under the rule of the Byzantine Empire for 600 years before the Turks and later the crusaders got a hold of the city. The island of Chios is still remembered for the Chios massacre, where, according to legend, approximately 80,000 Greek islanders of Chios were hanged, starved, or tortured to death; 50,000 Greeks were enslaved; and about 22,000 Greeks were exiled by Ottoman Empire troops in AD 1822. The island was devastated, and the few survivors that were dispersed throughout Europe became part of the Chian Diaspora. Ancient coins from Chios are rare.

Samos, Island off Ionia

The island of Samos is located roughly about fifty miles south of Chios in the Aegean Sea off Ionia province. Samos is one of the most important and most fertile of the islands of the Aegean Sea.

Samos. Greek Ionia. 460-453 BC. AR Diobol (9.5 mm, 0.9 gr.) forepart of winged boar/lion's head right. Very Rare.

Samos. Roman Ionia. Claudius, 41-54 AD. AE (26 mm, 7.93 gr.) Laureate head/statue of Hera Samia. Very Rare.

Samos. Greek Ionia. 408-380 BC. AE (14 mm, 2.42 gr.) head of Hara/head of lion. Rare.

A great portion of the island is covered with vineyards, and its high-quality wines give the island its reputation. Samos became one of the leading commercial centers in Greece due to the island's location on trade routes between the Black Sea, Asia Minor, and Egypt. The island of Samos went through three big wars between 600 and 400 BC and several political revolutions, which ended in the establishment of a democracy. After Alexander the Great's death, Samos served as a base for the Egyptian fleet of the Ptolemies in 275–270 BC. The island came under Rome and became a Roman province in 133 BC. Samos was occupied by the Turks and belonged to the Ottoman Empire from AD 1533–1821. Ancient coins from Samos are rare.

Miletus, Ionia

Miletus is an ancient city on the western coast of Asia Minor and in the southern tip of the province of Ionia. Based on archaeological evidence, Miletus was inhabited by the Neolithics in 3500–3000 BC. The city was recorded in the Hittite records around 1300 BC.

Miletos. Greek Ionia. circa 500 BC.
AR 1/12 Stater (10 mm, 1.15 gr.)
head of lion roaring/Stellite pattern
within an incuse square. Rare.

Miletos. Greek Ionia. circa 500 BC.
AR 1/12 Stater (10 mm, 1.25 gr.)
head of lion roaring/Stellite pattern
within an incuse square. Rare.

Miletos. Greek Kings of Macedon.
Alexander the Great, 336-323
BC. AE (17mm, 3.53 gr.) head
of Apollo/horseman riding.

The Persians occupied Miletus during their invasion to Asia Minor, and it was later liberated by Alexander the Great in 334 BC. The city came under the Roman rule, just like any other province in Asia Minor. The Apostle Paul met the elders of the church of Ephesus near the end of his third missionary journey in Miletus, and according to legend, he sat on the steps of the great harbor monument while he visited with them and bid them farewell on the nearby beach. The thing that made them sad the most was his last statement that they would never see his face again. Most scholars believe that Paul came to Miletus one more time before his death, as mentioned in the books of 2 Timothy and 1 Corinthians. Most scholars also believe that Paul came to Miletus on the way back from visiting Spain.

Cos, Island off Caria

Cos is a Greek island off the shore of the southern tip of the Caria province. Caria is a province located in southwest Asia Minor (modern-day Turkey). The island of Cos's history goes back to the eleventh century BC, where inhabitants from Cos participated in the war of the city of Troy.

Cos. Greek Caria. 167-88 BC. AE(23 mm, 8.43 gr.) head of Apollo/ Lyre within wreath. Rare.

Cos. Greek Caria. 167-88 BC. AE(24 mm, 9.2 gr.) head of Apollo/Lyre within wreath. Rare.

During the Hellenistic period, the island received its fame from its great wine and later from its silk manufacture. During the same period, the city attained the zenith of its prosperity and was valued by the kings of Egypt, who used it as an outpost for their navy fleets to protect the Aegean Sea. Cos became a provincial branch of the museum of Alexandria, Egypt, and became a well-known spot for education of the princes of the Ptolemaic dynasty. According to Josephus, King Mithridates was sent to Cos to fetch the gold deposited there by Queen Cleopatra of Egypt. According to the same source, Herod the Great had provided an annual stipend for the benefit of prizewinners in the athletic games in Cos, and a statue was erected there to his son, Herod the Tetrach. The Ottoman Empire ruled Cos for 400 years until right before World War 1 in 1912. The island of Cos is known to be the birthplace of Hippocrates, the ancient Greek physician, 460–370 BC. He was considered one of the most outstanding figures in the history of medicine. He is referred to as "the father of medicine." Ancient coins from Cos are rare.

Rhodes, Island off Caria

Rhodes is the largest of the Dodecanese Islands in both area and population. It is located about forty miles offshore south of the province of Caria. The city of Rhodes is the island's capital located at the northern tip of the island, as well as the site of the ancient and modern commercial harbors. Based on archeological evidence, the city was inhabited in the sixteenth century BC, and the Achaeans invaded the island in the fifteenth century BC. The Persians occupied the island and were defeated by the forces from Athens in 48 BC. At that time, the island joined the Athenian league.

Rhodos. Greek Caria. 229-205 BC. AR Didrachm (20 mm, 6.63 gr.) radiate head of Helios/ rose with bud, anchor. Scarce.

Rhodos. Greek Caria. 188-170 BC. AR drachm (16 mm, 2.7 gr.) radiate head of Helios/rose.

Rhodos. Greek Caria. 188-170 BC.
AR drachm (15 mm, 2.71 gr.)
radiate head of Helios/rose.

Rhodos. Greek Caria. 170-150 BC.
AR drachm (17 mm, 2.76 gr.)
radiate head of Helios/rose.

Alexander the Great conquered the island, and after his death, Ptolemy, Seleucus, and Antigonus succeeded in dividing the Greek kingdom. Rhodes played a strong role, having commercial and cultural ties with the Ptolemies in Alexandria, Egypt. Rhodes schools of philosophy, science, and literature were famous throughout the Mediterranean and the ancient world. Demetrius, son of Antigonus, besieged Rhodes in 305 BC by creating huge siege engines, and a year later, he signed a peace treaty, leaving behind a huge store of military equipment. The Rhodians sold it and used the money to build a statue of their sun god, Helios. The statue is now known as Colossus of Rhodes. The Apostle Paul brought Christianity to the island during his teaching in the area. The city reached her zenith in the third century AD and became one of the most civilized and beautiful cities in Hellas. The Byzantine Empire began in Rhodes when the Roman Empire was divided to Eastern and Western empires, and gradually, the Eastern half became a Greek Empire.

Patara, Lycia

Patara is a natural harbor city located in the southwest corner of the province of Lycia in modern-day Turkey. It was said that the city was founded by Patarus, a son of Apollo, and was noted in antiquity for its temple and oracle of Apollo.

Patara. Roman Lycia. Gordian III, 238-244 AD.
AE (29 mm, 18.43 gr.) draped bust/Apollo,
branch,bow,eagle,serpent. Extremely Rare.

Like most cities in Asia Minor, it was ruled by the Greeks when Alexander the Great defeated the Persian armies in 333 BC. King Ptolemy Philadelphus of Egypt enlarged the city and gave it the name of Arsinoe, after Queen Arsinoe II of Egypt—his wife and his sister—but the city continued to be called by its ancient name, Patara. The Romans occupied the city, and it was formally annexed by the Roman Empire in AD 43 and attached to Pamphylia. The Apostle Paul, according to Acts 21, changed ships in Patara to sail to Phoenicia. The city was Christianized early, and several early bishops are known to be from this city. Patara is located in the region of the Turkish Riviera on the coast of the Mediterranean. The Turkish Riviera, throughout history, was a unique landscape that attracted many heroes, kings, and warriors. Mark Antony of the Roman Republic chose the Turkish Riviera as the most beautiful wedding gift for his beloved Queen Cleopatra of Egypt. According to legend, the Turkish Riviera is the birthplace of the most important figures of history. St. Nicholas (later known as Santa Claus) was born in Myra, a small town close to Patara. Ancient coins from Patara are rare.

Tyre. Roman Phoenicia.
Time of Trajan, 112- 113 AD.
AE (22 mm, 6.67 gr.) Tyche/legend.

Ptolemais-Ace. Roman Phoenicia.
Caracalla,198-217 AD.
AR Tetradrachm (26 mm, 12.94 gr.)
Laureate head/eagle. Scarce.

Caesaraea Maritima. Roman Judaea.
222-235 AD, Severus Alexander.
AE (21 mm, 8.29 gr.) Laureate
head/eagle, wreath"SPQR". Scarce.

Jerusalem. Roman Judaea. Aelia
Capitolina. Antoninus Pius, 138-161 AD.
AE (24 mm, 9.27 gr.)
draped bust/Tyche in temple. Scarce.

Paul's Journey to Rome (AD 57–62)

Paul was warned several times not to go to the Holy City of Jerusalem. As the Bible tells us, he was warned by the disciples in Tyre and by the brothers in Ptolemais-Ake. All the efforts made by the disciples to discourage Paul from going to Jerusalem had failed, and he went to Jerusalem, saying, "The Lord's will be done" (Acts 21:14, NIV). He told the elders of Jerusalem church of all the success he had achieved in converting the Jews and Gentiles during his trips in Asia Minor. At the Feast of Pentecost, some Jews from Ephesus were there and caused a big stir by accusing Paul for defiling the temple by bringing along Gentiles and teaching the Jews to turn away from the Law of Moses. Paul was almost murdered by Jewish mobs in the temple of Jerusalem. The Roman soldiers rescued Paul, and they took him to the barracks in the fortress Antonia.

According to the Bible, forty Jewish men formed a plot and promised themselves, with an oath, not to eat or drink until they had killed Paul. The Roman commander heard about the plot and immediately ordered two of his centurions to guard Paul and take him to Caesarea. Since Paul was a Roman citizen, they put him under guard in Herod's palace, awaiting his accusers to present their cases to the Roman governor of Judaea, Antonius Felix (AD 54–59). For various reasons, Paul stayed as a prisoner for two years in Caesarea. At the end of two years, Felix was succeeded by Porcius Festus in AD 59/60, before whom the Apostle Paul was again heard. Paul invoked his right as a Roman citizen to appeal to the emperor and to be tried in Rome. As the Bible tells us, Festus told Paul, "You have appealed to Caesar, and to Caesar, you shall go" (Acts 25:12 NIV).

Therefore, Paul was taken to Rome from Caesarea, which is about a 1,700–1,800-mile journey.

Jerusalem. Roman Judaea. Aelia Capitolina.
Antoninus Pius, 138-161 AD. AE (22 mm, 10.19 gr.)
draped bust/Dioskouroi, eagle between them. Scarce.

Caesaraea Maritima. Roman Judaea.
98-117 AD, Trajan. AE (27 mm, 13.23 gr.)
Laureate head/Emperor sacrificing on altar. Rare.

Sidon. Greek Egypt. Ptolemy II, 285-246 BC.
AE (23 mm, 11.34 gr.)
Laureate head of Zeus/eagle, double cornucopia. Scarce.

They sailed to Sidon on a ship from Adramyttium, avoiding the open sea. The ship sailed along the coast of Antioch, Syria; on the southern shore of Cilicia; and around the northeast tip of Cyprus until they arrived to Myra in the province of Lycia. In Myra, they took an Egyptian vessel, with a cargo of wheat, bound from Myra to Italy. The ship hugged the shore of Asia Minor until they arrived at Cnidus in the province of Caria. The captain of the ship decided to sail through the open sea instead of fighting the strong winds through the Greek islands.

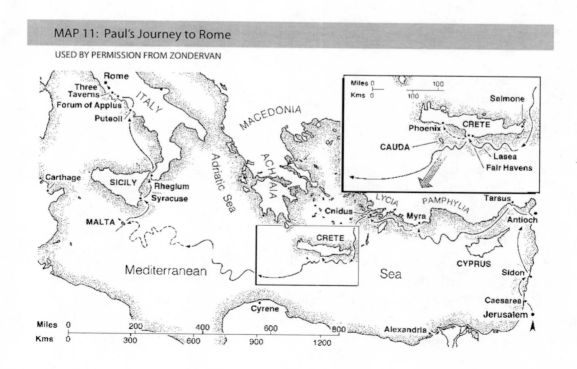

MAP 11: Paul's Journey to Rome

USED BY PERMISSION FROM ZONDERVAN

They sailed south, passing the eastern tip of Crete Island, and sailed along the southern shore of Crete until they came to a place called Fair Havens near the town of Lasea. Fair Havens was not a suitable place to anchor. They sailed west, but the ship was caught by the northern wind and was driven south, southwest, and west. The violent storm continued for several days, and finally, the ship broke down in the shallow water on the coast of Malitus (Malta). The Bible tells us the chief official of the island, Publius, welcomed Paul and his group, and during Paul's three-day stay, he cured the official father, who was suffering from fever and dysentery. The shipwrecked passengers spent three months on the island of Malta, and finally, they sailed on another Egyptian ship bound for Italy. They arrived to Syracuse, on the island of Sicily, and after three days there, they sailed north, touching Italy at Rhegion (Rhegium). Three days later, they arrived to the port of Puteoli (Neapolis), one of the largest commercial ports in Italy today on the west shore of Campania. In Puteoli, Paul stayed with brothers and elders for a week before he went to Rome. The brothers in Rome heard that Paul was coming to Rome. They went out and met him at Forum of Appius and at the Three Taverns, which are well-known rest stops (way stations), forty miles and ten miles, respectively, just south of Rome. Paul finally arrived to the imperial city of Rome probably in AD 61/62.

Cities that are mentioned in the Bible for Paul's journey to Rome are shown below:

Started from Jerusalem, Judaea*
Caesarea, Samaria*
Sidon, Phoenicia*
Myra, Lycia
Cnidus, Caria
Lasea (Priansos), Crete
Malitus, Malta
Syracuse, Sicily
Rhegion, Bruttium
Puteoli, (near Neapolis), Campania
Arrived to Rome, Latium
*Only different coins are presented in this section, as these cities were previously described.

Myra, Lycia

Myra is a coastal town located on the Turkish Riviera on the coast of the Lycia province. The city became the largest town in the Lycian alliance in 168 BC. In ancient time, the citizens in the city worshiped Artemis, who became the city goddess, along with Zeus and Tyche. The city came under the rule of the Persians, Greeks, and Romans, and today, most of the ancient theaters and Roman baths have been partly discovered.

Myra. Roman Lycia. 238-244 AD,
Gordian III. AE (29mm, 17.46 gr.) Diademed
bust/Tyche standing, head left. Extremely Rare.

Myra was one of the largest producers of purple dye, which was used exclusively with Roman court and royal families' clothing. The Apostle Paul came to this city when he changed ships in its harbor when he was prisoner on his way to Rome. Myra became the capital of the Byzantine Eastern Church under Theodosius II, who reigned the Byzantine Empire from AD 408 to 450. The city of Myra fell to the Islamic troops after siege of AD 809 under Caliph Harun Al-Rashid. The city was again taken by Islamic invaders—this time, the Seljuk Turks—and the city went into a decline afterward. According to legend, Myra is the birthplace of some of the most important figures of history. St. Nicholas (later known as Santa Claus) was born in Myra. Saint Nicholas was the bishop of Myra in AD 325. The earliest church of St. Nicholas at Myra was built in the sixth century AD. Later, a monastery was added to the church, in the eleventh century AD. Ancient coins minted in Myra are extremely rare.

Cnidus, Caria

Cnidus is an ancient city located at the extreme southwestern end of the province of Caria.

Cnidos. Greek Caria. circa 350 BC.
AR Drachm (14 mm, 3.03 gr.)
bust of Aphrodite/lion. Scarce.

Cnidos. Greek Caria. 350-330 BC.
AR Drachm (16 mm, 2.84 gr.)
bust of Aphrodite/lion. Scarce.

The city lies on the coast of a narrow peninsula that extends out into the Aegean Sea about thirty miles southeast of the island of Cos (Kos). The Athenians defeated the Spartans in a naval battle in and around Cnidus in 394 BC. The city and the whole province of Caria today is famous in exporting fruits, nuts, and figs to the Mediterranean Sea and beyond.

Lasea, Crete

Lasea is a town located on the southern shore of the island of Crete. There is very little known about this city.

Crete. Roman Crete. Augustus, 27 BC-14 AD.
AE (25 mm, 9.44 gr.) radiate head/victory. Rare.

Based on *A Bible Handbook to the Acts of the Apostles,* Lasea was about a few miles from the harbor town of Fair Havens, about the halfway point on the southern shore of the island. The ruins of Lasea are adjacent to the city of Priansos, located about five miles from Lasea. Coins were minted for the city of Priansos but not for Lasea, because recent discoveries suggest that Lasea seems to have served more as a fortress than a harbor. The city was not mentioned by ancient geographers, and as of today, the place is not well known. However, new surveys found ancient ruins on the shore beside Priansos that may be identified with Lasea.

Malitus

Malitus, modern-day Malta, is an island in the Mediterranean Sea approximately sixty miles south of the coast of Sicily. The island's history goes back to the Stone Age and was inhabited in about 5200 BC. The culture disappeared from the island around 2500 BC, historians think because of a famine or disease. However, the culture appeared again in around 1500 BC—a culture that is known to have cremated its dead and introduced much smaller religious structures. The Phoenicians invaded the island in around 600 BC, and they used the island as an outpost for their trade routes from the east Mediterranean Sea.

Malitus. Greek Island off Sicily. 150-146 BC.
AE(26 mm, 9.86 gr.) head of Isis wearing Uraeus/
male figure with four wings. Extremely Rare.

The island came under the Roman Empire in 117 BC. The Bible tells us that the Apostle Paul was shipwrecked on the shore of Malta and stayed there three months, introducing Christianity and performing various miracles. Paul cured Publius's father, the governor of the island, on this place. Today, we can see the Cathedral of St. Paul on the island, and according to legend, it was built on the site where Governor Publius was reported to have met St. Paul following his shipwreck on the Maltese coast. When the Roman Empire split into Eastern and Western divisions in the fourth century AD, Malta fell under the Greek-speaking Byzantine Empire, which was ruled from Constantinople. Ancient coins minted in Malitus are extremely rare.

Syracuse, Sicily

Syracuse is a historic city located on the southeastern shore of the island of Sicily. According to historians, Syracuse was founded in about 730 BC by settlers from Corinth and Tenea. Syracuse has very fertile land, and the settlers were hardworking people. Along with the native tribes, they made the city the most prosperous and powerful Greek city around the Mediterranean. The city continued to expand in Sicily, fighting against the rebellious Siculi. In the late fifth century BC, Syracuse found itself at war with Athens and, one hundred years later, was again at war against Carthage, a North African province on the southern shore of the Mediterranean.

Sicily. Greek Sicily, Kainon. Circa 365 BC.
AE (21 mm, 10.84 gr.) Griffin/bridled horse.

Sicily. Greek Sicily, Gela. 490-475 BC.
AR Didrachm (22 mm, 8.7 gr.) nude horseman/
forepart of man headed bull. Rare.

Sicily. Greek Sicily, Mamertinoi. 264-241 BC.
AE(28 mm, 18.83 gr.) head of Ares/eagle.

Sicily. Greek Sicily, Mamertinoi. 264-241 BC.
AE(29 mm, 16.27 gr.) head of Ares/eagle.

Sicily. Greek Sicily, Syracuse. 367-357 BC.
AE (23 mm, 7.87 gr.)Griffin/Bridal horse.

Sicily. Greek Sicily, Syracuse. 317-289 BC.
AE (22 mm, 10.05 gr.) Bust of Artemis/thunderbolt.

Sicily. Greek Sicily, Syracuse. 317-289 BC.
AE (21 mm, 10.63 gr.) Athena/Pegasos.

Sicily. Greek Sicily, Syracuse. 275-215 BC.
AE (19 mm, 6.1 gr.) Poseidon/trident, two dolphins.

Island off Sicily. Greek Kossura. 50-1 BC.
AE (24 mm, 10.87 gr.) Nike flying/
symbol of Tanit above "cossvra". Rare.

Carthage. Greek Carthage. 300-264 BC.
AE (20 mm, 5.90 gr.)
Head of Tanit/horse. Scarce.

Carthage. Greek Carthage. 264-241 BC.
AE(23 mm, 8.4 gr.) Head of Tanit/horse. Scarce.

Finally, Syracuse defeated the Carthaginians in 339 BC. In about 275 BC, Hieo II seized power, and he introduced a period of fifty years of peace and growth in which Syracuse became one of the most renowned capitals of antiquity. The city fell to the Romans in 212 BC. The Byzantine Empire took it over in AD 668, and later, it fell under the Muslim rule in AD 876 for almost 200 years. In modern day, the city exhibits spectacular temples, churches, and Roman amphitheaters.

Rhegion, Bruttium

Rhegion is a city located on the toe of Italy's boot, across from the island of Sicily.

Rhegion, Greek Bruttium. 260-215 BC.
AE (20 mm, 6.62 gr.) head of Apollo/Tripod.

Rhegion, Greek Bruttium. 260-215 BC.
AE (22 mm, 6.11 gr.) head of Artemis/Kithara. Scarce.

The general area has been influenced by several earthquakes and tsunami floods over the centuries. The city history of Rhegion goes well over 2,700 years old when the Greek settlers founded the region around 720 BC. The city became part of the Roman Republic and later under Byzantine Empire rule. In the twelfth century AD, it became part of the kingdom of Sicily and later became part of the kingdom of Naples. The city was hit by bad earthquakes in 1783 and 1908. The latter quake was the worst, where 80 percent of the city collapsed and thousands were killed. This quake remains the worst recorded earthquake in modern Western European history, and it took Rhegium generations to fully recover.

Puteoli, Campania

Puteoli is about six miles west of Neapolis on the bay of Naples. The city was founded by the Greeks in 594 BC and became a Roman colony in 194 BC. Puteoli was one of the largest cities for importing and distributing Egyptian wheat off the coast of the Campania province.

Neapolis. Greek Campania. 275-250 BC.
AR Nomos (19 mm, 7.27 gr.) head of Nymph/
man-headed bull crowned by Nike. Scarce.

It was said that Roman dictator Sulla built a villa in Puteoli and died in it in 78 BC. A story was told about Roman Emperor Caligula before he became an emperor. An astrologer in Puteoli predicted that Caligula had no more chance of becoming emperor of Rome than riding a horse across the Gulf of Baire, which was about two miles. To our surprise, Caligula built a temporary floating bridge over two miles long and crossed it, riding on his horse, in defiance of the astrologer. Ancient coins were never minted in the city of Puteoli; therefore, coins for Neapolis are presented here instead, since Neapolis is in the immediate vicinity of Puteoli.

Rome, Latium

Rome is the capital of Italy and is Italy's largest and most populous city.

Rome. Roman Republic. after 211
BC. AR Denarius (20 mm, 3.6 gr.)
helmeted head of Roma/the Dioscuri riding.

According to Roman tradition, the city of Rome was founded by the twins Romulus and Remus in 753 BC on the Palatine Hill, built in the area of the future Roman Forum. The Palatine Hill was the location of the cave where Romulus and Remus were found by the she-wolf that kept them alive. According to the same legend, the shepherd Faustulus found the infants and, with his wife, Acca Larentia, raised the children. When the boys were grown, Romulus killed his twin, Remus, and the city was called Rome ever since. Romulus would become ancient Rome's great conqueror, adding large areas of territory and population to his new city.

The original settlement developed into a large kingdom, and they were undefeated until Gauls occupied the city in 386 BC, but the Romans recovered Rome back a year later. During the reign of

Constantine the Great, the bishop of Rome had the authority of the political and religious concepts, eventually becoming known as the pope, establishing Rome as the center of the Catholic Church. In AD 410, Germanic barbarians sacked the city of Rome, which caused the fall of the Western Roman Empire in AD 476.

Paul's Journey to Spain
(Fourth Missionary Journey, AD 62–68)

According to scholars, Paul stayed in Rome for about two years after the Romans brought him from Caesarea as a prisoner. As a prisoner, he had his own hired house (at his own expense), but he was under constant guard. He was accorded this privilege because he was a Roman citizen. He welcomed everyone who came to see him, preaching the good news and teaching about Jesus Christ. He had the opportunity of preaching the gospel to the soldiers who kept guard over him, and it spread among the imperial guards, even in Caesar's household. His two years of imprisonment turned rather to the benefit of the gospel, and his hired house became the center of a great influence that spread over the whole city of Rome. During this period, Paul probably wrote most of his Epistles to the Colossians, Hebrews, Philippians, and Ephesians.

Paul's imprisonment ended when he was heard by the emperor of Rome, and he was found not guilty, and he was set free. Once more, his old dream of evangelizing came alive by going west to Spain, as mentioned in the book of Acts 13:1–21 and the book of Romans 15:24, 28. Also a convincing statement from Clement of Rome showed that Paul did go to Spain, as mentioned in his early Christian literature. Pope Saint Clement I, also known as Saint Clement of Rome, was listed as one of the first bishops of Rome (AD 96). According to the NIV Bible, scholars believe that Paul went to Spain, and a map is given in 1 Timothy, showing the route that Paul took going to Spain from Rome.

Rome. Roman Republic. 148 BC.
AR Denarius (19 mm, 4.0 gr.)
helmeted head of Roma/the Dioscuri riding.

He left Rome and headed west through the small channel just adjacent to the northern shores of Sardinia Island before he arrived at Tarraco, Spain. The Bible did not give much detail where Paul traveled in Spain, except that he entered Spain at the coastal city of Tarraco and went to the interior to the city of Toletum. Further examination to the route he took in Spain suggests that Paul followed the route drawn in the biblical map, and for him to leave Spain from the southern end, he had to pass through the most populated coastal cities before he left Spain. All the cities that Paul traveled to, from Rome to Spain and back to Rome, are shown below.

Cities that are mentioned in the Bible for Paul's Spain journey are as follows:

Started from Rome, Italy*
Sardinia, Sardinia
Tarraco, Spain (see additional cities in Spain below)
Crete, Crete*
Miletus, Ionia*
Colossae, Phrygia
Ephesus, Ionia*
Pergamum, Mysia
Alexandria, Troas*
Philippi, Macedonia*
Nicopolis, Epirus
Brundisium, Calabria
Neapolis, Campania
Back to Rome, Italy*
*Only different coins are presented in this section, as these cities were previously described.

Cities in Spain, as suggested by the route drawn on the biblical map of the scholars plus a few more cities suggested by the author:

Entered Spain: Tarraco, Spain
Celsa, Spain
Bilbilis, Spain
Catagurris, Spain
Totetum (no coins minted; it is believed that this city is located near Emerita)
Ercavica, Spain
Irippo, Spain
Illici, Spain
Carthago-Nova, Spain
Carteia, Spain
Out of Spain: Julia Traducta, Spain

MAP 12: Paul's Fourth Missionary Journey

USED BY PERMISSION FROM ZONDERVAN

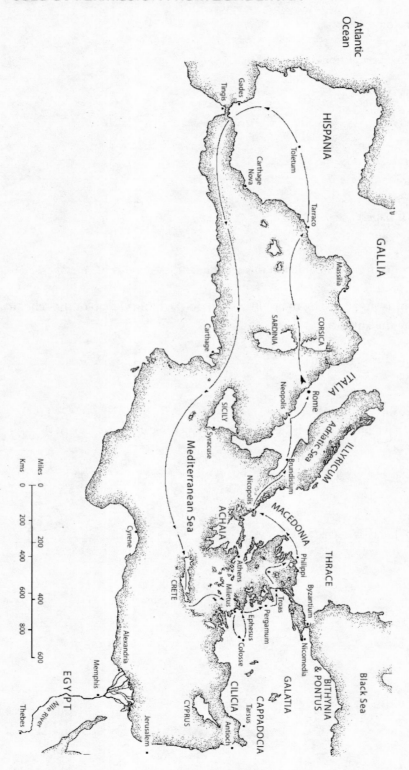

MAP 13: Western Mediterranean Area

COURTESY OF CNG (WWW.CNGCOINS.COM)

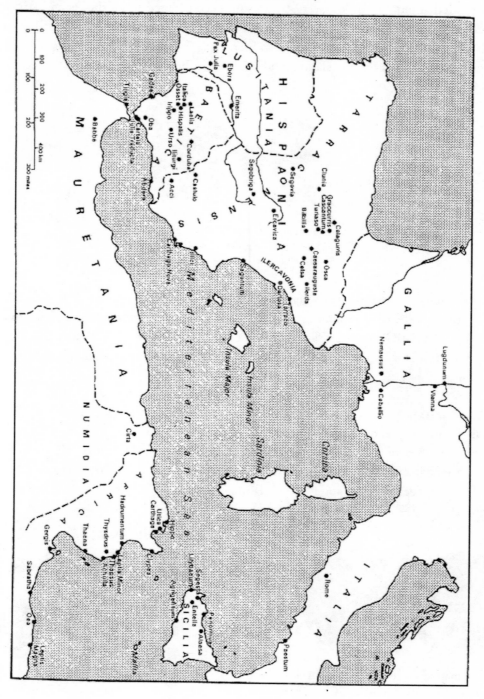

Sardinia Island, Sardinia

Sardinia is located about 150 miles west of Italy and is considered to be the second largest island in the Mediterranean Sea. The island was inhabited by humans around 6000 BC. The Phoenicians from the east Mediterranean came to this island with increasing frequency and settled in around 1000 BC. The Phoenicians expanded on the island, and by 500 BC, the native Sardinians started to attack the Phoenicians.

Sardinia. Greek Island off Sicily.
218-201 BC. AE (18 mm, 4.10 gr.)
head of Tanit/bull, star above. Extremely Rare.

The Phoenicians called upon Carthage for help, and the Carthaginians defeated the Sardinians and occupied most of the island for almost 300 years. The Romans defeated the Carthaginians in their first Punic War in 238 BC, and the island became a Roman province. The Roman Empire dominated the Island of Sardinia for almost 700 years. Ancient coins minted in Sardinia are very rare.

Tarraco, Spain

Tarraco was the most splendid coastal city in Spain. It is located on the northeast shore of Spain on the Mediterranean Sea. The history of Tarraco goes back to the third century BC when it was populated as an Iberian village. Emperor Augustus used the city of Tarraco to carry many war missions into Hispania. The city became the capital of the Roman province Tarragona, one of the largest on the Iberian Peninsula.

Tarraco. Roman Spain. Tiberius, 14-37 AD.
AE AS (25 mm, 7.8 gr.) Laureate head/confronting
busts of Livia and her grandson Drusus. Rare.

Tarraco. Roman Spain. Tiberius, 14-37 AD.
AE AS (22.4 mm, 6.79 gr.) Laureate head
of Augustus/bare head of Tiberius. Rare.

The Germanic barbarians invaded the city the third century AD and the Muslims in the seventh century AD, which caused the city to decline. The city reemerged and began to grow after the Christian conquest in the twelfth century AD. Many Roman ruins and amphitheaters can still be seen today. Ancient coins minted in Tarraco are rare.

Celsa, Spain

Celsa is a town located about fifty miles northwest of Tarraco in the Roman province of Celsa. Very little is known about this town, and there is no evidence that this town still exists today.

Celsa. Roman Spain, Lepida-Celsa.
27 BC-14 AD, Augustus. AE(29 mm, 12.0 gr.)
Laureate head/bull standing.

Calagurris. Roman Spain, 14-37 AD, Tiberius.
AE (30 mm, 12.4 gr.)Laureate head/bull.

Bilbilis, Spain

Bilbilis is a town in north Spain, approximately seventy-five miles from the coastal city of Tarraco. The city is located on the banks of the River Jalon in the middle of the Sistema Iberico mountain range.

Bilbilis. Greek Spain. 2nd-1st century BC.
AE (26 mm, 12.31 gr.) male head/horseman.

Bilbilis. Roman Spain. 27 BC-14 AD, Augustus.
AE (29 mm, 15.75 gr.) bare head/horseman.

Bilbilis. Greek Spain. 2nd-1st century BC.
AE (30 mm, 14.70 gr.)male head/horseman.

The Muslims (Moors) built the new Bilbilis about two miles to the north and called it Calatayud in AD 716. This name came from the Arabic word *Qalat Ayyub* (the fort of Job). The city contained large Jewish communities and, of course, large Arab (Muslim) populations. Both survived all conquests until the expulsion of all the Jews and Arabs from Spain in AD 1492. King Ferdinand of Spain and his wife, Queen Isabell, deported all the Arabs and Jews from Spain the same year they sent Christopher Columbus to discover a different trade route to India.

Emerita, Spain

Emerita was founded by Roman Emperor Augustus, and he called it Emerita Augusta.

Emerita. Roman Spain. 27 BC–14 AD,
Augustus. AE (31 mm, 16.3 gr.) radiate head/
two-towered and double-arched city gate

Ercavica. Roman Spain. 27 BC–14 AD, Augustus.
AE (28 mm, 13.5 gr.) Laureate head/bull standing.

The city soon became the most important city in Roman Spain, and today, the city preserves more important ancient Roman monuments than any other city in Spain. Pope Paul brought the diocese great wealth, making it the wealthiest diocese in Spain.

Irippo, Spain

This city was located in the southwestern region of Spain, about fifty miles from the coast of modern Gibraltar. The city was populated during the Apostle Paul's visit to Spain, and it is believed that he went through this town before reaching Carteia and Julia Traducta upon his departure from the southern coast of Spain. There is very little history known about this town.

Irippo. Roman Spain. 30 AD, Octavian.
AE(22 mm, 3.86 gr.) bare head/woman seated.

Illici. Roman Spain. 14-37 AD, Tiberius.
AE (27 mm, 11.4 gr.) bare head/inscribed altar.

Carthago Nova. Roman Spain. 14-37
AD, Tiberius. AE (28 mm, 12.72 gr.)
bare head/draped busts of Nero and Drusus.

Carthago Nova. Roman Spain.
27 BC-14 AD, Augustus. AE(29 mm, 14.90
gr.) Laureate head/Aspergillum & Simpulum.

Obulco. Greek Spain. late 2nd century BC.
AE (29 mm, 14.85 gr.)
female head/legend in two lines. Scarce.

Castulo. Greek Spain. mid 2nd century BC.
AE (30 mm, 20.76 gr.) male head/Sphinx. Scarce.

Carteia, Spain

Carteia is a coastal city on the southern tip of Spain just to the north of the Gibraltar Peninsula.

Carteia. Greek Spain. 1st century BC.
AE(22 mm, 6.48 gr.)Tyche/Neptune sitting. Scarce.

It is widely believed that the Apostle Paul departed from Spain from this coastal city or from Julia Traducta. The city of Carteia has been inhabited since prehistoric time and was the oldest known settlement in the area. The city was conquered by the Phoenicians in 228 BC. The Romans captured Carteia in 206 BC, and it came under the Roman Republic. About thirty years later, the Iberian-born children of Roman soldiers requested from the Roman Senate a town to live in and were given Carteia, and they named it Colonia Libertinorum Carteia. In AD 711, the Arabs invaded the city and the surrounding areas under the Ummayed conquest of Spain, led by Tariq Ibn Ziyad, and made Carteia part of the Andalusia region. In mid-fourteenth century AD, Alfonso XI, king of Spain, took the area back from the Muslims, and later, most of the population was gradually Christianized.

Julia Traducta, Spain

Julia Traducta is the southernmost city in Spain, and it has occupied a strategic position on the Strait of Gibraltar since antiquity. This city was originally captured by the Phoenicians, and they made it a trade post for their commerce. At the port gate today, one can see two signs—on the east it says, "Mar Mediterranean" (the Mediterranean Sea), and on the west, it says, "Oceanis Atlantico" (Atlantic Ocean)—that describe the importance of the city's strategic position.

Julia Traducta. Roman Spain.
27 BC-14 AD, Augustus. AE (16 mm, 2.3 gr.) bare head left/sacrifical implements. Rare.

The port is also the point of departures for the fast ferry to Tangiers. Also, it widely believed, in ancient time, that the Apostle Paul departed Spain bound for Asia Minor from this port. The Romans found this city, but the Moors—and later the Christians, during the Byzantine Empire—developed the town.

Crete. Roman Crete. Gortyna. 37-41 AD, Caligula. AE(21mm, 5.71 gr.) Laureate head of Caligula/ Laureate head of Germanicus. Rare.

Miletos. Greek Kings of Macedon. 336-323 BC. AR Drachm (16 mm, 4.22 gr.) Herackles/Zeus.

Colossae, Phrygia

Colossae is located about 120 miles east of the city of Ephesus in the Lycus River Valley in the ancient province of Phrygia in Asia Minor. Colossae is located about eleven miles south of Laodiceia ad Lycum, the sister city that is mentioned in the book of Revelation.

Colossae. Greek Phrygia. mid -1st century BC.
AE(20 mm, 7.34 gr.) Zeus/thunderbolt. Scarce.

Ephesus. Greek Ionia. 202-133 BC.
AE (18.2 mm, 2.42 gr.) Bee/stag standing. Scarce.

It is believed that the Apostle Paul addressed an epistle from Rome to the inhabitants of Colossae, who had perhaps been evangelized by him. The city of Colossae was the home of Paul's two companions, Archippus and Philimon, and also of Onesimus and Epaphras, who probably founded the church of Colossae.

The Persians occupied the city of Colossae in 396 BC, and they gave it the name of Colossinus based on the wool color that is similar to the cyclamen flower. During the Hellenistic period, the town was a very important commercial center. Based on the biblical narratives, the Apostle Paul had not visited Colossae when he wrote his epistle to the Colossians, since he told Philimon of his hope to visit it upon being freed from prison. This is another reason that scholars believe that Paul visited Colossae on his way back from Spain after he was released from prison. According to legend, the city fell into decay after a devastating earthquake.

Pergamum, Mysia

Pergamum is a city located in the northwest region of Asia Minor in the Mysia province. It is approximately fifteen miles from the coast of the Aegean Sea. The city of Pergamum became the center of a large kingdom in the third century BC, and it kept the leadership in the cultural and political status up to and during the early period of the Byzantine Empire.

Pergamum. Roman Mysia. 27 BC-14 AD,
Augustus. AE (20 mm, 4.77 gr.) togate figures
standing facing/statue of Augustus. Rare.

Pergamum. Greek Mysia. 188-133 BC.
AE(22 mm, 8.5 gr.) Helmeted Athena/trophy. Scarce.

A complex of the god of healing, Aesclepius, was built in Pergamum in the fourth century BC and became the cultic center around the Greek and Roman world. Emperor Hadrian expanded the complex, which was included on the list of "wonders of the world" in the second century AD. The city of Pergamum built a library, which housed more than 200,000 volumes and was the second largest library in the ancient world after Alexandria, Egypt. A century later, Mark Antony gave the volumes to Cleopatra VII as a wedding present to be added to the collection of the library in Alexandria. The Greeks built a theater on the edge of the city Acopolis. It was later modified by the Romans, and it was the steepest theater in Asia Minor with a seating capacity over 10,000 people. The city of Pergamum is one of the seven churches addressed in Revelation.

Alexandria Troas. Roman Troas. 235-238 AD,
Maximinus I. AE(25 mm, 6.2 gr.) head/Apollo.

Philippi. Roman Macedon. Claudius, 41-54 AD.
AE(25 mm, 10.09 gr.) bust/Augustus, Genius.

Nicopolis, Epirus

Nicopolis is a coastal city located on the western shore of Greece in the Epirus province. The city was founded by Octavian to celebrate the victory over Mark Antony and Cleopatra at the battle of Actium in 31 BC. The city was considered at one time the capital of southern Epirus.

Nicopolis. Roman Epirus. Caracalla, 198-217 AD.
AE (21 mm,3.79 gr.) Laureate bust/
Caracalla on horse. Very Rare.

According to legend, the city was built where Octavian (Augustus) pitched his tent the first time he landed there, and he built a monument adorned with the beaks of the captured galleys. Major highlights of the city were the building of the seventy-seven-row Roman theater and the aqueduct, which brought water to the town from a distance of twenty-seven miles. The Apostle Paul, as mentioned in Titus 3, planned to spend the winter in Nicopolis, where he invited his coworker, Titus, to join him from Crete about AD 66/67.

From Nicopolis, Paul sailed along the shore of Corcyra Island on his way to Brundisium. Ancient coins minted in Nicopolis are very rare.

Corcyra, Island off Epirus

Corcyra (Korkyra) is a Greek Island in the Ionian Sea close to the west shore of Epirus province. The history of this island goes hand in hand with the Greek mythology from the beginning. Its Greek name was Korkyra, which came from two powerful water gods: Poseidon is the god of the sea, and Asopos is river god.

Corcyra. Roman Korkyra.
1st-2nd centuries AD. AE(18 mm,5.3 gr.)
Zeus enthroned/Agreos. Rare.

Corcyra. Greek Korkyra. 229-48 BC.
AE (19mm, 6.61 gr.) Herakles/prow of galley. Rare.

According to myth, Poseidon fell in love with nymph Korkyra, daughter of Asopos, and river nymph, Metope. Poseidon abducted her and brought her to an unnamed island and offered her name to the place. They had a child together called Phaiak, after whom the people on the island were named, Phaiakes, and his name translated later via Latin to Phaeacians.

Brundisium, Calabria

Brundisium is an ancient city on the coast of Calabria province, the furthermost region on the eastern shore of the Italian peninsula. Brundisium's history goes back probably to the Illyrian settlement pre-dating the Roman expansion. After the Punic Wars (series of three wars fought between Rome and Carthage from 246–146 BC), the city became a major center of Roman naval power and maritime trade. Sulla the Roman general (138–78 BC) made the inhabitants Roman citizens and made the city a free port.

Brundisium. Greek Calabria. 200-89 BC.
AE (22 mm, 7.51 gr.) head of Poseidon/Taras holding Nike and lyre on a dolphin. Scarce.

Brundisium. Greek Calabria. circa 215 BC.
AE (23 mm, 8.96 gr.) head of Poseidon/youth holding Nike on dolphin,globe below. Scarce.

However, Julius Caesar sieged the city in 49 BC, and it was attacked twice in 42 BC and 40 BC. The city became the chief point of embarkation for Greece and the east. There was a major road that connected the city to Rome via Neapolis, and it is widely believed that this is the road Apostle Paul took when going back to Rome after he visited Spain and Asia Minor on his last trip. The city fell to the Byzantine rule, and soon after that, it was conquered and destroyed by the Lombards (Germanic people) in AD 674. Since the city was a very important and strategic port, it was soon rebuilt.

Neapolis, Campania

Neapolis (Naples) is a coastal city located on the western shore of Italy in the Campania province.

Neapolis. Greek Campania. 300-275
BC. AR Nomos (20 mm, 7.41 gr.)
female head/man-headed bull. Scarce.

The history of the city goes back to the seventh century BC when the ancient Greeks found the city and called it Neapolis, meaning "new city." Later, the whole region grew bigger, and many communities were built on the coast and the new and old cities on the gulf of Naples merged together and became one. Neapolis was an ally of the Roman Republic against Carthage, where they stopped Hannibal (Carthaginian military commander) from invading the city. Neapolis was greatly respected by the Romans as a place of Hellenistic culture and where the people maintained their Greek language and customs and elegant villas, aqueducts, public baths, and theaters were built. Tiberius and Claudius, two powerful Roman emperors, chose Neapolis to be a vacation or holiday city for them. Both Apostle Paul and Apostle Peter are said to have preached in this city during their missionary journeys. The city was occupied by the Byzantine Empire (also known as the Eastern Roman Empire) in AD 536. This city had a long history of wars and occupation between the Germanic, Spanish, and Austrians. The black plague, or the Black Death—the deadliest pandemic in human history—hit Neapolis and killed over half of the 300,000 inhabitants. Neapolis (Naples) was the most bombed Italian city in World War II, though Neapolis was the first Italian city to rise up against German military occupation and free their city completely by October 1943.

Rome. Roman Republic. 145 BC. AR Drachm
(18 mm, 4.0 gr.) Roma/the Dioscuri riding.

PAUL'S FINAL DAYS

After Paul's trip to Spain, he came to Rome, as mentioned earlier. He kept on preaching and writing to the churches all over Asia Minor until the Christians were blamed for the disaster of Rome under Emperor Nero (AD 54–68). Some scholars believe that no one heard from Paul after he settled in Rome the second time (knowing Paul, he did not just disappear). According to some tradition, he was caught and tried along with Christians in Rome. This time, the charge did not break down, and Paul was condemned and was delivered over to the executioner. Since Paul was a Roman citizen, his death penalty would have been by beheading.

The Apostle Paul labored his body and his soul many years for the good of men and the glory of God. I could not be any more disturbed and devastated than seeing Paul kneeling beside the block in front of the executioner. This order came from Emperor Nero, a man with the reputation of being the very worst and meanest human being the history ever known. His body and soul immersed in every nameable vice, and his purple robe was stained with the blood of the innocents. Most scholars believe that Paul died in AD 67/68.

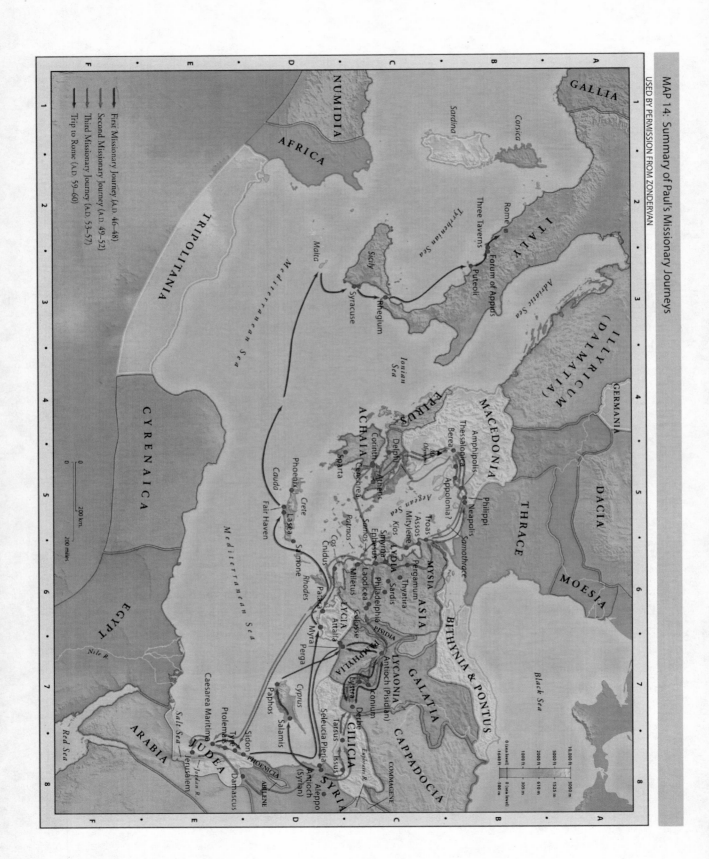

First Missionary Journey (A.D. 46–48)
Second Missionary Journey (A.D. 49–52)
Third Missionary Journey (A.D. 53–57)
Trip to Rome (A.D. 59–60)

Apostle John and the Seven Churches in Revelation

The Apostle John, according to Christian scholars, was the author of several New Testament books: the Gospel of John, the epistles of John, and the book of Revelation. John was one of the sons of Zebedee, and his mother's name was Salome (Salome is believed to be a sister of Jesus's mother, Mary). John was born around AD 6, and he and his brother the Apostle James, the Apostle Peter, and his brother Andrew were all partners in a fishing business in the Sea of Galilee prior to their call by Jesus to follow him. John, the apostle, was a faithful disciple of Jesus during his early Judaean ministry. John moved to Ephesus shortly before the destruction of Jerusalem by the Romans in AD 70, and later, he became the pastor of the church in Ephesus and had special relationships to other churches in the area.

During the reign of Roman Emperor Domitian, Apostle John was exiled to an island off the shore of Ionia called Patmos. On the island, there was a cave called the "Cave of the Apocalypse," where the sacred text of the book of Revelations was given to the Apostle John by Jesus through a vision. When he was released from exile, he returned to Ephesus, and it is said that John founded and built churches throughout Asia Minor. John died peacefully in Ephesus at an advanced age around AD 100. The purpose for John to write to the seven churches was to encourage the faithful to resist the demands of the emperor worships. He emphasized that the believers are sealed against any spiritual harm and the wicked are forever destroyed when Christ returns.

As the Bible tells us, "write on a scroll what you see and send it to the seven churches: to Ephesus, Smyrna, Pergamum, Thyatira, Sardis, Philadelphia and Laodicea." (Revelation 1:11, NIV).

The cities of the seven churches mentioned in the Bible:

Ephesus, Ionia*
Smyrna, Ionia
Pergamum, Mysia*
Thyatira, Lydia
Sardis, Lydia
Philadelphia, Lydia
Laodicea ad Lycum, Phrygia
*Only coins are presented here; the city's brief history was discussed earlier.

Ephesus. Roman Ionia. 81-96 AD, Domitian.
AE (32mm, 19.75 gr.) draped bust/
two Amazons clasping hands. Rare.

Pergamum. Greek Mysia. 133-30 BC.
AE(23.7 mm, 7.4 gr.) head of Asklepios/eagle. Scarce.

Pergamum. Greek Mysia. 133-27 BC.
AE(20.0 mm, 8.55 gr.)
head of Athena/Nike. Rare.

Smyrna, Ionia

Smyrna (Izmir) is a coastal city on the shore of the Aegean Sea in west Asia Minor in the province of
Ionia. The initial settlement was found around the eleventh century BC—first as an Aeolian settlement, and later by the Ionians around 680 BC. The city was enlarged by Antgonus (316–301 BC) and
Lysimachus (301–281 BC), carrying out the idea that was conceived by Alexander the Great before
his death. In about 200 BC, the city became an ally to Rome and created a cult of Roma, and the cult
became widespread through the whole Roman Empire. In 195 BC, the city of Rome itself started to
be defied in the cult to the goddess Roma. In 133 BC, the city fell under the Roman rule and became
a leading city in the newly constituted province in Asia Minor.

Smyrna. Greek Ionia. 2nd-3rd centuries BC.
AE (19mm, 4.47 gr.) draped bust of the
Amazon Smyrna/prow of quinquereme. Scarce.

Smyrna. Roman Ionia. 27 BC-14 AD, Augustus.
AE (19mm, 3.32 gr.) bare head of Augustus
and Tiberius/Livia as Aphrodite. Scarce.

Smyrna. Roman Ionia. 27 BC-14 AD, Augustus.
AE (20mm, 5.44 gr.) cojoined heads of Augustus
and Livia/Aphrodite, Nike, dove. Scarce.

Smyrna. Greek Ionia. 145-125 BC.
AE (20mm, 7.99 gr.)
Apollo/the Poet Homer seated. Scarce.

Smyrna is known to have large Jewish communities from early times. According to legend, a big portion of the Jewish communities became Jewish Christians in Smyrna after AD 150. The Byzantine Empire ruled Smyrna, and the city began to lose its importance, and Smyrna declined, especially when the seat of government moved to Constantinople. The Seljuk Turks took it over many times, and it finally came under the Ottoman Empire.

Thyatira, Lydia

Thyatira is located in the extreme northern region of Lydia province, almost standing on the border between Lydia and Mysia. The city was famous in ancient times for its dyeing industry and was a center of the indigo trade. Thyatira was the most contemporary town in the province of Asia Minor in dyers, woodworkers, potters, bronze smiths, and linen workers.

Thyatira. Roman Lydia. 2nd century AD.
AE (21mm, 4.68 gr.) bust of Athena/
Athena holding Nike. Scarce.

Thyatira. Roman Lydia. Elagabalus,218-222 AD.
AE (21mm, 3.7 gr.) bust of Elagabalus/
prize Urn containing two palms.

Lydia. Roman Lydia, Bagis. 190-240 AD.
AE (27mm, 9.23 gr.) youthful Senate/Tyche.

The city is one of the seven churches that were mentioned in Revelation, and Apostle Paul visited many small, unnamed towns in the general vicinity during his preaching in Asia Minor. Paul and Silas were helped in Philippi by a woman named Lydia from Thyatira, and she continued to help them, even after they were released from jail. In the vicinity of Thyatira, Roman Emperor Valens defeated the army of Roman usurper Procopius in AD 366. The city of Thyatira had many churches erected by the late fourth century AD.

Sardis, Lydia

Sardis is a city in west Asia Minor, almost in the middle of the province of Lydia. It is located about forty-five miles east of Smyrna. The history of Sardis goes back to Persian Empire time when they captured the city in the seventh century BC, the Athenians in the sixth century BC, and it finally fell to the Seleucid dynasty in late third century BC. The city of Sardis stayed under Persian rule until it surrendered to Alexander the Great in 334 BC. The city was destroyed by an earthquake in AD 17 and was rebuilt and became one of the great cities in western Asia Minor until the later Byzantine period.

Sardis. Roman Lydia. 14-37 AD, Tiberius.
AE (18mm, 3.83 gr.) Tiberius raising up
kneeling Tyche of Sardis/Livia seated. Scarce.

Again, just like the city of Thyatira, Sardis was the center of manufactures for dyeing of delicate wool and carpets. The city became very wealthy after discovering that the streams flowing around the city carried golden sand, which was gold dust coming out of Mount Timolos. Later, they refined the gold dust, and the city became the center of gold manufactures in the province and was ranked the third city in Asia Minor after Ephesus and Smyrna. The city was conquered by the Seljuk Turks and started to decline. Many Christian churches and Jewish synagogues were built in the city of Sardis, where the largest synagogue was situated in a large bath-gymnasium complex used for 500 years before it was destroyed by the Sasanians in AD 616.

Philiadelphia, Lydia

Philiadelphia is located about twenty-seven miles east of Sardis in the province of Lydia in Asia Minor. The city was founded by Attalus II, king of Pergamon, in 159–138 BC. Attalus II's loyalty and good deeds gave him the nickname Philadelphos, which literally means "one who loves his brother." When the king died, he gave his kingdom—including Philadelphia—to his Roman allies in 133 BC. In AD 17, the city had a severe earthquake, and Roman Emperor Tiberius rebuilt and repaired the damages and further relieved the inhabitants of having to pay taxes. Philadelphia is the sixth church of the seven listed in the book of Revelation.

Philadelphia. Roman Lydia. 177-192 AD, Commodus.
AE (23mm, 7.81 gr.) Laureate head/
Herakles holding lion's skin. Very Rare.

According to the letter written by Apostle John, Christians in the city were suffering persecution at the hands of local Jews, whom Revelation calls "the synagogue of Satan." The city was taken by the Byzantine Empire and became very prosperous. It was called "little Athens," about AD 600, the Basilica of St. John was built. The Basilica still remains the main archaeological attraction in the modern city. By the fourteenth century AD, Philadelphia was surrounded by Turkish emirates but maintained nominal allegiance to the Byzantine Emperor, and the city remained prosperous through trade and its strategic location.

Laodicea ad Lycum, Phrygia

Laodicea ad Lycum is located about fifty-five miles southeast of Philadelphia in the Phrygia province in Asia Minor (modern-day Turkey). There were eight Laodiceas in the ancient world. This city is defined as Laodicea ad Lycum, meaning it was built on the Lycum river in western Anatolia. The city was originally called Diospolis, "city of Zeus," and later was called Rhoas. The city was called Laodicea by Antiochos II Theos (261–253 BC) in honor of his wife, Laodice. The city is only eleven miles northeast of Colossae.

Laodicea Ad lycum. Greek Phrygia. 133-88 BC. AR Tetradrachm (28mm, 11.46 gr.) Pyronos, son of Apollanos with serpent/bow-case.

Laodicea Ad lycum. Roman Phrygia. 54-68 AD, Nero. AE (27mm, 11.50 gr.) Laureate head/ Demoi of Laodicea and Smyrna, clasping hands and holding scepter. Very Rare.

Laodicea was not originally a place of much importance, but toward the end of the Roman Republic, the city—benefiting from its location on a trade route—became one of the most important and flourishing commercial cities in Asia Minor. Laodicea became a very wealthy city, and the wealth of its inhabitants created among them a taste for the arts of the Greek, as is manifest from its ruins. The inhabitants built a medical school, synagogues, and beautiful monuments. According to legend, Antiochus the Great transported about 2,000 Jewish families from Babylonia to live in Laodicea. At a very early period, the city became one of the chief seats of Christianity—the domain authority of bishops. It is said that the Laodicean church was probably founded by the Colossian Epaphras, who shared the care of it with Nymphas, in whose house the Apostle Paul asks the Colossians to communicate to the church of Laodicea in the letter he sent to them. In modern day, all the ruins of ancient Laodicea—the stadium, theaters, ancient buildings, synagogues, churches, caves carved in stone, and aqueduct—can be seen near the city of Denizli.

PART IV
CHRISTIANITY AFTER PAUL

The Jewish Nation under Rome

By the time of the apostles' deaths, the Hebrews were still around for approximately 1,900 years, from the time God told Abraham to move to the promised land and had a covenant with him in Shechem. Since that time, the Hebrews had their rises and falls, invaded their neighbors and their neighbors invaded them, and they were in constant hostility and turmoil during biblical history. They had some peaceful, prosperous periods during the reign of kings, notably Persian King Cyrus, Greek King Alexander the Great, and some early emperors of the Roman Imperial period. During these peaceful times, the Jews moved all over the ancient world (the Diaspora) to Egypt, North Africa, Greece, Asia Minor, Rome, and the largest settlement was in Judaea. The Jewish people considered that Jerusalem in Judaea was their Holy City built by their ancestors, and the temple of Jerusalem was the core of their holy shrine that was built by King David and later continued by his son, King Solomon, in approximately 1100 BC.

The Roman province of Judaea was more troublesome to the Romans than any other province in the Roman world. As mentioned in part two in this book, the Romans sent fourteen procurators between AD 6 and AD 66 to govern Judaea. These procurators were supposed to run the affairs of the province and act as governors, but unfortunately, it did not happen that way. The first procurator, Coponius, began his rule by calling for a census of the Jews for the purpose of imposing stiff taxes. All the procurators after him were not any better for the Jews. During this period, robberies, ransoms, theft, bribery, and very high taxes were on the rise in Judaea, and the Jews were very oppressed. After Herod Agrippa I died in AD 44, each Roman procurator sent to govern Judaea seemed to be more oppressive, corrupt, and disrespectful to the Jewish traditions than the one before him. Under this kind of rule, the Jews were forming underground revolts, by a group known as Zealots, against the Roman oppression. The Jewish in Judaea were on the verge of war.

THE FIRST JEWISH REVOLT (AD 66–70)

The straw that broke the camel's back and the deadly spark occurred when the cruel procurator Gessius Florus (in AD 66) demanded the Jews had to pay a very heavy tribute of gold from the temple treasury for his own use. When the Jews protested and refused his demand, he sent his soldiers to the marketplaces and gave the freedom to kill the Jews. According to legend, about 3,600 Jews were killed. The whole city of Jerusalem was enraged. Rebels were fighting, and they gained control of the temple area. Some of the Zealots went to Roman army stations in Masada, captured their arms, and transported them back to Jerusalem. The procurator Florus escaped, and the Roman soldiers were killed. Two months later, the city of Jerusalem and the surrounding area were in the hand of the rebel, and rebellion had spread to many provinces in the ancient world. In addition to the number of Jews initially killed in Jerusalem, there were, according to the same legend, 20,000 Jews killed in Caesarea and 10,000 in Damascus and similar numbers in Antioch and Alexandria.

First Jewish Revolt. Roman Judaea. 66-70 AD.
AE (17mm, 2.9 gr.) vine branch/amphora.

First Jewish Revolt. Roman Judaea. 66-70 AD.
AE(16.5mm, 3.1 gr.) vine branch/amphora.

First Jewish Revolt. Roman Judaea. 66-70 AD.
AE(17.0mm, 2.7 gr.) vine branch/amphora.

First Jewish Revolt. Roman Judaea. 66-70 AD.
AE (17.0mm, 3.0 gr.) vine branch/amphora.

First Jewish Revolt. Roman Judaea. 66-70 AD.
AE (17.5mm, 2.7 gr.) vine branch/amphora.

First Jewish Revolt. Roman Judaea. 66-70 AD.
AE 1/8 Shekel (20mm, 6.48 gr.) year 4, bundle
of Lulav, two Etroges/Chalice. Scarce.

Rome decided that rebellion in the Jewish nation had to stop. Rome asked General Cestus Gallus, governor of Syria, to go to Judaea and suppress the uprising. The Roman suffered many loses by the rebels on the way to Jerusalem, and he did not think much about the small bands of defenders resisting his powerful Roman army. Unexpectedly, General Gallus was defeated after losing most of his men and his siege artillery gears. This action was a great victory for the Jewish nation.

When the word of the Jewish revolt and the defeat of the Roman general reached Emperor Nero in Rome, he ordered his distinguished General Flavius Vespasian to take care of the rebels in Judaea.

Vespasian. Roman Imperial. 69-79 AD.
AE AS (27mm, 10.10 gr.) head left/Victory standing.

General Vespasian led Rome's armies to victory in many places, including the Gauls in Germany and Britain. He was given the best fighting forces and unlimited power to go to Judaea. Vespasian departed for Judaea, and within two months, he captured the area of Galilee, where the Jewish commander Flavius Josephus surrendered to Vespasian, and he tried to challenge the Roman military in open battle. He survived the entire war and became a Roman court follower and later became a Roman citizen and Jewish historian. In mid-AD 68, Vespasian's army succeeded in crushing the revolt throughout Judaea, except Jerusalem, and the fortress of Masada remained in the hands of the rebels. Vespasian was ready to besiege Jerusalem, but the news about Emperor Nero committing suicide delayed his plans. However, Vespasian became the emperor of Rome and later assigned his capable son, Titus, to take over the operation of the campaign against Jerusalem and Masada.

Titus moved south to Jerusalem with a strong Roman army—according to Josephus, he had about 80,000 men. Jerusalem was the most heavily fortified city in Judaea. Titus was successful in breaking the outer wall around Jerusalem, and two months later, he sealed off Jerusalem completely with a wall of their own, and those Jews that attempted to escape were crucified. According to Josephus, sometimes the daily crucifixions reached 500, and the crosses were never left bare. Bodies were by the thousands were stacked in houses or thrown over the walls into the wilderness. Titus finally went to Masada, the last Jewish stronghold in Herod the Great's former mountaintop fortress, and he conquered it.

Titus. Roman Judaea, Caesarea
Maritima. 79-81 AD.
AE(20 mm, 8.10 Gr.)laureate head/Nike.

After the invasion, the Roman army found almost every inhabitant of Masada. Almost a thousand men, women, and children had committed suicide rather than stay alive under Roman rule. Titus's troops burned the temple in Jerusalem and took many holy implements from the temple to Rome. A month later, the temple was destroyed and was nothing more than a pile of ruins in AD 70.

About thirty-five years later, under Roman Emperor Trajan (AD 98–117), the Jewish started to rebel again against the Roman Empire in Jewish communities living in the Diaspora, such as Cyprus, Alexandria, Egypt, southern Mediterranean coast, Mesopotamia, and Cyrene in North Africa.

Trajan. Roman Imperial. 98-117 AD.
AE (27mm, 12.04 gr.) Laureate head/Victory flying.

Trajan. Roman Imperial. 98-117 AD.
AR Denarius (18mm, 3.1 gr.)
Laureate head/Victory advancing.

The Romans did not forget the first Jewish revolt, and fearing another revolt, Emperor Trajan's response was devastating. The rebels were crushed after bloody battles. Thousands of Jews were killed in those provinces, and the Jewish religious practices were restrained.

Roman Emperor Hadrian (AD 117–138) became the emperor of Rome after Trajan.

Hadrian. Roman Imperial. 117-138 AD.
AE (27mm, 10.6 gr.) Laureate head/
Salus feeding snake coiled around altar.

Hadrian. Roman Imperial. 117-138 AD.
AE (29mm, 11.9 gr.) Laureate head/Fortuna.

He visited the temple in Jerusalem as he was going to rebuild the city of Jerusalem and restoring the temple. The Jewish people had great hope that more prosperous times were ahead. Emperor Hadrian was not what the Jews had in mind. He wanted to rebuild Jerusalem as a Roman city and rename it to Aelia Capitolina and rebuild the temple for the worship of the Roman god Jupiter instead of the God of the Jews.

THE SECOND JEWISH REVOLT (AD 132–135)

Emperor Hadrian's decision created a lot of uprising between the Jewish in Judaea and in the Diaspora. Based on legend, this revolt was caused not only by renaming Jerusalem and the worship of Jupiter in the temple, but it was caused by more important factors, such as forbidding castration of males, and he put circumcision in the same category, and violators would be punished by death. The spiritual leader of the second revolt was Rabbi Akiba, and the military leader was Simon Ben Kosiba, also known as Bar Kochba. Bar Kochba proved himself as a dedicated and inspiring leader who put his name on a revolt that shocked the Roman Empire. The Bar Kochba rebels were, unlike the first revolt rebels, better prepared for battle with the ancient world-leading military strength.

Bar Kochba rebels were attacking the Roman soldiers in Jerusalem, and Roman Governor Tinnius Rufus found that the rebel forces were too strong to defeat. So he withdrew from Jerusalem and moved to Caesarea. The Roman governor of Syria, Publicius Marcellus, marched down with his troops along with enforcement troops from Egypt to Jerusalem to crush the rebellion before it got any larger. To his surprise, the Roman troops were defeated, and all Judaea was again in the hands of the rebels. Emperor Hadrian then recalled his most experienced and skilled general, Julius Severus, from Britain. In AD 134, Severus, with his massive army, opened a full-scale war against Judaea, and Bar Kochba was forced to withdraw.

Bar Kochba. Roman Judaea. 132-135 AD. AE (25mm, 8.45 gr.) grape leaf/palm tree. Rare.

Bar Kochba. Roman Judaea. 132-135 AD. AE (25mm, 9.75 gr.) grape leaf/palm tree. Rare.

According to Roman historian Dio Cassius, very few of the Jews survived, and about fifty of their most important outposts and their villages were burned to the ground. In AD 135, the Romans finally broke through the walls of Jerusalem and slaughtered the rebels, and Simon Bar Kochba was killed. The survivors of the rebels escaped and dwelled in caves, and some died from starvation, and some were killed by the Romans, and others committed suicide. By late AD 135, the Simon Bar Kochba revolt was over, and Judaea was destroyed beyond repair.

The victory of the Romans was a turning point in the history of "God's chosen people," the Jewish nation. Roman Emperor Hadrian ordered that all Jews in Jerusalem who did not manage to flee should be killed or enslaved in order to eliminate the slightest possibility of any future Jewish uprising. Other Jewish communities around the ancient world gained strength from the influx of refugees from Judea. The Jews were not allowed to come back to Judaea ever again. Jerusalem was renamed Aelia

Capitolina, and Judaea was renamed Syria-Palestina. Jerusalem became a Roman city full of Gentiles, with a statue of Hadrian in the temple and one of Jupiter placed on the site that once was the holy of holies.

The military power of the Rebels had been broken, and Jews scattered all over the ancient world, and they were forbidden to come back to Jerusalem. Even though they went through one disaster after another, their religion remained strong and united. All throughout the Mediterranean world (the Diaspora), the Jewish practices and teachings of their Torah and ancient faith continued. Many Jews believed that a messianic leader would appear one day and rule their land, and they were conditioned to be ready for that day.

After the Jewish revolts, the Jews lost their promised land that Abraham gave them 2,000 years before, and they lost their shrine, the temple, their spiritual hub that David and Solomon had built 1,000 years before. The Jews became a people without a homeland in AD 135 and remained without a homeland for the next 1,800 years until AD 1948 where the modern state of Israel was established. Even after this date, they still are in conflict with their neighbors until this day, just like they have always been for the last 4,000 years.

JUDAEA CAPTA

The massive, powerful Roman Empire had conquered the tiny province of Judaea and killed or enslaved all the Jews and destroyed their Holy City and their spiritual shrine. The war was over. Now the superpower needed to advertise their victory.

The Judaea Capta coins were originally issued by Roman Emperor Vespasian to celebrate the capture of Judaea and the destruction of the Jewish temple in Jerusalem by his son, Titus, in AD 70. It is clear from their coinage that Vespasian and his sons intended for their victory over the Jews to be spread all over the empire.

Judaea Capta. Roman Judaea. 69-79 AD, Vespasian. AR Denarius (18mm, 3.12 gr.) Laureate head/Judaea mourning, trophy.

Judaea Capta. Roman Judaea. 79-81 AD, Titus. AE (24mm, 11.26 gr.) Laureate head/ Judaea mourning, trophy, shield.

Judaea Capta. Roman Judaea. 81-96 AD,
Domitian. AE (19mm, 6.5 gr.)
Laureate head/Nike in flowing gown.

Judaea Capta. Roman Judaea. 81-96 AD, Domitian.
AE (21mm, 8.91 gr.) Laureate head/Minerva
advancing, trophy, shield and spear.

Judaea Capta. Roman Judaea. 81-96 AD,
Domitian. AE (22.9mm, 11.02 gr.)
Laureate head/Minerva advancing, trophy and shield.

Judaea Capta. Roman Judaea. 81-96 AD,
Domitian. AE (26.4mm, 14.62 gr.)
Laureate head/Minerva advancing, trophy and shield.

Judaea Capta. Roman Judaea. 81-96 AD,
Domitian. AE (24mm, 11.10 gr.)
Laureate head/Victory holding wreath and palm.

The coins of Judaea Capta were struck mainly in Rome, although some of them were issued locally in the land of Israel, being struck in Caesarea, and inscribed with Greek legends. Judaea Capta carried legends, such as "IVDAEA CAPTA," "IVDAEA DEVICTA," "IVDAEA," or "VICTORIA AVGVSTI," and some of them had no legend. Usually, if not all, Judaea Capta coins show a weeping Jewess who sits mourning beneath a palm tree—the symbol of Judaea. Some of the coins show a victorious emperor wearing war gear with armor, and sometimes broken swords and shields were scattered around the dejected mourner. Judaea Capta coins struck in the land of Israel usually carried the legend "IOYAAIAE EAAWKYIAE," which means "Judaea vanquished."

Most scholars relate conquering Judaea and the female figure on the coins to the fulfillment of the prophecy of Isaiah 850 years earlier, "Your men will fall by the sword, your warriors in battle. The gates of Zion will lament and mourn, destitute, she will sit on the ground" (Isaiah 3:25–26, NIV).

Christianity under Rome

It has been a little over 700 years since Daniel had his vision of the four beasts, Lion, Bear, Leopard, and terrifying and frightening beast. According to biblical scholars, these four beasts would rule the ancient world, as was explained in this book. The lion was the Babylonian Empire, the bear was the Persian Empire, the leopard was the Greek Empire, and the terrifying and frightening beast was the Roman Empire. The first three empires and a portion of the fourth were discussed. The Jewish nation, unfortunately, had the worst fate under Rome—more than any other empire in the past. But soon the Christians would receive their fate under the far more brutal imperialism, the reign of the Roman Caesars and their empire.

During the end of Emperor Tiberius's reign and the very beginning of Emperor Caligula's reign, Jesus Christ was crucified by the Romans.

Tiberius. Roman Syria, Seleucia Pieria. 14-37 AD. AE(26mm, 15.31 gr.) bare head/legend.

Caligula. Roman Phrygia, Amorium. 37-41 AD. AE (20mm, 5.34 gr.) bare head/eagle standing.

The Jewish high priests handed Jesus over to the Roman procurator Pontius Pilatus, and he (in most opinions) gave them his blessing to crucify Jesus. The apostles took over by spreading and proclaiming the word of God shortly after Jesus's death. In a period of less than five years, the apostles Paul, Peter, and James and others were put to death by the Romans under the reign of Emperor Nero. Early Christianity had begun to expand beyond Jerusalem and outside the orbit of Peter and Paul. In the late first century, the Christian communities were rapidly growing throughout the Roman Empire. Some of the Romans were very impressed by the behavior and compassion of the Christians when they would help the poor and care for sick and love their neighbors. There were not any formal church organizations; it was limited to small group meeting in house-churches focusing on the teaching of Jesus Christ.

The Roman authorities wondered for a long time over how to deal with this new religion (they called it a cult). The Romans had many gods and goddesses, from the god of wine to the goddess of wisdom in their beliefs, and did not understand nor tolerate the idea of one God over the universe like the Christians believed. The majority of the Romans, especially the royals, considered Christianity as potentially dangerous religion. By the end of the Apostle Paul's life, the new religion was flourishing not only in the Holy Land but also in Syria, Phoenicia, Asia Minor, Egypt, Greece, Rome, and all the way west to Spain.

In AD 64, a great fire broke out in the city of Rome, destroying a big portion of the city and economically devastating the Roman population. Nero was rumored of having intentionally started the fire himself, and he blamed it on a class he hated the most, the Christians.

Nero. Roman Syria, Antioch. 54-68 AD.
AE (21mm, 7.65 gr.) Laureate head/large SC.

Nero ordered that Christians be burned alive and crucified, and he fed them to lions and other wild beasts. Thousands and thousands of Christians died, and it is widely believed that the apostles Paul and Peter were martyred in Rome during Nero's persecution.

Christianity was not a tolerated religion like Judaism was. During the end of the first century and the beginning of the second century, the Christians were suffered from Roman hostility, and it was always an active oppression. The Christians refused to perform Caesar worship, and this, in the Roman mind, demonstrated their disloyalty to their rulers.

Domitian. Roman Imperial. 69-96 AD.
AR Tetradrachm (25mm, 11.06 gr.) Laureate
head/ligionary Aquila, two standards. Scarce.

Roman Emperor Domitian did not officially order Christian persecutions, but he issued anti-Christian policies. Supposedly, Domitian, who, upon hearing that the Christians refused to perform Caesar worship, sent investigators to Galilee to inquire on the reasons. The fact, however, that the

Roman emperor should take an interest in this group proves that the Christians were no longer an obscure little sect.

During the second century AD, Christians were persecuted for their beliefs largely because they did not resign to sacrificing to the Roman gods. Trajan set new anti-Christian rules that Christians were forbidden to meet in any house secretly.

Trajan. Roman Imperial. 98-117 AD.
AR Denarius (19mm, 3.45 gr.)
Laureate head/Vesta seated holding patera and torch.

Trajan. Roman Imperial. 98-117 AD.
AR Denarius (19mm, 3.2gr.)
Laureate head/Spes.

The martyrdom of several prominent church leaders occurred under Trajan's reign, including bishop Ignatius of Antioch. The bishop was torn apart by wild animals in a Roman arena.

The anti-Christian policy and rules stayed the same and were generally followed in the reigns of Hadrian an Antoninus Pius. Hadrian actively persecuted the Jews severely but not the Christians, showing that, by that time, the Romans were distinguishing between the two religions.

Hadrian. Roman Imperial. 117-138 AD.
AR Denarius (19mm, 3.3 gr.) draped bust/
Concordia seated, patera, figure of Spes.

Hadrian. Roman Imperial. 117-138 AD.
AE (34mm, 24.52 gr.) Laureate bust/Annona
holding cornucopia, Modius at foot. Rare.

Antoninus Pius. Roman Imperial. 138-161 AD.
AE (32mm, 26.3 gr.)
Laureate head/Antoninus sacrificing over altar.

Antoninus Pius. Roman Imperial. 138-161 AD.
AR Denarius (18mm, 3.9 gr.)
Laureate head/Equity holding scale and spear.

Antoninus Pius. Roman Imperial. 138-161 AD.
AR Denarius (18mm, 3.2 gr.) Laureate head/
Salus, snake around altar.

Faustina Junior. Roman Imperial. 138-141 AD.
AE (33mm, 23.87 gr.) draped bust/Salus.

Faustina Junior. Roman Imperial. 138-141 AD.
AR Denarius (18mm, 3.4 gr.) draped bust/
ceres holding sceptre and corn ears.

Nonetheless, Christianity was still not officially tolerated, and all the Christians were liable. If they broke the emperor's rules, they could be arrested at any time, put in prison, tortured, beaten, have their property taken away from them, exiled, and even executed. These rules were set by Emperor Trajan and were followed officially by all emperors during the second century AD.

During the late second century AD, Roman attitudes toward Christians hardened once again. By that time, the Christian faith grew stronger and more meaningful, and the Christians refused to renounce their faith in the face of persecution. Philosopher Emperor Marcus Aurelius considered the Christian doctrine to be vicious and dangerous to the welfare of the Romans.

Marcus Aurelius. Roman Imperial. 161-180 AD.
AE (30mm, 21.5 gr.) Laureate head/Victory attaching
shield (VIC/GER) to tree. Scarce.

Marcus Aurelius. Roman Imperial. 161-180 AD.
AR Denarius (18mm, 3.2 gr.)
Laureate head/Fortune seated.

Marcus Aurelius passed a law punishing everyone with exile who should try to influence anyone's mind by fear of the divinity. The law of Trajan was still in effect and was sufficient to justify very severe punishment against the followers of the "forbidden" religion of Christianity. Marcus Aurelius's reign was a nightmare to the Christian church, and his policy was criticized by many scholars that criminals were normally tortured to confess their crimes, while Christians were tortured to renounce their faith in Christ. One of the best-recorded acts of violence against Christians in Marcus Aurelius's reign was the persecution of Lyons in 177 AD. According to legend, more than forty-eight Christians were tortured and executed because they did not renounce their faith. Although he did not order this persecution, but did not prevent it form happening.

The Christianity continued to spread, even without designated churches. Most Christian communities were centered in homes, "house-churches," where the Christians usually gathered on Sunday to study the scriptures. The earliest house-church was known to be in eastern Syria on the Euphrates River in the town of Dura-Europos dating back to 232 AD. The town started as a Seleucid fortress in 300 BC, and the ruins are still standing today where the name changed to modern As Salihiyah. Christianity was portrayed as the religion of the poor, slaves, and the needy, but this was not the true picture.

Commodus. Roman Imperial. 177-192 AD.
AE(25mm, 11.5 gr.) Laureate head/legend.

Commodus. Roman Imperial. 177-192 AD.
AE (26mm, 14.73 gr.) radiate head/Libertas.

Commodus. Roman Imperial. 177-192 AD.
AR Denarius (18mm, 2.7 gr.)
Laureate head/Providence standing.

From the beginning, there appeared wealthy and influential figures, even some members of the royal court were believers and at least tolerated the Christians. According to legend, Marcia, the concubine of Emperor Commodus, for example, used her influence to achieve the release of Christian prisoners from the mines.

During the reign of Emperor Septimius Severus, the Christians suffered terribly between AD 193–211. According to the historian Clement of Alexandria, many martyrs were burned, cut to pieces, and beheaded on a daily basis. The Christians were gaining power, making converts, and growing in numbers, which made the Romans to have these anti-Christian feelings.

Septimius Severus. Roman Imperial. 193-211 AD.
AR Denarius (19mm, 3.23 gr.)
bare head/funeral pyre of five tiers.

Septimius Severus. Roman Imperial. 193-211 AD.
AR Denarius (20mm, 3.06 gr.) head right/
Severus sacrificing over altar.

Septimius Severus. Roman Imperial. 193-211 AD.
AR Denarius (19mm, 3.8 gr.) head right/
Victory holding wreath and palm.

Septimius Severus. Roman Imperial. 193-211 AD.
AR Denarius (19mm, 3.1 gr.) draped bust/
Fortuna holding rudder and Cornucopia.

Julia Domna. Roman Imperial. Wife of Severus.
Died in 217 AD. AR Denarius (19mm, 3.4 gr.)
draped bust/Pietas at altar raising hands.

During his reign, Christians were persecuted in most of the biblical world in Carthage, Alexandria, Rome, Corinth, and many other places. Emperor Septimius Severus allowed his government to pursue persecution policy during his reign. In AD 202, the emperor enacted a law prohibiting the spread of Christianity and Judaism, and that was the first universal decree forbidding conversion to Christianity. Many prominent Christian figures wrote *Apologia* or "Defense of the Faith" to Roman authorities stating that there was no argument between the Roman political system and Christian theology. Violent persecutions broke out in Egypt, where the father of origin, the Christian apologist, was beheaded. According to scholars, thousands of Christians were tortured, cut to pieces, burned, or thrown to wild animals during the reign of Emperor Septimius Severus.

After Septimius Severus's death, his son, Caracalla, became the emperor of the Roman Empire. He became joint ruler with his brother, Geta, in AD 209. He caused his brother's death in AD 212, at which time he became the sole emperor of Rome.

Caracalla. Roman Imperial. 198-217 AD.
AR Denarius (19mm, 3.3 gr.)draped bust/Salus.

Caracalla. Roman Imperial. 198-217 AD.
AR Denarius (19mm, 3.1 gr.) radiate bust/Mars.

Caracalla was the common enemy of all mankind. He spent his reign traveling from province to province so that everyone could feel his cruelty. He was one of the most wicked of Roman emperors. In AD 212, Caracalla had his brother, Geta, his father-in-law, his wife, his second cousin, and her brother assassinated, and he persecuted all his brother Geta's supporters.

Emperor Caracalla, in spite of his cruelty, gave the Roman Empire a legacy. He was a good military man and good to his soldiers. He granted Roman citizenship to all free men throughout the Roman Empire in order to increase taxation. His reign was full of cruelty and severity, and many Christians were put to death.

Upon the sudden death of Caracalla in Mesopotamia, Emperor Elagabalus became emperor of Rome in AD 218. Elagabalus was barely fourteen years old when he came to imperial power and began a reign that was marred by controversies. Elagabalus was married and divorced five times during his short reign. His most stable relationship seems to have been with his chariot driver, who he referred to as his husband.

Elagabalus. Roman Imperial. 218-222 AD.
AR Denarius (20mm, 3.35 gr.) draped bust/
eagle between two standards.

According to Augustan history, he also married a man, an athlete from Smyrna, in a public ceremony in Rome. According to Cassius Dio, Elagabalus would paint his eyes and wear wigs before prostituting himself. Besides Emperor Nero, Elagabalus was the shame of the Roman Empire, and his name appeared in history above all other Roman emperors because of his unspeakably shameful life. Finally, he was assassinated, along with his mother, by his own guard in AD 222 when he was eighteen years old. Christianity, under the reign of Elagabalus, remained with the same rules as previous emperors, and no persecutions for the Christians were reported during Emperor Elagabalus's reign, mainly because he was a kid, and secondly, the Christians were not on his mind.

Severus Alexander took over the Roman Empire in AD 222 after the death of his cousin, Elagabalus. Emperor Severus Alexander also was about fourteen years old when his reign started.

Severus Alexander. Roman Imperial.
222-235 AD. AR Denarius (19mm, 3.3 gr.)
Laureate bust/Jupitar.

Severus Alexander. Roman Imperial.
222-235 AD. AR Denarius (19mm, 3.16 gr.)
Laureate bust/Perpetuitas holding globe and sceptre.

He was a young, well-meaning emperor and was entirely under the dominion of his mother, Julia Avita Mamaea, who was a woman of many virtues, and she surrounded the young emperor with wise counselors. The reign of Alexander was prosperous until the rise of the Sasanids in the east. The

Germanic tribes also invaded from the north. This drove the army to look for a new leader. Severus Alexander was assassinated, along with his mother, in AD 235, and Maximinus became Emperor. Christian persecution during Severus Alexander's reign was not reported to exist, although the Trajan laws were still in effect. The Christians experienced softer and more forgiving times during Emperor Severus Alexander's reign.

Maximinus I was elected as the new emperor of Rome in AD 235. Many historians said that Maximinus was the first barbarian who wore the imperial purple and the first emperor never to set foot in Rome. His reign was considered to mark the beginning of the crisis of the third century. He inherited some of the problems from Severus Alexander. The crisis, also called the Imperial Crisis, is the commonly applied name for the crumbling and near collapse of the Roman Empire between AD 235 and AD 284 and was caused by many factors, such as internal civil war, economic collapse, and external invasions from the east and north. The year AD 238 is known as "the Year of the Six emperors" when Maximinus I was assassinated, along with his son and his chief ministers, by his guards. Their heads were cut off, placed on poles, and carried to Rome.

Maximus. Roman Imperial. 236-238 AD.
AR Denarius (19mm, 2.88 gr.) draped bust/
Lituus, knife, jug, simpulum and sprinkler.

Maximinus reversed Severus Alexander's policy of forgiving the Christians and being softer toward them. Maximinus considered the Christians as unsupportive enemies of the Roman Empire. He persecuted Christians ruthlessly. Pontian, the bishop of Rome, and his successor, Anterus, are said to have been martyred. The Roman Senate elected the thirteen-year-old Gordian III as an emperor.

Gordian III was elected emperor in AD 238 after the death of Maximinus and after five emperors reigned in one year. Due to Gordian III's age (thirteen years old), the Imperial Senate was surrendered to the aristocratic families that controlled the affairs of Rome.

Gordian III. Roman Imperial. 238-244 AD.
AE (30mm, 21.49 gr.) Laureate bust/Mars.

Gordian III. Roman Imperial. 238-244 AD.
AE (30mm, 20.5 gr.) Laureate bust/Victory.

Gordian III. Roman Imperial. 238-244 AD.
AR Antoninianus (23mm, 4.6 gr.)
radiate bust/Naked Hercules.

Gordian III. Roman Imperial. 238-244 AD.
AR Antoninianus (24mm, 4.8 gr.)
radiate bust/Sol holding globe.

Gordian III had a war with the Sasanids and drove them back over the Euphrates and defeated them in the battle of Rhesaena in AD 243. Gordian III joined the army at a young age and was planning an invasion of the enemy's territory when his father-in-law died of an unknown cause. Marcus Julius Philippus, also known as Philip the Arab (Philip I), stepped in at this moment, and the campaign proceeded. Some sources claimed that the battle was fought in Misiche (modern Fallujah, Iraq) and ended with a major defeat to the Roman army and the death of young Gordian III. The cause of death of Gordian III is still unknown; however, ancient sources discovered Philip I, who succeeded Gordian III as emperor, as having murdered Gordian III in the battle.

In AD 234, Philip I married Marcia Otacillia Severa, and they had a son named Marcus Julius Philipus Severus (Philip II). In AD 248, Philip I had the honor of giving a celebration of the one thousandth birthday of Rome, which, according to legend, was founded in 753 BC by Romulus.

Philip I. Roman Imperial. 244-249 AD.
AR Antoninianus (23mm, 3.2 gr.)
radiate bust/Philip seated on curule chair.

Philip I. Roman Imperial. 244-249 AD.
AR Antoninianus (23mm, 4.6 gr.)
radiate bust/Fides holding standard.

Otacilia Severa, Wife of Philip I. 244-249 AD.
AE (30mm, 14.62 gr.) Diademed bust/Pudicitia seated.

Otacilia Severa, Wife of Philip I. 244-249 AD.
AR Antoninianus (23mm, 4.2 gr.)
Diademed bust/Concordia seated.

Otacilia Severa, Wife of Philip I. 244-249 AD.
AR Antoninianus (23mm, 3.8 gr.)
Diademed bust/Concordia seated.

Philip II. Roman Imperial. 247-249 AD.
AR Antoninianus (23mm, 4.2 gr.)
radiate bust/Philip II holding globe.

Philip II. Roman Imperial. 247-249
AD. AR Antoninianus (22mm, 4.8 gr.)
radiate bust/Philip II holding globe.

This celebration was wonderful and included many games, and more than 1,000 gladiators were killed, along with hundreds of animals, including leopards and lions. This event was recorded in literature as "history of a thousand years." Trajan Decius was proclaimed emperor by the army in AD 249. Dacius was discontent with the Roman economy and the army, and he marched to Rome. The army of Philip I met Decius near Verona, and Decius won the battle, and Philip I was killed, and later Philip's eleven-year-old son (Philip II) and heir was murdered. According to the historian Eusebius, Philip I was the first Christian Roman emperor. Based on the same historian, Philip I had once entered a

Christian service on Easter after having been required by a bishop to confess his sins. Saint Quirinus of Rome was, according to tradition, the son of Philip the Arab.

Trajan Decius became an emperor of Rome in AD 249, and he ruled for three years, and those were the worst three years for the Christians. In AD 250, Decius issued an edict for the suppression of Christianity.

Trajan Decius. Roman Imperial. 249-251 AD.
AR Antoninianus (22mm, 4.8 gr.)
radiate bust/Uberitas standing.

Trajan Decius. Roman Imperial. 249-251 AD.
AR Antoninianus (21mm, 4.0 gr.)
radiate bust/Uberitas standing.

Herennia Etruscilla, Wife of Trajan Decius.
Roman Imperial. 249-251 AD.
AR Antoninianus (22mm, 4.3 gr.)
Diademed bust/Pudicitia standing.

Herennia Etruscilla, Wife of Trajan Decius.
Roman Imperial. 249-251 AD.
AR Antoninianus (21mm, 4.1 gr.)
Diademed bust/Pudicitia seated.

The edict was loud and clear: All the inhabitants of the empire were required to sacrifice, and they would obtain a certificate that they had complied with the order. Most Christians and bishops reacted to it in different ways, and it was further said that the bishops and high priests refused to offer the pagan sacrifice and they were killed, including Pope Fabian himself, in AD 250. At this time, in addition to Christians' persecution, there was a plague (smallpox) that killed over five million people in Europe between AD 251 and AD 266. The Roman army was considerably weakened, and while Decius was fighting the barbarians across the Danube, he got killed on the field of the battle. It was said that Decius was the first emperor to die in battle against a foreign enemy. The Christian church never forgot the reign of Decius, whom they labeled as the "fierce tyrant."

Valerian I was elected emperor after Decius's death. Decius edicts were renewed under his reign from AD 253–260. All Christians were required to sacrifice to the Roman gods.

Valerian I. Roman Imperial. 253-260
AD. AE (21mm, 3.5 gr.) Radiate head/
The Orient presenting wreath to Valerian.

The punishment was exile in AD 257, and the punishment was death in AD 258. Many Christians were forced to sacrifice to Roman gods under pain and later death. Finally, all Christians were forbidden to visit their dead in cemeteries. Among the thousands executed under Valerian were St. Cyprian, bishop of Carthage, and Sixtus II, bishop of Rome. The Christian persecution ended with the capture of Valerian by the Sasanians, and he was murdered in AD 260. Valerian's son and successor, Gallienus, revoked the edicts of his father.

Gallienus ruled the Roman Empire as co-emperor with his father, Valerian I, from AD 253–260 and then as the sole Roman emperor from AD 260–268. Gallienus won many victories for the Roman Empire but this time, as the empire started to deteriorate and he was unable to keep much of his realm from seceding.

Gallienus. Roman Imperial. 253-268 AD.
AR Antoninianus (21mm, 4.15 gr.)
radiate bust/Diana Lucifera advancing.

Gallienus. Roman Imperial. 253-268 AD.
AR Antoninianus (20mm, 3.83 gr.)
radiate bust/Mercury standing.

However, in AD 261, Gallienus issued nationally the first decree of toleration to all religions. During the next four decades, the bloodletting was stopped, and the Christian communities appeared from Britain in the west to Mesopotamia in the east. The Christians made great progress by making converts, building churches, and installing bishops in larger numbers than ever before. This glory was brought to an end in AD 303.

Roman Emperor Diocletian (AD 284–305) came to power with the idea of dividing the Roman Empire into four military regions. The pressure of invaders from all directions forced him to open many fronts for wars, and it was impossible for one ruler to control all fronts.

Diocletion. Roman Imperial. 284-305 AD.
AE (28mm, 9.9 gr.) Laureate head/Genius.

Diocletion. Roman Imperial. 284-305 AD.
AR Antoninianus (22mm, 4.09 gr.)
Radiate head/statue of Hercules
with lion's skin and club.

The Germanic invasions increased, and the trade route fell to barbarian conquests, causing the trade and the Roman markets to disappear. Diocletian, toward the end of his long reign, became ever more concerned about the high positions held by Christians in Roman society and even in the palace court and the army. There were three co-emperors on the throne during the reign of Diocletian, Maximianus (Maximian), Constantius I, and Galerius. On February 23, AD 303, on the Roman day of the gods of boundaries, Diocletion enacted what was to become the last most violent and greatest persecution of Christians under Roman rule.

Maximianus. Roman Imperial. 286-305 AD.
AE (28mm, 10.02 gr.) Laureate head/Genius.

Constantius I. Roman Imperial. 293-305 AD.
AE (29mm, 8.5 gr.) Laureate head/Genius.

Galerius. Roman Imperial. 293-305 AD.
AE (27mm, 10.6 gr.) Laureate head/Genius.

Diocletion, the ablest emperor since Hadrian, who saved the Roman Empire from many catastrophes, also almost succeeded to rid the empire of Christianity. Diocletian considered the Christian faith as a threat to his authority. Diocletian and his co-emperors, mainly Galerius, ordered all members of the court to perform a sacrifice to Roman gods to purify the place. He also sent letters to the military commanders ordering the entire army perform the sacrifice or face discharge.

Of course, the Christians refused to sacrifice to the Roman gods, and they were protesting, and Diocletian was displeased at what he called "the arrogance of the Christians." He ordered that the deacon Romanus have his tongue removed in Caesarea and be sent to prison and finally executed for defying the order of the courts. In AD 303, the edict against the Christians ordered the destruction of Christian scriptures and places of worship across the Roman Empire and prohibited Christians from gathering for worship. According to some historians, Galerius convinced Diocletian that the Christians burned the imperial palace. History is very clear about this great persecution, which is called "the Diocletianic persecution." Thousands of Christians were slaughtered, boiled, or burned alive, and hundreds of churches were destroyed. Unfortunately, historical records sometimes are not so clear, where reliable estimates are difficult to make. However, recent scholars believe huge numbers, even millions, were martyred. In any case, early martyrs lie not in their numbers but in the impact that their courage and faith had on countless others from then until now.

Both Diocletian and Maximian abdicated in AD 305, plunging the Roman Empire into disorder. Licinius I (AD 308–324) and his son, Licinius II (AD 317–324), became emperors of the Roman Empire. The Licinius family was close friends and comrades of arms of Emperor Galerius and accompanied him on his expedition against the Christians.

Licinius I. Roman Imperial. 308-324 AD.
AE (22mm, 4.2 gr.) Laureate head/Jupiter.

Licinius II. Roman Imperial. 317-324 AD.
AE (19mm, 3.5 gr.) Laureate head/camp-gate.

Some of the laws were that he prevented bishops from communicating with each other, and he prohibited men and women from attending services together and young girls from receiving instruction from their bishop. Finally, he gave orders that Christians could hold services only outside of the city walls. Additionally, he deprived officers in the army of their commissions if they did not sacrifice to the Roman gods. In AD 306, Constantine I (the Great) became the emperor of the Roman Empire, and the Christians began to see the light at the end of the tunnel.

Christianity under Constantine the Great (AD 306–337)

In AD 306, Constantine I (the Great) was proclaimed emperor of the west by his troops. It took almost six years before he took undisputed possession of the title of emperor. This happened when he defeated his only rival then, Maxentius, in the historic battle of Milvian Bridge over the Tiber River. The night before the battle, according to tradition, Constantine had a dream and saw a fiery cross in the sky, and some tradition said that he had a vision of the sign of Christ with the Greek letters Chi and Rho, which they are the first two letters of the Greek word *Christos*. Constantine was to have the symbol inscribed on his helmet and ordered all his soldiers to paint it on their shields. He went to the battle and defeated his opponent in a crushing victory in AD 312.

Constantine the Great. Roman Imperial.307-337 AD. AE (18mm, 3.2 gr.) Draped bust/Camp-gate.

Constantine the Great. Roman Imperial.307-337 AD. AE (22mm, 3.5 gr.) Draped bust/Jupiter holding Victory.

Constantine the Great. Roman Imperial.307-337 AD. AE (19mm, 3.8 gr.) Draped bust/Sol holding globe.

Constantine the Great. Roman Imperial.307-337 AD. AE (21mm, 3.2 gr.) Draped bust/Sol holding globe.

Constantine the Great. Roman Imperial.330-346 AD. AE (17mm, 2.8 gr.) commemorative issues. helmeted bust of Roma/she-wolf suckling Romulus and Remus

Constantine the Great. Roman Imperial. 330-346 AD. AE (18mm, 2.4 gr.) commemorative issues. helmeted bust of Constantinopolis/Victory.

Constantine declared that he owed his victory to the God of the Christians. Constantine was known as the first Christian emperor in the Roman Empire. In AD 313, the emperor issued the edict of Milan, which announced the toleration of Christianity, and removed all penalties for professing Christianity and returned all confiscated church property created by previous emperors. Constantine I granted the Christians unlimited freedom to worship, and Christian citizens who had been in exile were free to come back. After his victory, Constantine I took over the role of the patron for the Christian faith and set a precedent for the position of the Christian emperor within the church that would be followed for centuries. Constantine I built the Basilica on the Vatican Hill, where reputedly St. Peter had been martyred (he was crucified on an inverted cross). He chose the Roman synagogues archetype to build the Basilica. In AD 1506, the Basilica was torn down of old age and was rebuilt to the Basilica known today, which took, according to sources, 120 years to build.

Nicomedia. Roman Bithynia. 222-235 AD,
Severus Alexander. AE (22mm, 4.57 gr.)
Laureate head/Octastyle temple. Scarce.

He built hundreds of churches, including the great churches of St. John, later in Rome and rebuilt the great church of Nicomedia (Bithynia), which had been destroyed by Diocletian. Between AD 324 and AD 330, he built, virtually from scratch, a new imperial capital at Byzantium on the Bosphorus and called Constantinople after himself. The city employed overtly Christian architecture, contained churches within the city walls, and had no pagan temples. The city became his imperial residence and remained the capital of the Byzantine Empire for over a thousand years.

In the same year that Constantine I achieved supremacy over the empire, the Christian faith itself suffered a notable crisis of Arianism, a heresy that confronts the church definition of the Holy Trinity. History tells us that Constantine I invited 300 bishops at the city of Nicaea (Bithynia) to discuss this controversy that was threatening the church's existence.

Nicaea. Roman Bithynia. 253-268 AD, Gallienus.
AE (25mm, 7.7gr.) Radiate head/Athena standing. Scarce.

The bishops voted and arrived at a resolution that the Christians believe in one God, the Father, and in Jesus, the Son, would remain the principle of Christian doctrine. This declaration of faith is known to this day as the Nicene Creed. The other pillar of the trinity, the Holy Ghost, was endorsed and accepted by the council in Theodosius's reign some forty-five years later.

In May AD 326, Constantine I had his eldest son, Crispus, seized and put to death. In July AD 326, Constantine had his wife, Empress Fausta, killed at the request of his mother, Helena.

Crispus. Roman Imperial. 317-326 AD.
AE (21mm, 3.0 gr.) Helmeted bust/altar.

Crispus. Roman Imperial. 317-326 AD.
AE (20mm, 3.0 gr.) Laureate bust/camp-gate.

During history, many reasons and rumors were written about this subject. At the time of the executions, it was commonly believed that Empress Fausta was either in a relationship with Crispus or was spreading rumors to that effect. The common opinion was that Constantine I killed Crispus and Fausta for their immoralities. Based on other legend, Fausta told Constantine that Crispus raped her and bribed several officials to stay silent about the story. After Constantine killed his son and his wife, he was so very depressed that he never returned to the western half of the empire in his lifetime. Constantine I became very ill, and he summoned the bishops and told them of his hope to be baptized in the Jordan River, where Christ was written to have been baptized. He requested the baptism right away, promising to live a more Christian life should he live through his illness. He was baptized on his deathbed, and it was thought that Constantine put off baptism as long as he did so as to be absolved from as much of his sins as possible. Constantine the Great died on May 22, AD 337. His body was buried in the Church of the Holy Apostles. He was succeeded by his three sons: Constantine II, Constans, and Constantius II.

Constantine II. Roman Imperial. 337-340 AD.
AE (19mm, 2.6 gr.) Laureate bust/VOT.X.

Constantine II. Roman Imperial. 337-340 AD.
AE (19mm, 3.3 gr.) Laureate bust/VOT.X.

Constantine II. Roman Imperial. 337-340 AD.
AE (19mm, 3.0 gr.) draped bust/two soldiers.

Constantine II. Roman Imperial. 337-340 AD.
AE (19mm, 3.2 gr.) draped bust/camp-gate.

Constantine II. Roman Imperial. 337-340 AD.
AE(17mm, 2.3 gr.) draped bust/two soldiers.

Constans. Roman Imperial. 337-350 AD. AE
(17mm, 1.7 gr.) draped bust/two soldiers.

Constantius II. Roman Imperial. 337-361 AD.
AE (19mm, 3.0 gr.) draped bust/camp-gate.

Constantius II. Roman Imperial. 337-361 AD.
AE (17mm, 2.5 gr.) draped bust/
Soldier spearing fallen horseman.

Constantius II. Roman Imperial. 337-361 AD.
AR Siliqua (17mm, 1.97 gr.) draped
bust/legend in four lines.

Constantine I earned his honorific of "the Great" from Christian historians after he died. He could have claimed this title on his military conquests and victories alone. Two hundred years later, the Byzantine Empire considered Constantine I its founder, and the Holy Roman Empire recognized him among the venerable figures of its tradition. During his life and those of his sons, Constantine I was presented as a perfect example of virtue. Even pagans showered him with praise. It became a great honor for emperors after him to be hailed as a "New Constantine."

The long fight and misery for the Christians was over. The Christian faith was firmly planted and outlasted the Roman Empire that had tried to eliminate it. The Christian religion was still the minority religion and existed mainly in the cities throughout the Roman Empire. The apostles and those after them had labored long and well by going out and proclaiming the word and preaching their Master's gospel, and in the triumph of the church under Constantine the great, it could be seen as fulfillment of the mission once begun in Jerusalem 300 years earlier.

In AD 361, Julian the Apostle (so named later for his pro-pagan stance) came to power upon the death of Constantius II and was determined to stop the expansion of Christianity and officially renounce it. Julian tried to go back to the ancient religion to the people in the Roman Empire, but it was a little too late for him to succeed in an empire in which Christianity, by then, dominated.

Julian II, the Apostate. Roman Imperial. 360-363 AD.
AE (26mm, 8.89 gr.) head/bull.

Therefore, Julian avoided open violence against the Christians and encouraged the growth of non-Catholic sects, but he tolerated Christianity in spite of his disagreement with it. By this time, paganism was a dying part of the dominant culture. In fact, in the east of the empire, Christian mobs went on riot and vandalized some of the pagan temples that Julian had established. If Julian's reign had been a little setback to the Christian movement, it had only given more proof that Christianity was here to stay.

After Julian died in AD 363, matters went back to normal and Christianity remained as the powerful religion. The final destruction of the pagan faith came about twenty years later when Theodosius I (AD 379–395) took the final stage and made Christianity the official religion of the Roman Empire in AD 380. With his western counterpart, Gratian, both sponsored the growth of Christianity.

Theodosius I. Roman Imperial. 379-395 AD.
AE (23mm, 5.72 gr) pearl-diademed, helmetd
bust/Gratian standing on galley. Scarce.

Gratian. Roman Imperial. 367-383 AD.
AE (19mm, 2.3 gr.) Draped head/Concordia.

In AD 390, Theodosius I ordered the massacre of Thessalonica against the inhabitants of the city. According to legend, 7,000 were killed there. According to some sources, the order, by the emperor, took place in response to the assassination of his military governor stationed in the city. Ambrose, bishop of Milan, had excommunicated Theodosius, and this incident showed that the church was not the highest authority of the empire, but it proved that the church was sufficiently confident to challenge the Roman Emperor himself on matters of moral authority.

Theodosius I died in AD 395, and his elder son, Arcadius, and his brother, Honorius, jointly became the Western Roman Emperors. Arcadius was severely dominated by his wife, Delia Eudoxia, who convinced her husband in many court and consulate matters, and most people felt that she had used her family's wealth to gain control over the emperor.

Arcadius. Roman Imperial. 383-408 AD.
AE (17mm, 1.7 gr.) Draped head/
Arcadius, Victory.

Arcadius. Roman Imperial. 383-408 AD.
AE (22mm, 4.7 gr.) Draped head/Arcadius.

Honorius. Roman Imperial. 393-423 AD.
AE (22mm, 4.3 gr.) Draped head/Honorius.

Honorius. Roman Imperial. 393-423 AD. AV
Solidus (21mm, 4.42 gr.) Draped bust/Honorius
holding Victory on globe, captive.

Honorius. Roman Imperial. 393-423 AD.
AV Solidus (21mm, 4.40 gr.) Draped bust/Honorius
holding Victory on globe.

Arcadius was more concerned with appearing to be a Pious Christian that he was with political or military matters. He died only nominally in control of his empire in AD 408. The reign of Honorius was characterized by erosion of the Western Empire and its territories. Honorius died in AD 423 AD and left an empire on the verge of collapse.

After the death of Arcadius in AD 408 and Honorius in AD 423, Theodosius II (AD 427–450 AD), the eldest son of Arcadius, became emperor.

Theodosius II. Roman Imperial. 408-450 AD. AV Solidus (21mm, 4.44 gr.) Helmeted bust/Theodosius holding Victory on globe .

Theodosius II. Roman Imperial. 408-450 AD. AV Solidus (22mm, 4.39 gr.) Helmeted bust/Victory holding long jeweled cross.

Theodosius II. Roman Imperial. 408-450 AD. AV Solidus (21mm, 4.24 gr.) Helmeted bust/ Theodosius holding Victory on globe.

Theodosius II. Roman Imperial. 408-450 AD. AV Solidus (22mm, 4.47 gr.) Helmeted bust/ Theodosius holding Victory on globe .

Because of his minority, the real power was exercised by the governor of the east, Anthemius, and was heavily influenced by his eldest sister, Pulcheria. Theodosius II was mostly known for the law code bearing his name, the "Codex Theodosianus" and the "Theodosian Walls of Constantinople." In AD 429, Theodosius II appointed a group of historians to collect all of the laws since the reign of Constantine I and create a full formalized, documented system of law. These laws were summarized and used during future emperors for the next one hundred years.

The Fall of Rome

The Roman Empire was born when Julius Caesar and Augustus transformed the republic into a monarchy. The Roman Empire reached its peak during the twelve Caesars' reigns up to the end of the second century AD. The empire started to decline slowly, and the population, in some provinces, started to vanish as a result of the barbarian invasions. The decline of the Roman Empire was a gradual decline that cannot precisely be dated. The traditional date of the fall of the Roman Empire is (as agreed by many historians) September 4, AD 476, when the last Emperor of the Roman Empire, Romulus Augustus, was disposed of by Odoacer. Odoacer was a Germanic general and the first non-Roman ruler of Italy after AD 476. Odoacer continued to rule first as a nominal client of Julius Nepos and after Nepos' death in AD 480 as a client of the emperor in Constantinople. Many historians put the fall of Rome at AD 480, at the end of Julius Nepos's reign, and the others put it at AD 476, at the end of Romulus Augustus's reign. For the purpose of writing this book, the fall of the Roman Empire happened in AD 476. Although Roman Emperor Zeno (AD 474–491) was in the middle of the fall of the Roman Empire, he contributed much to stabilize the Eastern Empire. Zeno was an Isaurian, a people who lived on the southwestern Mediterranean coast of Anatolia.

Zeno. Roman Imperial. 474-491 AD.
AV Solidus (21mm, 4.46 gr.) Helmeted
bust/Victory holding long jeweled cross.

Zeno continued to be unpopular with the people and Senate because of his foreign origins. Some historians put Zeno as a Byzantine emperor; however, for the purpose of writing this book, he is considered to be a Roman emperor, and the Byzantine period starts with Anastasius I (AD 491–518).

Many historians gave hundreds of reasons for the collapse of the Roman Empire, and for this book, it will be kept to minimum. During the third century AD, many crises occurred which caused the empire to be near collapse between AD 235 and AD 284 from many invasions on all fronts: the civil war, the plague, and economic collapse. During the reign of Emperor Diocletion, from AD 284–305, the empire witnessed many substantial political and economic reforms (not all of them helped the empire), many of which carried on into the next centuries. During Constantine the Great's reign, from AD 306–337, the Roman Empire was split in half—the Western Roman Empire based in Rome and the Eastern Roman Empire (Byzantine Empire) based in Constantinople, the city that the emperor built from scratch. At the end of the fourth century, AD 376–382, a series of civil wars with the Visigoths, East Germanic tribes, resulted in a massive defeat for the Roman army. Finally, the Visigothic army, under Alaric I, eventually moved into Italy and famously sacked Rome in AD 410. Migration of the Huns, nomadic tribes from the east, into Italy did not do the Romans any better than driving one more nail in the coffin of the Roman Empire.

Emperor Theodosius (AD 379–395) made Christianity the official religion of the empire, and he continued and intensified the policies against paganism of his predecessors, eventually outlawing it. This action caused a lot of friction and uprising throughout the Roman Empire, since Christianity was only a minority religion when compared with paganism. In AD 455, the Vandals, Barbarian tribes from the north, fought the Roman army, and as a result, the Vandals defeated the Romans and went and sacked Rome for the second time in AD 455. Future Roman emperors had several wars with the Vandals, and they were defeated. The last campaign against the Vandals was a naval expedition sent by Roman emperors Leo I and Anthemius. Both were defeated by the Vandals in AD 468.

As can be seen above, the deterioration of the Roman Empire was piece by piece over a period of 300 years. However, most historians believe that the war with Rome's biggest enemies, the Sasanids, was a major reason for the fall of the Roman Empire.

The Sasanian Dynasty

As mentioned earlier, under the Parthian Empire section, the Parthians were conquered by force from the east under King Ardashir, king of Persia. The Parthians were the biggest threat to Rome's eastern territories in the first and second centuries AD, and the Romans considered them as the second Persian Empire. The defeat of the Parthians by Ardashir in AD 224 marked the beginning of the Sasanian dynasty, and they were also a big threat to the Roman Empire. The Romans, in turn, called them the third Persian Empire.

Ardashir II. King of Persis. Late 1st century BC.
AR Hemidrachm (15mm, 1.93 gr.) Draped
bust/king standing in front of altar. Rare.

The Sasanid Empire conquered many Roman provinces in the east or part of provinces encompassing all of today's Iran, Iraq, Armenia, southeastern central Asia, western Afghanistan, parts of Turkey, parts of Syria, and parts of the Arabian Peninsula. Most of these areas were under the Roman Empire in the third century AD. The Sasanids called their empire Eranshahr, or the Iranian Empire.

The empire reached its golden period in the fourth and fifth centuries AD when, during King Kavadh's reign, the empire had a long, peaceful period with the Romans interrupted only by two brief conflicts.

Kavadh. Sassanian Empire. 488-497 AD.
AR Drachm (28mm, 3.9 gr.) bearded
bust/fire altar with attendants.

After Kavadh, his son, Khosrau I (531–579), ascended to the throne, and he was the most celebrated of the Sasanid rulers. Khosrau I is most famous for his reforms that introduced a rational system of taxation based upon a survey of land possessions that refer to a property that generate income for the owner without the owner having to do the actual work of the estate. He tried, in every way, to increase the welfare and the revenues of his empire.

Khursu I. Sassanian Empire. 531-579 AD.
AR Drachm (30mm, 3.5 gr.) bearded
bust/fire altar with attendants.

Hormazed IV. Sassanian Empire. 579-590 AD.
AR Drachm (31mm, 4.1 gr.) bearded
bust/fire altar with attendants.

The empire reached its second golden age under his reign. After Khosrau I died, Hormazd IV (AD 579–590) took the throne. Hormazd had many wars with the Byzantine Empire that caused many revolts. He was eventually overthrown by a palace coup, and his son, Khosrau II (AD 590–628), was placed on the throne. Khosrau II faced a rebellion with his own realm, and he in, an unexpected move, turned to the Byzantine Empire's King Maurice—his former enemy—for help. In AD 602, King Maurice was overthrown and killed by Phocas. Khosrau II used the murder of his benefactor as an excuse to launch a new invasion called the war of revenge. Khosrau II's generals advanced on the Byzantine Empire territories and occupied the frontier cities of Byzantine Mesopotamia and Armenia.

Khursu II. Sassanian Empire. 590-627 AD.
AR Drachm (33mm, 4.0 gr.) bearded
bust/fire altar with attendants.

Khursu II. Sassanian Empire. 590-627 AD.
AR Drachm (33mm, 3.9 gr.) bearded
bust/fire altar with attendants.

Khursu II. Sassanian Empire. 590-627 AD.
AR Drachm (29mm, 4.1 gr.) bearded
bust/fire altar with attendants.

Khursu II. Sassanian Empire. 590-627 AD.
AR Drachm (32mm, 4.2 gr.) bearded
bust/fire altar with attendants.

Khosrau II's army reached Palestine and occupied Jerusalem in AD 614, Alexandria in AD 619, and all of Egypt in AD 621. Jerusalem was in great peace for the last 300 years before the Sasanid invasion. Roman shrines and temples were demolished in the city, and they destroyed every Christian structure on the surrounding hills, and according to legend, more than 65,000 Christians were killed during the second invasion. Many churches were burned to the ground, including the Church of the Holy Sepulchre. They carried the true cross that Constantine the Great's mother, Helena, identified 300 years before to Persia. This victory lasted only a few years when Byzantine Emperor Heraclius defeated the Sasanian army in the battle of Nineveh. The impact of Heraclius's victory of the devastation of the richest territories of the Sasanid Empire, and the humiliating destruction of high-profile targets, undermined Khosrau's II prestige and his support among his people. He was overthrown and murdered in AD 628. In AD 630, Byzantine Emperor Heraclius solemnly returned the true cross to Jerusalem. The Sasanian Empire was defeated by the Islamic invasion to Persia, and they murdered the last Sasanian king, Yazdgard III, in AD 651, and most of its territory was absorbed into the Islamic caliphate.

PART V
THE SPREAD OF CHRISTIANITY

Note to Reader

This part of the book is not directly related to the Bible, as was the case for the previous parts discussed earlier in this book. It was added to show the reader the effects and influence that coins had on the Christian faith and how far the Christians reached after the Romans, as well as to show the fate of the Holy City of Jerusalem with the crusaders trying to liberate it from the hands of the Islamic forces. The roads were rough and arduous, but the success was smooth through few paths. After the Romans, some roads led east, where the Eastern Orthodox Church became well known in Constantinople. By the turn of the fifth century AD, Christianity got a foothold in southern Europe and Asia Minor and reached westward to Spain and Britain. Along with their faith, these visionaries carried symbols of their beliefs that not only strengthened their courage and determination but enabled them to identify and find comfort with fellow Christians. Coins are effective witnesses to our forefathers' trials and struggles to promote the beliefs that gave them strength to continue. These tangible bits of history should be seen, touched, and appreciated for what they tell us of the past and what they can assure us today.

There are many books written about the Byzantines, Muslims, and the crusaders. These books ranged from 200 to 800 pages, and what you see in the following pages is a very, very brief history of them all. Also, hundreds and hundreds of coin varieties were minted during the reigns of these dynasties, but again, for the scope of this book, relatively few coins are presented.

The Byzantine Empire

The Byzantine Empire and the Eastern Roman Empire are traditional names to describe the Roman Empire during the Middle Ages, with its capital being Constantinople. Constantine I, in AD 330, founded Constantinople as a second Rome that was well positioned on the trade routes between the east and west of the ancient world. Constantine I built the city based on the administrative reforms created by Emperor Diocletian. He stabilized the coinage of the empire, making the gold solidus a highly prized and stable currency. Under Constantine I, the Roman Empire gained most of its military strength and enjoyed a period of stability and prosperity. The Western Roman Empire collapsed about 150 years after Constantine the Great's death, and the Roman Empire capital was moved and centered in Constantinople under the name of the Byzantine Empire. This empire shaped the known world with art, literature, and government during the period usually called the Dark Ages. They converted much of the area to Christianity, enacted codes that form the basis of today's legal system, and produced a fascinating array of coinage.

The Byzantine Empire's coinage was Christian-oriented issues, they show Jesus Christ, saints, and the cross appeared on most of their coinage. The coinage showed the cross figure of Jesus Christ, the Virgin Mary, and an inscription, such as "Servant of Christ" or similar Christian religious wordings. Also, some coins showed a cross on steps, now called "cross calvary," for the site of Jesus Christ's execution. The empire assured an active role of the emperor in the affairs of the church. The Byzantines thought of the emperor as a messenger of Jesus Christ that was responsible particularly for the propagation of Christianity among pagans and its finances after the decline of Rome. The church of Constantinople became the richest and most influential center of Christendom during the era of AD 500–800. Even when the empire was reduced to only a shadow of itself, the church, as an institution, had never exercised so much influence both inside and outside the imperial frontiers. By the time of the Byzantine Empire collapsed, Christianity was spreading rapidly from Spain in the west to Mesopotamia in the east and to Egypt in the south. The Byzantine Empire kept the Islamic invader out of western Asia Minor and the Balkans for almost 300 years.

The coinage of the Byzantine Empire was a constant reminder of Christianity on a daily basis for both the pagans and Christians. The copper follis and its fractions were used on a daily basis for everyday transactions. There were almost one hundred emperors that ruled the Byzantine Empire over a span of 800 years. For the purpose of this book, only the prominent emperors and their coinage are presented.

Anastasius I (AD 491–518) became the first Byzantine emperor after the fall of Rome. History tells us that Anastasius I had one eye black and one blue. For this reason, he was called Dicorus, which means "two pupiled." Anastasius I proved himself to be an able emperor and was said to have held a very high character. He married Emperor Zeno's widow in AD 491. His reign was disturbed by foreign wars and religious distractions. In spite of this, he displayed a great interest and energy in administrating the affairs of the empire.

Anastasius I. Byzantine Empire. 491-518 AD.
AV Solidus (21mm, 4.37 gr.) Helmeted
head/victory holding jeweled cross.

Anastasius I. Byzantine Empire. 491-518 AD.
AE (12mm, 1.1 gr.) Draped bust/large E.

Anastasius I. Byzantine Empire. 491-518 AD.
AE (13mm, 1.9 gr.) Draped bust/large E.

Anastasius I. Byzantine Empire. 491-518 AD.
AE (32mm, 14.2 gr.) Draped bust/large M.

Anastasius I had several wars with the Sasanid Persians, which made him build the strong fortress of Daras in Nisibis. Anastasius I was childless, and he could not decide which of his three nephews should succeed him, but this issue was decided for him after his death. Anastasius I died in AD 518 after he introduced the coinage reform, which involved three denominations of gold coins (solidus and its half and third) and five copper coins (the follis, forty nummi and its fraction, down to anammus). Anastasius I was buried at the Church of the Holy Apostles. At the end of his reign, according to sources, he left the Imperial Treasury richer by twenty-three million solidus (300,000 pounds of gold).

Justin I (AD 518–527) became an Emperor in AD 518 through the ranks of the Byzantine Empire army.

Justin I. Byzantine Empire. 518-527
AD. AE (12mm, 1.5 gr.) Draped bust/
Tyche of Antioch seated left,large E .

Justin I. Byzantine Empire. 518-527 AD.
AE (24mm, 7.6 gr.) Draped bust/large K.

Justin I. Byzantine Empire. 518-527 AD.
AE (30mm, 10.7 gr.) Draped bust/large M.

He was about seventy years old at the time of accession and was said to be illiterate. He found the Justinian dynasty, which deemphasized the influence of the old Byzantine nobility. Justin repealed a law that prohibited a member of the senatorial class from marrying women from the common or lower class of society. Justin I died of poor health and also of old age (he was ninety-seven years old) in AD 527.

Justinian I (AD 527–565) took over the throne after the death of his uncle, Justin I. Justinian I was considered to be a saint among the Orthodox Christians and also by some Lutheran Churches. His reign witnessed the prosperity of the Byzantine culture, and his building plans yielded such a masterpiece as the Hagia Sophia, which was to be the center of the Eastern Orthodox Christianity for many centuries to come. Justinian I was full of energy, as he was known as the emperor who never slept. He came from a common and low provincial background; therefore, he did not have the old power base in the traditional aristocracy of Constantinople. He was able to marry Theodora, who was a courtesan, after his uncle, Justin I, had passed a law permitting intermarriage between social classes. The marriage caused a big scandal, but she would prove to be very intelligent, a good judge, and became Justinian's greatest supporter.

Justinian I. Byzantine Empire. 527-565 AD.
AV Solidus (21mm, 4.48 gr.) Helmeted bust holding globus Cruciger/angel holding long crossed staff.

Justinian I. Byzantine Empire. 527-565 AD.
AE (24mm, 8.6 gr.) Helmeted bust/large K.

Justinian I. Byzantine Empire. 527-565 AD.
AE (32mm, 17.3 gr.) Draped bust/large M.

Justinian I. Byzantine Empire. 527-565 AD.
AE (31mm, 16.9 gr.) Draped bust/large M.

Justinian I. Byzantine Empire. 527-565 AD.
AE (35mm, 18.67 gr.) Helmeted bust/large M.

Justinian I. Byzantine Empire. 527-565 AD.
AE (37mm, 20.41 gr.) Helmeted bust/large M.

Justinian I. Byzantine Empire. 527-565 AD.
AE (39mm, 23.41 gr.) Helmeted bust/large M.

Justinian I. Byzantine Empire. 527-565 AD.
AE (41mm, 22.12 gr.) Helmeted bust/large M.

During his reign, he had several riots and wars: the Nika riots, which resulted in the death of 30,000 civilians; the war with the Sasanid Empire; the war with the Vandals in North Africa; and the war of Italy. Justinian I actively participated in the affairs of Christian doctrine, and he became more devoted to Christianity during the later years of his life. From the beginning of his reign, he made it proper to proclaim by law the church's belief in the Trinity and the incarnation and to threaten all heretics with severe penalties. Justinian I was the nursing father of the Eastern Orthodox Church. In AD 540, Justinian I was hit by a devastating plague. He recovered, but his wife, Theodora, died at a relatively young age. Justinian I died twenty years later, in AD 565, and was succeeded by Justin II, the son of his sister. Justinian I body was entombed in a specially built mausoleum in the Church of the Holy Apostle.

Justin II (AD 565–578) became the emperor of the Byzantine Empire after the death of Justinian I. Justin II was the nephew of Justinian I and husband of Sophia, the niece of the late empress Theodora. During the first part of his reign, Justin paid his uncle's debts, proclaimed universal religious toleration, and administered justice.

Justin II. Byzantine Empire. 565-578 AD.
AV Tremissis (16mm, 1.78 gr.) Draped bust/
Angel holdind cross, star below.

Justin II. Byzantine Empire. 565-578 AD.
AV Tremissis (18mm, 2.1 gr.) Draped bust/
Angel holdind cross, star below.

Justin II. Byzantine Empire. 565-578 AD.
AV Solidus (22mm, 4.14 gr.) Helmeted bust/
Victory holding cross and crossed staff.

Justin II. Byzantine Empire. 565-578 AD.
AE (11mm, 1.5 gr.) Seaby monogram/large E.

Justin II. Byzantine Empire. 565-578 AD.
AE (23mm, 5.5 gr.) Justin and Sophia, cross/large K

Justin II. Byzantine Empire. 565-578 AD.
AE (29mm, 13.3 gr.) Justin and Sophia/large M.

Justin II. Byzantine Empire. 565-578 AD.
AE (28mm, 12.3 gr.) Justin and Sophia/large M.

Justin II. Byzantine Empire. 565-578 AD.
AE (27.5mm, 13.3 gr.) Justin and Sophia/large M.

Justin II. Byzantine Empire. 565-578 AD.
AE (30mm, 12.7 gr.) Justin and Sophia/large M.

Justin II. Byzantine Empire. 565-578 AD.
AE (32mm, 12.9 gr.) Justin and Sophia/large M.

Justin II experienced many wars with Persia and with the Avars, which caused him to lose the greater part of Italy. The Persians took a big part of Syria that belonged to the Byzantine Empire, and he was losing, piece by piece, his empire to foreign invaders. He refused to pay tribute to the Persians, in combination with overtures to the Turks, which led to a war with the Sasanid Empire. Justin II, contrary to his uncle, completely relied on the support of the aristocratic part and his wife, Sophia. As history tells us, Justin II lost his mind and had fits of insanity. The last four years of his reign, he sank into growing insanity, and he finally died in AD 578.

Tiberius II Constantine (AD 578–582) became emperor after Justin II died. During the years of his reign, to increase his popularity, he began spending money that Justin II had reserved in the treasury, and it is said he gave away about 7,000 pounds of gold every year.

Tiberius II Constantine. Byzantine Empire. 578-582 AD.
AE (18mm, 3.9 gr.) Bust wearing crown/large
cross between ANNO.

Tiberius II Constantine. Byzantine Empire. 578-582 AD.
AE (19mm, 3.3 gr.) Bust wearing crown/large
cross between ANNO.

Tiberius II Constantine. Byzantine Empire. 578-582 AD.
AE (23mm, 5.8 gr.) Helmeted bust/large XX, cross above.

He had a disease where part of his brain was not properly functioning, which caused him to lose the use of his feet. He had peace with the Visigoths in Spain and defeated the Berbers in North Africa, but the Slavs began to migrate from the west. Tiberius II Constantine fell ill and died in AD 582, and Maurice was named his heir.

Maurice Tiberius (AD 582–602) took over the throne of the Byzantine Empire upon Tiberius II's death in AD 582. Maurice was one of the most important rulers of the early Byzantine Empire, and his reign was full of unending conflicts from all directions. From the beginning of his reign, wars broke out with Persia, with the Balkans, with the Avars, with the Slavs, and there were also riots of Italy and North Africa. Maurice's reign was considered to be the final era of classical antiquity, as the turmoil shattered the Byzantine Empire in the next four decades. Maurice's greatest weakness was his inability to judge how unpopular he was.

Maurice Tiberius . Byzantine Empire. 582-602 AD.
AV Tremissis (17mm, 1.8 gr.) Draped bust/Cross.

Maurice Tiberius . Byzantine Empire. 582-602 AD.
AV Tremissis (18mm, 1.9 gr.) Draped bust/Cross.

Maurice Tiberius . Byzantine Empire. 582-602 AD.
AV Solidus (22mm, 4.28 gr.) Helmeted bust holding
globus cruciger/angel holding long P headed cross.

Maurice Tiberius . Byzantine Empire. 582-602 AD.
AV Solidus (22mm, 4.23 gr.) Helmeted bust holding
globus cruciger/angel holding long P headed cross.

Maurice Tiberius . Byzantine Empire. 582-602 AD.
AV Solidus (22mm, 4.30 gr.) Helmeted bust holding
globus cruciger/angel holding long P headed cross.

Maurice Tiberius . Byzantine Empire. 582-602 AD.
AV Solidus (23mm, 4.41 gr.) Helmeted bust holding
globus cruciger/angel holding long P headed cross.

Maurice Tiberius . Byzantine Empire. 582-602 AD.
AV Solidus (24mm, 4.44 gr.) Helmeted bust holding
globus cruciger/angel holding long P headed cross.

He had too much confidence in his own judgment, without regard for his people's disagreement. Maurice's son, Theodosius (AD 590–602), shared the leadership with his father as a co-emperor for about twelve years. His army revolted against him when he made his announcement to cut military wages by 25 percent. He made peace with Persian King Chosroes II and paid tribute to him after a long war that weakened both nations. Maurice was murdered in AD 602 after he was forced to watch his three sons be executed before his eyes. Persian King Chosroes II used this murder of his patron as an excuse for a renewed war against the Byzantine Empire.

Phocas (AD 602–610) became the emperor of the Byzantine Empire in AD 602. At the beginning of his reign, Phocas was popular because he immediately reduced the taxes, which had been very high during the reign of Maurice. Phocas was in great support of the Christian Church, as he received many praise letters from Pope Gregory I. He supported the church heavily, and he realized that the church needed the money to operate and help the needy.

Phocas . Byzantine Empire. 602-610 AD.
AV Solidus (22mm, 4.47 gr.) Helmeted bust holding
globus cruciger/angel holding long P headed cross.

Phocas . Byzantine Empire. 602-610 AD. AV
Solidus (22mm, 4.49 gr.) Helmeted bust holding
globus cruciger/angel holding long P headed cross.

Phocas faced great opposition and was regarded by many of his followers as a populist. As a result, he seemed to have good relations with the papacy and tended to support the popes in many theological problems. Phocas experienced many wars and foreign invaders from all fronts. The traditional frontiers of the Byzantine Empire began to collapse during his reign. Persian King Khosrau II advanced from the east and waged war against the Byzantine forces in northern Mesopotamia, and by AD 607, he had advanced the Persian control to the Euphrates River. In AD 610, a coup was arranged by some prominent Byzantine aristocratic figures, and they crowned Heraclius as emperor. Heraclius, according to legend, killed and beheaded Phocas, and his body was paraded through the capital city.

Heraclius (AD 610–641) became the emperor of the Byzantine Empire and ruled for almost thirty-one years. His reign was marked by several military campaigns with the Persians and Arab Islamic forces. The Persians, as mentioned before, gained the biggest majority of Mesopotamia during Phocas's reign, and then they took advantage of the current civil war and internal conflicts to advance deep into Syria. By AD 613/614, the Persians took Damascus and Jerusalem, damaging the Church of the Holy Sepulcher and capturing the holy cross, and moved south and took Egypt.

Heraclius . Byzantine Empire. 610-641 AD. AV Solidus (22mm, 4.45 gr.) crowned busts of Heraclius and Heraclius Constantine/cross Potent on three steps.

Heraclius . Byzantine Empire. 610-641 AD. AV Solidus (22mm, 4.47 gr.) crowned busts of Heraclius and Heraclius Constantine/cross Potent on three steps.

Heraclius . Byzantine Empire. 610-641 AD. AV Solidus (22mm, 4.47 gr.) crowned busts of Heraclius and Heraclius Constantine/cross Potent on three steps.

Heraclius . Byzantine Empire. 610-641 AD. AV Solidus (22mm, 4.47 gr.) crowned bust/ cross Potent on three steps.

Heraclius . Byzantine Empire. 610-641 AD.
AV Solidus (22mm, 4.49 gr.) Heraclius
flanked by Heraclius Constantine and
Heraclonas/cross Potent on three steps.

Heraclius . Byzantine Empire. 610-641 AD.
AV Solidus (22mm, 4.47 gr.) crowned
busts of Heraclius and Heraclius
Constantine/cross Potent on three steps.

Heraclius began to build a strong army, and by AD 621, he had about a 70,000 man army; he led the battle himself and marched through Asia Minor and invaded Persia itself. Heraclius defeated the Persians at the battle of Nineveh in AD 627 and personally killed Rhahzadh, the commander of the Persian army. The Persians made a peace treaty with Heraclius by returning all the empires former territories, including Syria, Palestine, and Egypt. Heraclius marched barefoot as a pious Christian pilgrim into Jerusalem and restored the true cross to the Church of the Holy Sepulcher. Heraclius called himself the ancient Persian title of the "king of kings," which is a very similar rank to the traditional Roman Imperial title of Augustus. Heraclius fell ill after the long war with the Persians, and when the nomadic tribes of the Arabian Peninsula were united under the new conversion of Islam, he invaded part of the Byzantine Empire territories. In AD 634, the Muslim army captured Syria and Palestine, and Heraclius was too ill to fight them personally, so he sent his generals, and they were defeated in the battle of Yarmuk in AD 636. Syria and Palestine were lost again to the Muslim Arabs, and by the time of Heraclius's death, Egypt had fallen to the Muslim Arabs as well. Heraclius died in AD 641, leaving the empire to Constans II and Heraclonas, but the latter ruled only for six months.

Constans II's (AD 641–668) official name was Heraclius Constantine III, but this was popularly shortened to Constans, and he stayed by this name during his reign. He was also called "Constantine the Bearded." The Arab Muslims continued their advances into the Byzantine Empire territories, and they built their naval fleet and constituted a real threat to the Byzantine naval supremacy. The Byzantines completely withdrew from Egypt, which was now permanently lost but had once been one of the richest provinces of the empire.

Constans II . Byzantine Empire. 641-668 AD.
AV Solidus (22mm, 4.47gr.) crowned bust/
cross Potent on three steps.

Constans II . Byzantine Empire. 641-668 AD.
AV Solidus (22mm, 4.42 gr.) busts of
Constans and Constantine IV/
cross between Heraclius and Tiberius.

Constans II . Byzantine Empire. 641-668 AD.
AE (18x19mm, 5.0 gr.) beardless Constans/large M.

Constans II . Byzantine Empire. 641-668 AD.
AE (21mm, 5.0 gr.) crowned bust of Constans
holding globus cruciger/large M, S, C.

Constans II had wars with the Muslim army almost all of his reign. The Muslim army got stronger and stronger to a degree that they invaded most of the eastern province under the Byzantine rule. He finally had a peace treaty with them in AD 651. The Muslim army marched west to Rhodes, and they were preparing to attack Constantinople but did not carry out the plan due to a civil war between the Sunnis and Shiats, which broke out among them in AD 656. Constans II defeated the Slavs in the Balkans, and he established some notion of Byzantine rule over them. Constans II visited Rome in AD 663 when no Byzantine emperor had set foot in Rome for the last 200 years. He was received with great honor by Pope Vitalian, who he kept a long, friendly relationship with. Constans II moved his residence to Syracuse, Sicily, and stayed there until his assassination in AD 668. His son, Constantine IV, succeeded him.

Constantine IV (AD 668–685), Pogonatus, had been named a co-emperor with his father, Constans II, in AD 652 and became the sole emperor of the Byzantine Empire in AD 668. Before he did anything in his reign, he suppressed the military revolt in Sicily, which had led to his father's death.

Constantine IV . Byzantine Empire. 668-685 AD.
AV Solidus (21mm, 4.45 gr.) cuirassed bust/cross
on three steps flanked by Heraclius and Tiberius.

The Arab Muslims sent a large army to Asia Minor and captured Cyzicus and set up a base from which to launch further attacks into the heart of the Byzantine Empire. The Arabs attacked Carthage and Sicily and tried to siege Constantinople from the sea. Constantinople survived the Arab siege, and they withdrew and were defeated at the battle of Syllaeum in the Pamphylia province of Asia Minor. Constantine IV paid a lot of attention to the church torn between Monothelitism and orthodoxy. Monothelitism teaches that Jesus Christ had two natures but only one will, while the orthodoxy believes that Jesus Christ has two wills (human and divine). He reaffirmed the Orthodox doctrines, which, in turn, solved the controversy over Monothelitism; most of them were under the Umayyad Caliphate at the time. Constantine IV died of dysentery in September AD 685.

For the next 150 years, the Byzantine Empire tried to protect their borders from foreign invasions and tried to survive against the newly fresh army of the Arab Muslims. In the eighth and ninth centuries AD, the Byzantine Empire shrunk to only Asia Minor and northern parts of Greece. The rest of their provinces all over were taken by Slavic, Bulgars, and Arabs.

Leo V . Byzantine Empire. 813-820 AD.
AE (18mm, 3.1 gr.) facing bust of Leo,
star/facing bust of Constantine IV.

The period of Leo V was dominated by controversy and religious division over iconoclasm. Iconoclasm condemned the making of any lifeless image (painting, statue) that was intended to represent Jesus Christ or one of the saints. Icons were banned during the reign of Emperor Leo V in AD 787, leading to revolts throughout the empire. In AD 813, Leo V restored the policy of iconoclasm, and the empire stayed in conflicts over this for a long period of time.

During the reign of Basil II (AD 976–1025) and his brother, Constantine VIII (AD 1025–1028), the empire prospered. Since Basil II was only five years old and his brother, Constantine VIII, was too young to be emperors on their own. Therefore, their mother married one of the generals, Nikephorus II, to help running the empire, and he reigned as an emperor for six years, and then he was murdered. The mother married another general, John I Tzimisces (AD 969–976), and he reigned as an emperor for seven years until he died. By that time, Basil II was old enough, and he took over the throne and became emperor of the Byzantine Empire. During his time and the time from John I to Alexis I (AD 969–1092), the Byzantine Empire expanded well into Syria and defeated the emirs in Iraq, and they re-conquered Crete and Cyprus. Under Emperor Basil II, the Bulgarian territories that had been taken from the Byzantine Empire for the last 300 years were conquered back and became part of the Byzantine Empire. Between AD 800 and AD 1100, the Byzantine Empire developed a mixed relationship with the new state of Kievrus that appeared to the north of the Black Sea. They had good relationships with them after Christianizing the whole of the state of Rus. They accepted the Orthodox version of Christianity.

John I-ALexius I . Byzantine Empire. 969-1092 AD.
AE (30mm, 8.9 gr.) Jesus Christ holding
book of gospels/cross on three steps.

John I-ALexius I . Byzantine Empire. 969-1092 AD.
AE (31mm, 6.7 gr.) Jesus Christ holding
book of gospels/cross on three steps.

John I-ALexius I . Byzantine Empire. 969-1092 AD.
AE (33mm, 9.2 gr.) Jesus Christ holding
book of gospels/cross on three steps.

Basil II and Constantine VIII .
Byzantine Empire 976-1025 AD.
AE (33mm, 17.02 gr.) Jesus Christ raising hand
in Benediction/legend in four lines.

Basil II and Constantine VIII .
Byzantine Empire 976-1025 AD.
AE (36mm, 19.43 gr.) Jesus Christ raising hand
in Benediction/legend in four lines.

Constantine X . Byzantine Empire 1059-1067 AD.
AE (30mm, 8.3 gr.) Jesus Christ holding book of
gospels with both hands/Eudocia on
left and Constantine on right.

The Byzantine Empire reached its climax, then stretched to Armenia in the east, to Calabria in the south, and to Italy in the west. Basil II wanted to go to Sicily and capture it from Arab occupation. His death in 1025 put an end to this project. None of his successors had any particular military or political talent, and the administration of the empire increasingly fell into the hands of the civil service. The army was now seen as both an unnecessary expense and a political burden. The Byzantine Empire began to shrink again. During Constantine X, Ducas's reign, the Normans advanced into southern Italy and occupied what was Byzantine Italy.

In AD 1071, Michael VII, Ducas, became an emperor of the Byzantine Empire with his uncle, Romanos DioGenes, as co-emperor. Michael VII exhibited little interest in politics. He was mainly interested in academic pursuits, increasing taxes, and luxury spending without properly financing the army.

Michael VII . Byzantine Empire 1071-1078 AD.
AV Scyphate (30mm, 4.4 gr.) Jesus Christ
enthroned facing/Michael holding cross.

Michael VII . Byzantine Empire 1071-1078 AD.
AV Scyphate (29mm, 4.5 gr.) Jesus Christ
enthroned facing/Michael holding cross.

Michael VII . Byzantine Empire 1071-1078 AD.
AV Scyphate(31mm, 4.6 gr.) Jesus Christ
enthroned facing/Michael holding cross.

With his loss of Italy and many revolts in Balkans, the empire was in a big falling stage. In AD 1073, the Byzantine government sent a new army to contain the Seljuk Turks, but this army was defeated, and its commander was captured in AD 1073. Every expedition sent afterward failed, and the Seljuk Turks captured all of their commanders. Michael VII resigned from the throne and retired into the Monastery of Stoudios in AD 1078.

Nicephorus III (AD 1078–1081), Botaniates, became the emperor of the Byzantine Empire in AD 1078.

Nicephorus III . Byzantine Empire 1078-1081 AD.
AV Scyphate (30mm, 4.5 gr.) Jesus Christ
enthroned facing/Nicephorus holding cross.

Nicephorus III . Byzantine Empire 1078-1081 AD.
AV Scyphate (30mm, 4.6 gr.) Jesus Christ
enthroned facing/Nicephorus holding cross.

Nicephorus III . Byzantine Empire 1078-1081 AD.
AV Scyphate (30mm, 4.4 gr.) Jesus Christ
enthroned facing/Nicephorus holding cross.

He and his general, Alexius, could not drive the Seljuk Turks out of Asia Minor. In his reign, the Byzantine gold currency was devaluated, and he was interested mainly in court bureaucracy, and his administration did not win him much support. He became more dependent on the support of Alexius, who successfully defeated the rebellion in the Balkans. Since he was only in the background while Alexius I ran the affairs of the empire, Nicephorou III was forced to abdicate in AD 1081.

Alexius I (AD 1081–1118), Comnenus, became the emperor of the Byzantine Empire in AD 1081. The military, financial, and territorial recovery of the Byzantine Empire began in his reign, and he also witnessed the First Crusade, which he used to conquer their lands. Almost all of his thirty-seven-year reign was full of wars and struggle. He met the Normans in Italy, and with the help of German King Henry IV, after bribing him with 360,000 gold pieces, he won and drove the Normans from Italy and recovered most of the Byzantine Empire's losses. Next Alexius I went to Thrace and fought the rebels who took the province many years ago. Alexius I recaptured the territories in the Balkans from the Cumans in AD 1094. His biggest nightmare was the Seljuk Turks in Asia Minor.

Alexius I . Byzantine Empire 1081-1118 AD.
AV Scyphate (31mm, 4.6 gr.) Jesus Christ
enthroned facing/Alexius holding cross.

Alexius I . Byzantine Empire 1081-1118 AD.
AE (20mm, 2.2 gr.) Jesus Christ facing raising
hands in Benediction/figure of virgin orans.

Alexius had taken a new relationship toward the papacy with the intention of seeking western support against the Seljuk Turks. In AD 1095, Pope Urban II preached the First Crusade, and later that year, he gathered groups of men to help Alexius. Alexius dealt with the first disorganized group of crusaders, led by preacher Peter the Hermit, by sending them on to Asia Minor, where they were massacred by the Seljuk Turks in AD 1096. The second group of crusaders were more organized and were led in groups by Godfrey of Bouillon, Bohemund of Taranto, Raymond IV of Toulouse, and other important members of the western nobility. They went to Asia Minor and fought the Seljuk Turks, and they captured almost the entire western half of Asia Minor and returned it to the Byzantine Empire. Alexius I, Comnenus, died in AD 1118.

John II Comnenus (AD 1118–1143) became the emperor of the Byzantine Empire after the death of his father Alexius I. John II was a pious and dedicated emperor who was determined to repair all the damages the Byzantine Empire suffered the last fifty years. John made alliances with the Holy Roman Empire in Italy, and with their help, he defeated the rebels in the Balkans and personally led many campaigns against the Seljuk Turks in Asia Minor.

John II . Byzantine Empire 1118-1143 AD.
AV Trachy (31mm, 4.7 gr.) Jesus Christ facing
raising hands in Benediction/The virgin nimbate
on right and John on left cross in between them.

John II . Byzantine Empire 1118-1143 AD.
BI Trachy (28mm, 4.7 gr.) Jesus Christ
facing raising hands in Benediction/
bust of John holding cruciform scaptre.

John wanted to demonstrate the Byzantine emperor's rule as the leader of the Christian world. He led an army with combined forces of Byzantium and the crusader states and went into the Holy Land.

He was disappointed by the deceptive action of the crusader allies, who deliberately failed to fight against the Muslim army at the crucial moment. According to Latin historian William of Tyre, John II was very ugly and short, and his entire complexion was dark (eyes, hair, skin), which was common for the Moors, people of the Berbers in North Africa. During his twenty-five years of reign, he was known as John the Beautiful, not because of his look, but because of his soul. John II restricted his court to discuss serious subjects, his food at the emperor's table was frugal, and he lectured the individuals in his royal court that lived in excessive luxury. John II was an excellent strategist, he was gifted with self-control and personal courage, and through his many wars, he devoted himself to recover his empire. His reign was remarkably just and mild, and he was an exceptional example of a model ruler at a time when cruelty was the norm. John II was "accidentally" infected by a poisoned arrow while out hunting, and he died in AD 1143.

Manuel I Comnenus (AD 1143–1180) took over the throne of the Byzantine Empire after the death of his father, John II. He reigned for almost forty years, and his reign was very critical for the sake of the Byzantine Empire in particular and the Mediterranean countries in general.

Manuel I . Byzantine Empire 1164 1167 AD.
AV Trachy (31mm, 4.27 gr.) Jesus Christ
facing raising hands in Benediction/Manuel
holding Labarum and cross on globe.

He was very ambitious, and he wanted to restore the past boundaries of the Byzantine world again. Unfortunately, by the time of his death, the empire started to deteriorate and rapidly decline. Manuel I tried to communicate with the popes for the possibility of uniting the eastern and western churches. However, Pope Adrian IV and popes after him demanded recognition of their religious authority over all the Christians of the world and put themselves superior over the Byzantine emperor. Such demands would not be accepted by either side, and ultimately, the deal proved unrealistic, and the two churches have remained divided until this day. During his reign, taxes were raised to an unacceptable level, unlike his father. The money thus raised was spent lavishly at the expense of his people, and he spared no expense on military or any government affairs. All his subsidies poured into papal and the crusader states, and all the large sums spent on his many failed expeditions were pure financial loss to his empire. Manuel I died in AD 1180, and the Byzantine Empire began to fall and was subject to foreign invaders from all directions. The empire was ruled by many emperors after Manuel for a year or two at the time until the reign of John III, Ducas, which lasted thirty-two years.

John III, Ducas (AD 1222–1254), became the emperor of the Byzantine Empire in mid-December AD 1221. John III was a successful soldier, and he came from a military family.

John III . Byzantine Empire 1222-1254 AD.
Trachy (28mm, 4.7 gr.) Jesus Christ facing raising
hands in Benediction/the virgin crowning John.

John III was successful in maintaining generally peaceful relations with his powerful neighbors, Bulgaria and the Seljuk Turks, and his diplomatic relations extended to the Holy Roman Empire and the papacy. John III was credited with developing the internal prosperity and economy of his empire, encouraging justice and charity. He was known as an active leader in both peace and war in spite of his epilepsy. John III was canonized as a saint 500 years later under the name of "John the Merciful" and is still commemorated annually until this day.

After a long siege of the city of Constantinople under Ottoman Empire Sultan Mehmed II, the city walls were broken, and the Ottoman army went into the city in AD 1453. Hagia Sophia was converted into a mosque, although the Greek Orthodox Church remained intact, and the city of Constantinople was renamed to Istanbul, and that was the end of the Byzantine Empire.

The Venetians, France, and Bishops of Valence

In addition to the Byzantine Christian-oriented coinage, some of the dynasties in the medieval time struck coins that were considered to be Christian coins also. These coins were also circulated around the Byzantine Empire era and were a constant reminder of Christ and the Christian religion and played a good role between converts. The following are brief presentations of the provinces and their coinage.

The city of Venice, in northern Italy in the Gulf of Venice, originated as a collection of lagoon communities united together to defend themselves from the northern invaders, the Lombards. In the lagoon, the people elected their first leader, who was agreed upon by the Byzantine Empire and given the title "dux" (duke, doge). The city of Venice became independent under the name the Republic of Venice. The doge was the head magistrate and the leader of the most serene Republic of Venice for over 1,000 years.

Venice. The Venetians. 1253-1268 AD. Renier Zeno. AR Grasso (20mm, 2.1 gr.) The Duke receiving a flag from St. Mark/Jesus Christ seated holding the book of the Gospels.

Venice. The Venetians. 1289-1310 AD. Pietro Gradenigo. AR Grasso (20mm, 2.0 gr.) The Duke receiving a flag from St. Mark/Jesus Christ seated holding the book of the Gospels.

Venice. The Venetians. 1289-1310 AD. Pietro Gradenigo. AR Grasso (20mm, 2.1 gr.) The Duke receiving a flag from St. Mark/Jesus Christ seated holding the book of the Gospels.

Venice. The Venetians. 1311-1327 AD. Giovanni Soranzo. AR Grasso (21mm, 2.2 gr.) The Duke receiving a flag from St. Mark/Jesus Christ seated holding the book of the Gospels.

Venice. The Venetians. 1311-1327 AD.
Giovanni Soranzo. AR Grasso (21mm, 2.0 gr.)
The Duke receiving a flag from St. Mark/Jesus
Christ seated holding the book of the Gospels.

Venice. The Venetians. 1311-1327 AD.
Giovanni Soranzo. AR Grasso (21mm, 2.1 gr.)
The Duke receiving a flag from St. Mark/Jesus
Christ seated holding the book of the Gospels.

Venice. The Venetians. 1382-1400 AD.
Antonio Venier. AR Grasso (21mm, 1.8 gr.) The
Duke receiving a flag from St. Mark/Jesus Christ
seated holding the book of the Gospels.

Venice. The Venetians. 1382-1400 AD.
Antonio Venier. AR Grasso (21mm, 1.8 gr.) The
Duke receiving a flag from St. Mark/Jesus Christ
seated holding the book of the Gospels.

Venice. The Venetians. 1382-1400 AD.
Antonio Venier. AR Grasso (21mm, 1.8 gr.) The
Duke receiving a flag from St. Mark/Jesus Christ
seated holding the book of the Gospels.

Venice. The Venetians. 1382-1400 AD.
Antonio Venier. AR Grasso (21mm, 1.6 gr.) The
Duke receiving a flag from St. Mark/Jesus Christ
seated holding the book of the Gospels.

Venice. The Venetians. 1382-1400 AD.
Antonio Venier. AR Grasso (21mm, 1.9 gr.) The
Duke receiving a flag from St. Mark/Jesus Christ
seated holding the book of the Gospels.

Venice. The Venetians. 1382-1400 AD.
Antonio Venier. AR Grasso (21mm, 2.0 gr.) The
Duke receiving a flag from St. Mark/Jesus Christ
seated holding the book of the Gospels.

Venice. The Venetians. 1382-1400 AD.
Antonio Venier. AR Grasso (22mm, 1.7 gr.) The
Duke receiving a flag from St. Mark/Jesus Christ
seated holding the book of the Gospels.

Venice. The Venetians. 1423-1457 AD.
Francis Fosari. AR Grasso (20mm, 1.6 gr.) The
Duke receiving a flag from St. Mark/Jesus Christ
seated holding the book of the Gospels.

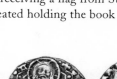

Venice. The Venetians. 1423-1457 AD.
Francis Fosari. AR Grasso (20mm, 1.5 gr.) The
Duke receiving a flag from St. Mark/Jesus Christ
seated holding the book of the Gospels.

Venice. The Venetians. 1423-1457 AD.
Francis Fosari. AR Grasso (21mm, 1.6 gr.) The
Duke receiving a flag from St. Mark/Jesus Christ
seated holding the book of the Gospels.

Venice. The Venetians. 1423-1457 AD.
Francis Fosari. AR Grasso (21mm, 1.6 gr.) The
Duke receiving a flag from St. Mark/Jesus Christ
seated holding the book of the Gospels.

Venice. The Venetians. 1478-1485 AD.
Giovanni Mocenigo. AR Grasso (21mm, 1.6 gr.)
The Duke receiving a flag from St. Mark/Jesus
Christ seated holding the book of the Gospels.

Venice. The Venetians. 1486-1501 AD.
Agostino Barbarigo. AR 16 Soldi (24mm, 3.1 gr.)
The Duke receiving a flag from St. Mark/
Jesus Christ seated on throne. Rare.

Venice. The Venetians. undated. .
AV 140 Soldi, Zecchino (21mm, 3.5 gr.) The Duke
kneeling before St. Mark/Jesus Christ standing

Venice coins

Ancient Coins Through the Bible   317

Venice. The Venetians. undated. .
AV 140 Soldi, Zecchino (19mm, 3.1 gr.)
The Duke kneeling before St. Mark/
Jesus Christ standing

Doges of Venice were elected for life by the republic's aristocracy and typically were the shrewd-est elder in the city. The doges of Venice minted an array of coinage ranging from silver and gold to bronze in later times. Coins presented here are a few as compared to hundreds that were minted at the time of doges. In the ninth century AD, the Republic of Venice began to establish its military power, and they dominated the Adriatic for centuries. In about AD 840, the Republic of Venice sent a fleet of sixty galleys to assist the Byzantines in driving the Arab Muslims from Crotone. In the late Middle Ages, Venice became very wealthy through its control of trade between Europe and the Levant and began to expand beyond the Adriatic Sea. Venice was involved in the Crusades almost from the beginning. Two hundred Venetian ships assisted in capturing the coastal cities of Syria after the First Crusade. The Venetian fleet was crucial to the transportation of the Fourth Crusade, where the crusaders could not pay for the ships. After the fall of Constantinople in AD 1453 to the Ottoman Empire, the discovery of America, and rerouting the trade route around the Cape of Good Hope, Venice declined due to lack of trading.

After the fall of the Roman Empire, the Gauls' eastern frontier along the Rhine River was overrun by Germanic tribes, principally the Franks, from whom the name of "France" was derived. The Franks were the first tribes among the German conquerors of Europe to convert to Catholicism, thus France obtained the title "eldest daughter of the church." France developed the feudalism system, along with many countries in Europe, around AD 1000.

Feudal France. Counts of Chartres.
Charles De Valois, 1293-1323 AD.
AR Denier (21mm, 1.2 gr.)
Chartraine head/Cartis Cavitas cross.

Feudal France. Counts of Chartres.
Charles De Valois, 1293-1323 AD.
AR Denier (21mm, 1.2 gr.)
Chartraine head/Cartis Cavitas cross.

Feudal France. Counts of Chartres.
Charles De Valois, 1293-1323 AD.
AR Denier (21mm, 1.2 gr.)
Chartraine head/Cartis Cavitas cross.

Feudal France. Counts of Chartres.
Charles De Valois, 1293-1323 AD.
AR Denier (21mm, 1.3 gr.)
Chartraine head/Cartis Cavitas cross.

Feudalism was characterized by giving the estate of land, mainly in the form of labor, in return for political and military service. The grantor was lord of the grantee, his vassal, but both were free men and social peers. When the Germans invaded the Western Empire, they destroyed the professional Roman army and substituted their own armies, which were made up of warriors who fought on foot and lived off the countryside. When other invaders, such as the Muslims, the Vikings, and the Magyars, came to invade them, they were forced to own horses, build forts, and live in castles to defend themselves. Now the estate given a vassal was commonly understood to be hereditary, provided he paid an inheritance tax called a relief. Thus feudalism was a political, as well as military, institution—one based upon a contract between two individuals, both of whom held rights in the fiefs. Feudalism reached its maturity and flourished in the thirteenth century AD. Its cradle was the region between the Rhine and Loirs rivers, where a part of modern France is located. Feudalism ended in the fifteenth century AD because the superior lords had difficulty obtaining the service to which they were entitled. Vassals typically preferred to give money to their lords instead of personal military service, and the lords themselves tended to prefer the money because it enabled them to hire professional troops that were better trained and disciplined than the vassals.

In addition to feudal France striking Christian-oriented coins, the bishops of Valence struck similar principle coinage. Valence is a town located in the southeastern part of France.

France. Bishops of Valence. 13th centyry AD.
AR Denier (18mm, 1.1 gr.) Cross/eagle.

France. Bishops of Valence. 13th centyry AD.
AR Denier (18mm, 0.83 gr.) Cross/eagle.

France. Bishops of Valence. 13th centyry AD.
AR Denier (18mm, 0.80 gr.) Cross/eagle.

France. Bishops of Valence. 13th centyry AD.
AR Denier (18mm, 1.1 gr.) Cross/eagle.

The town was the seat of a celebrated school prior to the Roman conquest, a colony under Augustus, and an important town under Valentinian. Its bishopric probably dates from the fourth century AD. The city was invaded by the Alani and other barbarian tribes and fell under the power of the Burgundians and the Franks. The bishops were often in conflict with the citizens and the dukes of Valentinois. Protestantism spread in the area, and Valence became the capital of the Protestants of the province in AD 1563.

The Birth of Islam

The Prophet Muhammad was born in Mecca in the Arabian Peninsula in about AD 570. Arabia was a Roman colony in the second century AD as a province that extended roughly to today's Sinai, all of Jordan, a piece of Syria and Lebanon, and the northernmost corner of Saudi Arabia. The Hejaz region, where the city of Mecca and Madina (then called Yathrib) are located, was the main caravan route of the spice trade, connecting Arabia to the Roman routes.

Muhammad was orphaned at the age of six and was sent to live with relatives. He grew up and became a dealer and was married to a widow called Khadija. When he was forty years old, or around AD 610, shortly before the Sasanian conquest of the Holy Land, he went alone to pray in a cave on Mount Hira (just outside of Mecca). He was visited by a supernatural being, which was later referred to as the angel Gabriel. The angel dictated to Muhammad various sacred texts that he was to memorize. The legend tells us that these visitations by the angel Gabriel continued until his death, and these texts were later made into the Islam Holy Book, the Koran. Muhammad began his preaching throughout Mecca, including to his wife's friends and relatives. A good friend of his, Abu Bakr, became the first convert to the new religion, Islam. Unfortunately, his preaching was not popular with the ruling classes of the city, mainly because it promoted monotheism (the belief in one God, Allah). In AD 622, soldiers were sent to arrest or murder Muhammad in Mecca, but he managed to escape with Abu Bakr and some disciples to Yathrib (Madina). The flight of Muhammad to Madina is semi-important to Muslim people, who call it "Hegira." The Hegira in AD 622 is the beginning date of the Islamic calendar. In AD 632, Muhammad died, and by this time, most of Arabia had become Muslim. After Muhammad's death, and by AD 649, the Muslim army pushed through the Byzantine and Persian empires. They invaded Syria, Palestine, Mesopotamia, Egypt, Persia, North Africa, and Cyprus, and they all fell to Islam. The Umayyad Caliphate (AD 661–750) is the second Arab Caliphate after the death of the Prophet Muhammad. The four dynasties that ruled the Islamic world are the Rashidun (right after prophet Muhammad), the Umayyads (in Damascus and later in Spain), the Abbasids (in Baghdad), and the last are the Turkish Ottomans (in Istanbul). The Umayyads, under Muawiya II, encouraged peaceful coexistence with the Christian communities in Syria. Abd Al-Malik became Umayyad Caliphate in AD 685–705. He reconsolidated the Umayyad control of the caliphate. His reign experienced many revolts from Shi'a Ali under Al-Mukhtar and Ibn Al-Zubayr, who was based in Kufa. In AD 691, the Umayyad troops re-conquered Iraq, and in AD 692, the same troops captured Mecca, and Ibn Al-Zubayr was killed in the battle. During Abd Al-Malik's reign, the Arabic language was established and became the official language of the kingdom, and he was also credited with centralizing the administration of the caliphate. During the Umayyad period, the Dome of the Rock was built in Jerusalem, along with the Great Umayyad Mosque in Damascus.

Omayyad Caliphate. 698-749 AD.
AR Dirhem (25mm, 2.8 gr.) there is no God except
Allah alone/Allah is one, Allah is the eternal.

Omayyad Caliphate. 698-749 AD.
AR Dirhem (27mm, 2.7 gr.) there is no God except
Allah alone/Allah is one, Allah is the eternal.

Omayyad Caliphate. 698-749 AD.
AE Fals. Hims mint (15mm, 2.19 gr.) Elephent,
Kalima around/continuation of Kalima. Rare.

Omayyad Caliphate. 698-749 AD.
AR Dirhem (27mm, 2.8 gr.) there is no God except
Allah alone/Allah is one, Allah is the eternal.

Omayyad Caliphate. 698-749 AD.
AR Dirhem (27mm, 2.9 gr.) there is no God except
Allah alone/Allah is one, Allah is the eternal.

Omayyad Caliphate. 698-749 AD.
AR Dirhem (24mm, 2.8 gr.) there is no God except
Allah alone/Allah is one, Allah is the eternal.

Omayyad Caliphate. 698-749 AD.
AR Dirhem (28mm, 2.7 gr.) there is no God except
Allah alone/Allah is one, Allah is the eternal.

Omayyad Caliphate. 698-749 AD.
AR Dirhem (25mm, 2.9 gr.) there is no God except
Allah alone/Allah is one, Allah is the eternal.

Omayyad Caliphate. 698-749 AD.
AR Dirhem (27mm, 2.8 gr.) there is no God except
Allah alone/Allah is one, Allah is the eternal.

Omayyad Caliphate. 698-749 AD.
AR Dirhem (25mm, 2.6 gr.) there is no God except
Allah alone/Allah is one, Allah is the eternal.

Omayyad Caliphate. 698-749 AD.
AR Dirhem (26mm, 2.9 gr.) there is no God except
Allah alone/Allah is one, Allah is the eternal.

Omayyad Caliphate. 698-749 AD.
AR Dirhem (26mm, 2.8 gr.) there is no God except
Allah alone/Allah is one, Allah is the eternal.

The Dome of the Rock was built in AD 691, it is an Islamic shrine and a major landmark, and it is considered to be the oldest extant Islamic building in the world. It is in the complex building where Al-Aqsa mosque is located and is one of the holiest sites in Islam. According to Islamic tradition, the rock is the spot from where the Prophet Muhammad ascended to heaven, accompanied by the angel Gabriel, even though the dome was not built until after Muhammad's death. Also, in Judaism, the location of the dome is considered to be the holiest spot on earth—the site of the holy of holies during the temple period. Legend tells us that this is also the site where God seized Abraham's arm as he was about to sacrifice his son, Isaac. In Christianity, it is believed that Constantine the Great's mother built a small church that later was called the Church of the Holy Wisdom. According to the New Testament, Jesus preached from this location on the eve of his arrest.

The other great structure that was built by the Umayyad dynasty was the Ummayed mosque in Damascus. The mosque also holds a shrine, which is said to contain the head of John the Baptist, who is honored as a prophet by Muslims and Christians alike. Also, the mosque is an important landmark for the Shi'a. It is said that the head of Husain (the grandson of Muhammad) was kept on display on that site by Yazed I. Also, the tomb of Saladin, the well-respected conqueror, was placed in the garden near the wall of the grand mosque. In AD 749, the Umayyad caliphate fell to the Hashimiyya (the Abbasid family), and Abu Al-Abbas was recognized as the new Abbasid caliphate in the mosque of Kufa. However, most of the Umayyad family in Syria were struck down and killed. The grandson of Hisham, Abd Al-Rahman, survived and established a kingdom in Al-Andalus (southern Spain), and they ruled this region for more than 700 years. The Arabs and the Jews were dismissed from Spain by King Ferdinand and Queen Isabella in 1492, the year Christopher Columbus discovered America.

The Abbasid caliphate (AD 750–1258) was the third of the Islamic caliphates of the Arab-Muslims Empire. The Abbasid initially focused on internal matters, and military operations during this time were minimal. The golden Islamic age was reached around the eighth century AD by transferring the capital from Damascus to Baghdad.

Abbasid Caliphate. 749-847 AD.
AR Dirhem (25mm, 2.9 gr.) there is no God except
Allah alone/Mohammad is the Prophet of Allah.

Abbasid Caliphate. 749-847 AD.
AR Dirhem (26mm, 2.9 gr.) there is no God except
Allah alone/Mohammad is the Prophet of Allah.

Abbasid Caliphate. 749-847 AD.
AR Dirhem (25mm, 2.7 gr.) there is no God except
Allah alone/Mohammad is the Prophet of Allah.

Abbasid Caliphate. 749-847 AD.
AR Dirhem (21mm, 3.0 gr.) there is no God except
Allah alone/Mohammad is the Prophet of Allah.

Abbasid Caliphate. 749-847 AD.
AR Dirhem (22mm, 3.0 gr.) there is no God except
Allah alone/Mohammad is the Prophet of Allah.

Abbasid Caliphate. 749-847 AD.
AV Dinar (18mm, 3.8 gr.) there is no God
except Allah alone/Mohammad is the Prophet
of Allah. Citing Ali Ibn Abi Talib. Scarce.

Islamic Gold. Ghaznavids Muhmud Ibn
Sebuktekin, independent ruler. 1000 AD.
AV Dinar (27mm, 3.83 gr.) Herat mint.
There is no God except Allah alone/
Mohammad is the Prophet of Allah. Scarce.

Islamic Gold. Ghaznavids Muhmud Ibn
Sebuktekin, independent ruler. 1017 AD.
AV Dinar (27mm, 4.27 gr.) Ghazna mint.
There is no God except Allah alone/
Mohammad is the Prophet of Allah. Scarce.

During this period, the Muslim world became the unrivaled intellectual center of science, philosophy, and education, as the Abbasids built "the House of Wisdom" in Baghdad, where both Muslim and non-Muslim scholars translated all the world's knowledge into Arabic. Many works of antiquity would otherwise have been lost were they not translated into Arabic and Persian and later into Hebrew, Turkish, and Latin.

In AD 1258, Hulagu Khan (grandson of Genghis Khan) attacked Baghdad in a critical battle in which the Mongols destroyed the greatest center of Islamic power. The city of Baghdad was captured, sacked, and burned, and that was the end of the Abbasid caliphate.

Mongoles.Great Khans Chingiz
(Genghis Khan), 1206-1227 AD.
BI Jital (16mm, 4.05 gr.) Titles of Genghis/
name of Caliph AL-Nasir. Very Rare.

Mongoles. Hulagu Ibn Tuluy Ibn Genghis Khan
(grand son of Genghis Khan), 1256-1265 AD.
AR Dirhem (27mm, 2.7 gr.) Acknowledging
the Suzerainty of the great Khan. Rare.

Mongoles. Hulagu Ibn Tuluy Ibn Genghis Khan
(grand son of Genghis Khan), 1256-1265 AD.
AR Dirhem (27mm, 2.7 gr.) Acknowledging
the Suzerainty of the great Khan. Rare.

Hulagu Khan conquered Syria with an army of 100,000 strong, destroying cities and irrigation work. Aleppo and Damascus fell in AD 1260, but then Hulagu needed to break off his attack to return to China to deal with a succession dispute.

The Crusaders

The Arabs conquered the east in the seventh century, and the Muslim presence in the Holy Land put increasing pressure on the Eastern Orthodox Byzantine Empire. Christians and Jews were tolerated during the Islamic rule and were allowed to worship, and the pilgrims easily visited the holy shrines in Palestine. The Islamic Empire of the eighth century AD stretched from Mesopotamia to Spain and controlled nearly the entire southern and eastern coasts of the Mediterranean Sea. The governing authority in Baghdad began to lose control of some of the provinces in this massive empire. In the early eleventh century, the Fatimid dynasty of Egypt ordered the destruction of the Church of the Holy Sepulcher, and later, the Byzantine Empire was permitted to rebuild the church after paying large sums to the Fatimid dynasty. This disrupted western Christians' pilgrim passage to Jerusalem, although pilgrimages were allowed to the Holy Land, but for a time, pilgrims were captured, and some of them were killed. In addition, the Seljuk Turks were on the borders of the Levant threatening the occupation of the Holy Land. These reasons, plus other political reasons, promoted the passion for the crusaders.

The Crusades were a series of religious-driven military campaigns created by most of Christian Europe. There were, altogether, nine crusader campaigns between AD 1095, the beginning of the First Crusade, and AD 1272, the beginning the Ninth Crusade. The Crusades had the aim, originally, of recapturing Jerusalem and the Holy Land from Muslim rule and also were launched in response to a call from the Eastern Orthodox Byzantine Empire for help against the expansion of the Muslim Seljuk Turks. The Crusades involved fighting mainly against Muslims, but some campaigns were directed to Muslims, Jews, Greek Orthodox Christians, and political enemies of the popes. The crusaders took vows and were promised by the pope that those who die in the endeavor would receive immediate remission of their sins. Not all the crusader campaigns went to liberate Jerusalem from the Muslims. For instance, the Fourth Crusade resulted in the sacking of Christian Constantinople and the attempt to divide the Byzantine Empire between the Venetians and the crusaders. The Sixth Crusade took off heading east without the official approval of the pope. The Seventh, Eighth, and Ninth Crusades were defeated by the Muslim army. One of the heartbreaking unofficial Crusade missions was known as the Children's Crusade. These children were idealistic youngsters who tried to accomplish what their elders could not, which Pope Innocent II interpreted as a reproof from heaven to their unworthy elders. Stephen led the French children army of 30,000 children, and Nicholas led the German children army of 7,000 children, and both headed to Jerusalem. The French mission sailed from Marseilles (Massalia), France, and the German mission traveled overland from Germany.

Massalia. Greek Gaul. 218-200 BC.
AR Obol (10mm, .66 gr) Bare head of Apollo/
MA within wheel of four spokes. Scarce.

History tells us that none of the children ever reached the Holy Land and they tried to return home or settle along the route to Jerusalem or died from shipwreck or hunger or were sold into slavery by their leaders in Egypt or North Africa.

The Principality of Antioch was the seat of the four Greek Orthodox patriarchs and contained a big population of Christians, even though it was under Muslim rule. Bohemond of Taranto, one of the leaders of the First Crusade, was proclaimed prince of Antioch in AD 1099. Two years later, he was captured by Turkoman Muslims, and he stayed captive for two years. Roger of Salerno (AD 1112–1119) acted as a regent of Edessa and went out and fought the Muslims, and he became a legendary figure in the area because of his military victories against the Turkomans.

Crusaders. Roger of Salerno. 1112-1119 AD.
AE Follis (21mm, 5.4 gr.) Virgin standing/
Lord help your servant Roger. Scarce.

In 1119, the Franks suffered a serious defeat by Al-Ghazi, and Roger of Salerno was killed. The village of Maguelonne found the earliest apostle in southeastern France. The first historically known bishop of Maguelonne to exercise the Papal Suzerainty, preached the first crusade in this town.

Feudal France. Bishops of Maguelonne.
Raimond I, 1125-1215 AD.
AR Denier (17mm, 1.1 gr.) Cross form/
four Annulets in cross. Rare.

The coins minted in Maguellone (Mel Gueil) were one of the most valued by the crusading armies. Baldwin III was king of Jerusalem from AD 1144–1162. He was thirteen years old when his father died, and the kingdom legally passed to his mother as the daughter of Baldwin II.

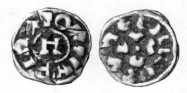

Crusaders. Heinrich III, 1039-1125 AD.
AR Denaro (16mm, 0.97 gr.) Big H/Enricvs. Rare.

Crusaders. Baldwin III, 1144-1162 AD.
AR Denier (13mm, 1.1 gr.) Castle/cross. Scarce.

Because of Baldwin III's minority, he was crowned as co-ruler and heir to his mother. In 1148, the Second Crusade came to Jerusalem, and Conrad III, one of the leaders of the Second Crusade, unwisely advised Baldwin III to attack Damascus to gain more wealth, despite the peace treaty between Damascus and Jerusalem. Baldwin III, the kid, perhaps was eager to impress the strong leaders of Europe who had arrived in his kingdom. The result was a big defeat to him after four days of siege. Baldwin III died in AD 1162. It was rumored that he had been poisoned by pills given to him by his Syrian Orthodox doctor.

Bohemond III (AD 1163–1201) was known as the prince of Antioch. He helped Raymond III of Tripoli to recover part of Antioch territory from the Muslim Nur Ad-Din. The battle was a disaster; Raymond III and Bohemond III were defeated and were taken prisoners. They were freed by the king of Jerusalem for a large ransom. Antioch was harassed by Saladin in AD 1183, and eventually, Antioch was captured by Saladin in AD 1189. Bohemond III died in AD 1201. From his death onward, the Bohemond family ruled the areas of Tripolis, Antioch, and the majority of territories in the Levant.

Crusaders. Bohemond III, 1163-1201 AD.
AR Denier (17mm, 0.94 gr.) Helmeted head/
cross patt'ee, crescent in second angle. Rare.

Crusaders. Bohemond V, 1233-1251 AD. AR Denier
(16mm, 0.6 gr.) cross patt'ee/eight pointed star. Scarce.

Crusaders. Bohemond V, 1233-1251 AD.
AR Denier (16mm, 0.6 gr.) cross patt'ee/
eight pointed star. Scarce.

Crusaders. Bohemond VI, 1251-1275 AD.
AR Gross (26mm, 4.2 gr.) cross within frame/
eight pointed star within eight arcs. Rare.

Crusaders. Bohemond VII, 1275-1287 AD.
AR Half Gross (19mm, 2.1 gr.) cross within
twelve arcs/triple towered gateway. Rare.

The Bohemond family ruled from the death of Bohemond III in AD 1201 to the death of Bohemond VII in AD 1287—a span of eighty-six years. The Bohemond rulers helped all the crusaders' missions in the Levant from AD 1201–1187, which corresponds from the Fourth Crusade to the Ninth Crusade.

In AD 1187, Saladin, sultan of Egypt, recaptured Jerusalem from the Christian crusaders following the battle of Hattin, where he defeated the Third Crusade army. Saladin was born in Tikrit, Iraq, to a family with Kurdish background. His full name was Yusuf Salah Ad-Din Ibn Ayyub. He founded the Ayyubid dynasty, and at the height of his power, he ruled over Egypt, Syria, Iraq, Arabia, and Yemen. In AD 1187, Saladin crushed the crusade army in what was a major disaster for the crusaders and a turning point in the history of Crusades. After taking Jerusalem, Saladin spared all civilians and, for the most part, left churches and shrines untouched. Saladin is remembered respectfully by both European Christians and Islamic sources as a man who always stuck to his promise and was loyal.

Saladin (Salah Al Din). Ayyubids Dynasty, 1169-1193 AD.
AE Dirham (27mm, 11.3 gr.) Dated AH
583(1187/1188 AD). Lion seated, four stars around/
name and title of Abbasid caliph. Extremely Rare.

He did not maim, kill, or retaliate against those whom he defeated, with notable exception of certain events following the battle of Hattin. After the battle, Saladin captured Raynald De Chatillon (French knight in the crusaders' army) and was personally responsible for his execution, because Raynald attacked Muslim caravans and insulted their prophet, Muhammad, before torturing and murdering the people in the caravan. Upon hearing this, Saladin swore an oath to personally execute Raynald, and he did.

The Third Crusade, financed in England under Richard I of England (Richard the Lionheart), set out to liberate Jerusalem. History tells us Richard I came to Acre and conquered it and executed 3,000 Muslim prisoners, including women and children. Saladin's army met Richard I's army in the battle of Arsuf in AD 1191, at which time Saladin was defeated.

Richard the lionheart. Britain. Plantagenet, 1189-1199 AD.
AR Penny (20mm, 1.49 gr.) bust of Henry II/
short cross, pellet. Very Rare.

All attempts made by Richard I to retake Jerusalem failed. Saladin's relationship with Richard was one of mutual respect, as well as military rivalry. According to legend, when Richard got sick, Saladin offered his personal doctor to treat him and sent him fresh fruits with snow to chill the drink as treatment. When Richard lost his horse, Saladin sent him two replacements. Finally, in AD 1192, Richard and Saladin came to an agreement whereby Jerusalem would remain in Muslim hands but would be open to Christian pilgrimages. Saladin was known by giving to the poor and helping charity. Saladin died in AD 1193 in Damascus, not long after Richard I's departure to Europe. Since Saladin had given most of his money away to charity, they found there was not enough money to pay for his funeral. He was buried in the garden outside the Grand Umayyed Mosque in Damascus. Jerusalem stayed in Muslim hands after Saladin's death until AD 1228, when the crusaders regained control of it. But the Egyptian Ayyubid's army retook Jerusalem in AD 1244, and it stayed in Muslim hands until World War I when the British invaded Palestine.

Another figure worth mentioning who appeared at the end of the Ninth Crusade campaign was Philippe IV (AD 1285–1314). He was called "Philip the fair," not by too many people, and became the king of France in AD 1285 after the death of his father, Philip III.

Crusaders. Philippe IV (the fair), 1285-1314 AD. AR Gross (25mm, 4.0 gr.) Cross Patt'ee/ Chatel Tournois, twelve Lis. Rare.

Crusaders. Philippe IV (the fair), 1285-1314 AD. AR Gross (26mm, 4.1 gr.) Cross Patt'ee/ Chatel Tournois, twelve Lis. Rare.

Crusaders. Philippe IV (the fair), 1285-1314 AD. AR Gross (26mm, 4.1 gr.) Cross Patt'ee/ Chatel Tournois, twelve Lis. Rare.

Crusaders. Philippe IV (the fair), 1285-1314 AD. AR Gross (26mm, 4.1 gr.) Cross Patt'ee/ Chatel Tournois, twelve Lis. Rare.

Philippe began to strip all of the king of England's possessions in France, thereby creating hostilities with England, and that was the trigger for the Hundred Years' War between France and England due to Philippe's greed. Philippe IV arrested Jews so he could seize their assets, and he expelled them from his French territories in AD 1306. He imposed taxes on the French clergy of one half of their annual income and caused many conflicts with the Roman Catholic Church and the papacy. Philippe IV was forming another Crusade mission to recapture Jerusalem and establish a worldwide Christian empire under French rule, and Henry II of Cyprus was eager to help him, but this never happened, because he died in a hunting accident in AD 1314.

Henry II (AD 1285–1324) was the last ruling and the first titular king of Jerusalem, and he also ruled as king of Cyprus. Henry had himself crowned king of Jerusalem in 1286, but he returned to Cyprus and appointed his uncle in his absence. He tried to stop Italian ships from trading with the Muslims, hoping to weaken their economy, and he wrote Pope Clement V twice, asking him to preach for a new Crusade. His reign in Cyprus was prosperous and wealthy, and he was very much involved in the administration of his kingdom. He had his brother Guy, the constable of Cyprus, put to death in 1303 for conspiring against him.

Crusaders. Henry II of Cyprus, 1310-1324 AD.
AR half Gross (21mm, 2.3 gr.) King seated on
curule chair/cross of Jerusalem. Very Rare.

Crusaders. Oshin, king of Armenia, 1308-1320 AD.
AR Takvorin (21mm, 2.1 gr.) King on
horse back/lion walking. Scarce.

Henry was disposed of by his brother, Amalric, in 1306, and he was exiled to Armenia. King Oshin of Armenia was Amalric's brother-in-law. King Oshin initiated his reign by raising an army and driving out the Mongols. In AD 1310, Amalric was assassinated, and King Oshin released Henry II, and he was restored to the throne of Cyprus. During Henry II and Hugh IV, the island enjoyed comparative peace and reached its zenith in prosperity. Henry II died from poor health and epilepsy in AD 1324.

Peter I (AD 1359–1369) took over the throne in Cyprus in AD 1359 after the death of his father, Hugh IV.

Crusaders. Peter I of Cyprus, 1359-1369 AD.
AR Gross (26mm, 3.8 gr.) King seated on
crude bench/cross of Jerusalem. Vary Rare.

He was a warrior and tried to get the crusaders' campaign in existence again, and he spent much of his time visiting kings in Europe to get enough enthusiasm for the Crusade. Finally, he led a Crusade army, formed from Cyprus, Rhodes, and Europe against Alexandria, Egypt. He captured and sacked Alexandria, but he was forced to evacuate it a week later. Peter I was assassinated in AD 1369.

Levon I (Leo I, AD 1198–1219) reigned during the Third Crusade and was the great-uncle of Raymond of Antioch.

Crusaders. Levon I, king of Armenia, 1198-1219 AD.
AR Tram (22mm, 2.9 gr.) King seated on throne/
long cross between two lions. Scarce.

He became the lord of Cilician Armenia in AD 1187 but later had himself crowned prince of Armenia in AD 1199. Levon was a powerful ruler and was remembered as "Leo the Magnificent." His court was cultured, and he was a supporter of calligraphy and the arts. He opened his commerce with Venice and Genoa and opened his port to the world. Levon died in AD 1219, and his daughter, Isabella, became the queen of Armenia.

The crusader armies took the city of Constantinople in AD 1204, and that was the end of the 700-plus years of the Byzantine Empire. According to historians and some scholars, after the crusaders stormed the city, it was left with the worst scenes of destruction, pillage, and massacre the ancient world had ever seen. However, the empire was divided up amongst the conquerors, the Byzantine capital was ruled by Latin princess, and what was left of the Byzantine aristocracy went into exile to Greece and Asia Minor. An attempt was made to recapture the Byzantine capital by John III of Nicaea (AD 1222–1254), but this dream was never accomplished.

Epilogue

In the course of history, the city of Jerusalem has been destroyed twice, besieged twenty-three times, attacked fifty-two times, and captured and recaptured forty-four times. In spite of all this, the three faiths—Christianity, Islam, and Judaism—remain in the city of Jerusalem at different numbers and social classes, but they all have one thing in common: conflicts. Based on recent statistics, the city of Jerusalem consists of 64 percent Jews, 32 percent Muslims, and only 2 percent Christians. The world statistics, based on one source, contains 33 percent Christians, 21 percent Muslims, and less than 1 percent Jews, and the remaining are other religions.

From the beginning of history to present day, religion continues to be the most influential aspect of human lives. There are countless religions in this world today, each different from the other, but they all serve the same purpose. In each religion, everyone seems to ask the questions: "What happens when I die? What should I do in my life, and why am I here on earth?" Religion helps people transmit their values from one generation to another and influences the way we interact with the natural environment. It teaches us how to see ourselves in light of the universe and gives purpose and meaning to life. With our complex society, it is very likely that, in our lifetime, we will meet people from every corner of this planet. Understanding the religious beliefs of these people is one of the many steps that mankind must take in order to someday prosper together in peace.

Appendices

Appendix I: Grading and Abbreviations

A. Grading Conditions:

English	German	French
(FDC) Uncirculated	Stempelglanz	Fleur De Coin
(EF) Extremely Fine	Vorzuglich	Superbe
(VF) Very Fine	Sehr Schon	Tres Beau
(F) Fine	Schon	Beau
(G) Good/Fair	Sehr Guterhaltent	Tres Bien Conserve

B. Abbreviations:

AV	Gold
AE	Copper/Bronze
AR	Silver
AD	Anno Domini
AH	Anno Hegira
BC	Before Christ
BCE	Before Common Era
BI	Billion
CE	Common Era
C/M	Countermark
CY	Civic Year
Cuir	Cuirassed
Diad	Diademed
DR	Draped
EL	Electrum
EX	Exergue
GR	Gram
IY	Indictional year
Laur	Lauereate
MM	Millimeter
Obv	Obverse
Rev	Reverse
RY	Regnal year
Rad	Radiate
SE	Seleukid era
VAR	Variety

There are two ends to each grade: low and high ends. Sometimes a coin does not fall within the normal grade; therefore, the objective "Good" (G) is given to the high end, and "Near" (N) is given to the low end, such as NVF or GVF and so on.

Appendix II: Patriarchs and Rulers of the Ancient World

All dates are approximate from 2165 BC to 650 BC, fairly accurate from 650 BC to 336 BC, and very accurate from 336 BC onward.

The Period of the Patriarchs

Abraham	2165–1990 BC
Isaac	2065–1885 BC
Jacob	2005–1860 BC
Joseph	1915–1805 BC
Moses	1525–1405 BC

The Period of Judges

From Moses to Solomon	1405–930 BC (period of judges)

The Period of Kings

From Solomon to exile	930–586 BC

Kings of Judah		Kings of Israel	
Rehoboam	930–913 BC	Jeroboam I	930–909 BC
Asa	910–869 BC	Baasha	908–886 BC
Jehoshaphat	872–848 BC	Omri	885–874 BC
Jehoram	853–841 BC	Ahab	874–853 BC
Athaliah	841–835 BC	Joram	852–841 BC
Joash	835–796 BC	Jehu	841–814 BC
Azariah	792–740 BC	Jeroboam II	793–753 BC
Jotham	750–735 BC	Menahem	752–742 BC
Ahaz	735–715 BC	Pekah	752–732 BC
Hezekiah	715–686 BC	Hoshea	732–722 BC
Manasseh	697–642 BC		
Josiah	640–609 BC		
Jehoiakim	609–598 BC		
Zedekiah	597–586 BC		

The Assyrian Empire

King of Assyria, Tiglath-Pileser III	745–727 BC

The Babylonian Empire

King of Babylonia, Nebuchadnezzar	604–562 BC
Destruction of Jerusalem by Nebuchadnezzar	586 BC

The Persian Empire

King Cyrus	559–530 BC
King Darius I	522–486 BC
King Xerxes I	486–465 BC
King Artaxerxes I	465–423 BC
King Darius II	423–404 BC
King Artaxerxes II	404–358 BC
King Artaxerxes III	358–338 BC
King Arses	338–336 BC
King Darius III	336–330 BC

The Greek Empire, starting only from Philip II

Philip II (Alexander's father)	359–336 BC
Alexander the Great	336–323 BC

Thrace/Macedonia Kingdom

Antigonus	319–301 BC
Cassander	305–297 BC
Demetrius I	294–288 BC
Lysimachos	288–281 BC
Pyrrhus	288–285 BC
Ptolemy Ceraunus	281–280 BC
Antipater Etesias	279 BC
Antigonus II	277–239 BC
Demetrius II	239–229 BC
Antigonus III	229–221 BC
Philip V	221–179 BC
Perseus	179–168 BC

Thrace/Macedonia kingdom fell to Rome in 168 BC

Isaac I, Comnenus	AD 1057–1059
Constantine X	AD 1059–1067
Eudocia	AD 1067
Romanus IV	AD 1068–1071
Michael VII	AD 1071–1078
Nicephorus III	AD 1078–1081
Alexius I	AD 1081–1118
John II	AD 1118–1143
Manuel I	AD 1143–1180
Alexius II	AD 1180–1183
Andronicus I	AD 1183–1185
Isaac, Usurper of Cyprus	AD 1184–1191
Isaac II	AD 1185–1195
Alexius III	AD 1195–1203
Isaac II, Angelus (restored), and Alexius IV, Angelus	AD 1203–1204
Alexius V, Ducas	AD 1204
	(only a little more than two months)